JAPAN

料理の旅日記

CLÉMENCE LELEU & ANNA SHOJI
ILLUSTRATIONS BY ADRIEN MARTIN

JAPAN

A CULINARY TRAVEL DIARY

PRESTEL
MUNICH · LONDON · NEW YORK

To my parents, Annie and Claude Leleu

OUR ITINERARY

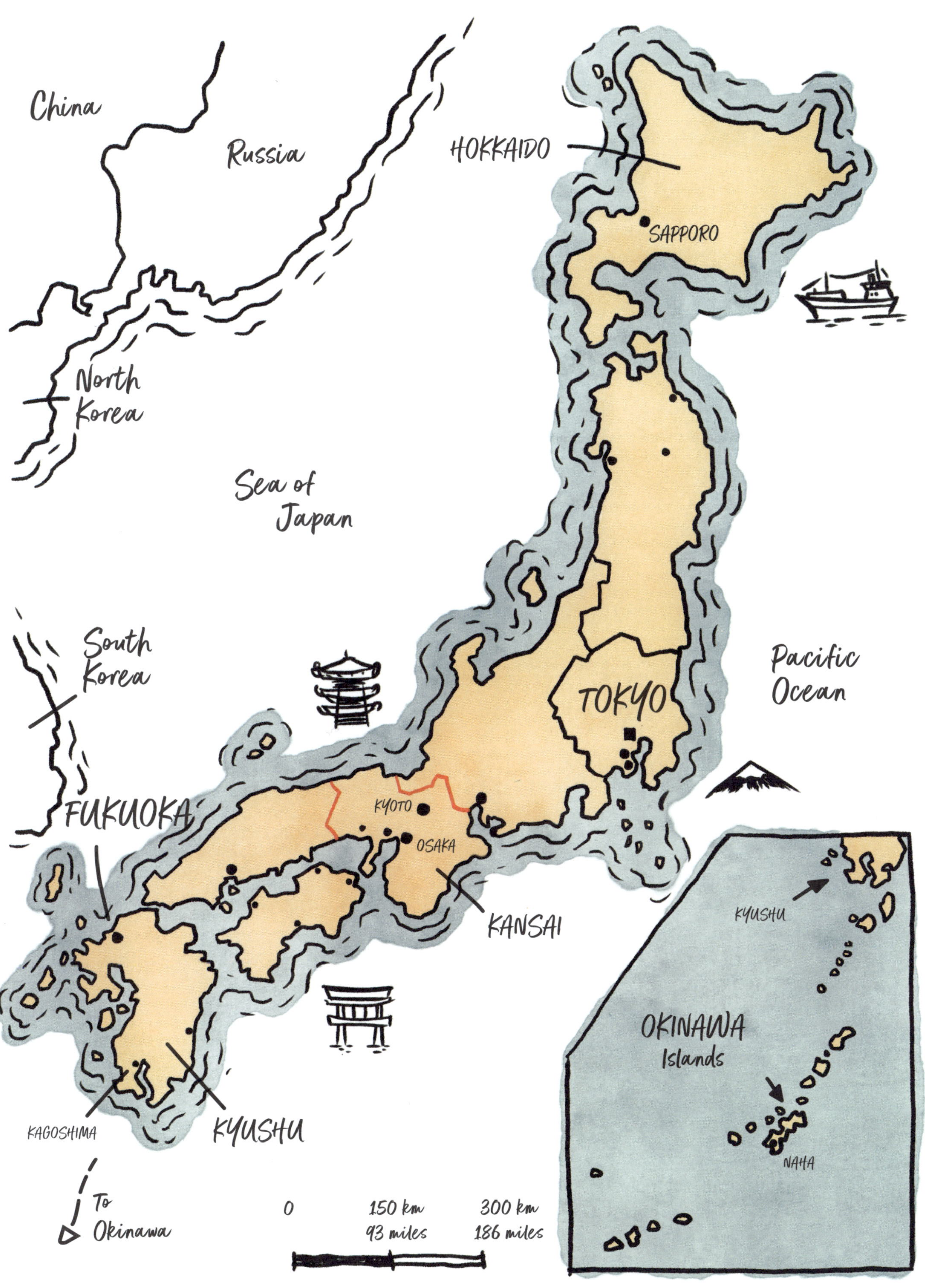
China
Russia
HOKKAIDO
SAPPORO
North
Korea
Sea of
Japan
South
Korea
Pacific
Ocean
TOKYO
FUKUOKA
KYOTO
OSAKA
KANSAI
KYUSHU
OKINAWA
Islands
NAHA
KAGOSHIMA
KYUSHU
To
Okinawa
0
150 km
93 miles
300 km
186 miles

INTRODUCTION

Join us on a culinary journey to the land of the rising sun

'To understand, you first have to eat, so please sit down.' Usa Teruyo's words still ring in my ears. Usa is of Ainu origin, an indigenous people from the island of Hokkaido. Before telling me about her ancestors and the ways in which she tries to preserve their customs and traditions, particularly the culinary ones, she insisted that we take the time to share a meal, together and in silence. So we enjoyed mashed sweet potatoes served in a wooden bowl, then sausages stuffed with *pukusa*, the wild onions found mainly in the mountains of the north island. 'If you go out of your way to experience new flavours, if you are interested in where they originate from, then you will understand those who cultivate and cook them. Cooking is the best way to understand a people, a country or a culture.'

My intention was for this book to be a kind of culinary travel diary which allows you to explore Japanese cuisine and everything it stands for - to understand what its best-liked ingredients, the way they are combined as well as the regional preferences and idiosyncracies say about its local and national cuisines, as well as about the whole country itself.

As Usa says, a country's cuisine is perhaps the best gateway to its culture. The best and also the least expensive. Most people can cook and choose their ingredients - interpreting, circumventing, even twisting recipes a little here or there to suit their own desires and means. Tasting the cuisine of another country allows you to visit the place for the duration of a meal, without the need to pay for a train or plane ticket.

A JOURNEY WITH FIVE STOPS

We selected five geographical areas, either because they are emblematic of the archipelago or because they possess their very own culinary identity. Each area is presented in one chapter, peppered with articles and features that cover subjects connected with Japanese cuisine in the broadest sense. My text is enriched with recipes written by Anna Shoji, my quintessential teammate. Anna has been a market gardener in the province of Touraine, France, since 2015. She grows vegetables, fruit and Japanese plants, while respecting the land and its produce.

This travel diary begins in Tokyo, the largest megalopolis in the world, where culinary influences from all over Japan and foreign cuisines mingle and merge. The Japanese capital digests them all and sometimes reinvents them in its own way. First, we discover a fish market the size of a continent, then we stroll down the famous Kappabashi-dori, also known as Kappabashi or Kitchen Town, the main street for food lovers. Next, we go behind the scenes of the *konbinis*, the famous small convenience stores which are a perfect mirror of Japanese society. Finally, who better than the poet and translator Ryōko Sekiguchi to tell us all about her city? She offers us a new perspective on this place that we may think is devoid of its own culinary identity.

The next destination on our trip is Kansai, a vast region full of contrasts, home to the historic city of Kyoto and the popular port city of Osaka. Here, fine vegetarian cuisine and gourmet street food intertwine. We push open the doors of the tearooms that remained locked in the 1960s. We stop every few metres to try a *takoyaki* or a *kushikatsu* street food snack before continuing to a traditional pastry shop where we will sample a traditional Japanese confection: the famous *wagashi*.

Our journey continues on the island of Kyushu, the most southerly of the archipelago's four largest islands, not counting Okinawa. This volcanic land is the country of market gardeners, who feast on the richness of its soil. Kyushu has long been the only Japanese gateway for trade with South Korea, as well as later on with Portugal and the Netherlands. The island's cuisine has been hugely enriched by these multicultural influences – *tonkotsu*, *tempura* and *kare raisu* grace plates on Kyushu. Before leaving the island, we must make a detour to Fukuoka to discover the local yatai. People come to chat and eat on the go at these mobile food stalls which set up everywhere from about 5 p.m., before disappearing again in the middle of the night.

We then head to Hokkaido, the northernmost island in the Japanese archipelago. Here, fishing rules supreme. Seafood, fish and seaweed are fished here and sold throughout the country. Locally, the menus feature stuffed squid, salmon roe, crab and shellfish. But Hokkaido is also the land of the Ainu, an

©Laurence Revol

indigenous people with multiple culinary traditions that have almost - but not entirely - disappeared.

Finally, the last leg of our culinary journey takes us to the tropics. Okinawa comprises a string of more than 150 islands, mainly known for their turquoise waters and sandy beaches. It is also a so-called 'blue zone' - people here live much longer than in most countries on Earth and the islands boast more centenarian women than any other place in the world ...

What would a meal be without a drink? In the final chapter of this book, we fill our glasses with sake, whiskey and *sochu*, three alcoholic drinks produced in the archipelago. We sneak into the sparsely decorated traditional teahouses with their tatami mats to discover how the tea ceremony is performed and how it has permeated Japanese culture (ceramics, horticulture, architecture and more). Finally, we need to find out about an essential part of Japanese life - the vending machine.

DISCOVERING JAPAN, A-SIDE AND B-SIDE

Japan. A Culinary Travel Diary explores the terroirs of the archipelago, their specificities and their multiple facets, all of which reveal that 'eating Japanese' actually means much more than it seems. It is obviously a story of country, tastes and seasons, of regionality and the relationship with nature and living creatures. But a country's cuisine also bears the traces, and sometimes the stigmata, of history. Japanese cuisine is a melting pot of multiple culinary cultures. It is the result of assimilation and of power struggles, featuring periods of conquest and periods of occupation. When we taste the dishes, we savour food infused with Chinese, Korean, but also Dutch and Portuguese influences. The meals are an infusion, sometimes constrained, but always reinterpreted with a flavour made in Japan. This will help us understand that what we eat is always much more political than we imagined - for example, how these dishes first saw the light of day, the care that is taken in growing the vegetables and in selecting the animals to ensure their sustainability, the fight to perpetuate the best ancestral know-how and the culinary customs of the indigenous peoples ...

This is why I simply could not write a book on Japanese cuisine without mentioning the history of the Ainu people and being interested in the influence exercised once - and still today - by the American occupation on the Okinawa Islands. Finally, it was difficult to ignore the depletion of fishery resources in Japanese waters, or not to mention the already very concrete impact of global warming on market gardening and marine life.

Finally, it was important to me that this book should offer recipes for home cooking that were accessible to everyone, using ingredients that can also be found in Europe and the United States, either because they are grown or produced there, or because they can easily be found on the shelves of a supermarket or an Asian grocery shop.

So, all that remains for me to do is wish you a good trip and *itadakimasu!*

Anna Shoji:
'The taste of Japan is the taste of our country. It seeps into our dishes so they will always remind us of Japan.'

A Japanese market gardener in the Touraine province of France, Anna Shoji is passionate about cooking and created all the recipes in this book. She is also the cofounder of an ecovillage dedicated to Japanese food, in the Île-de-France region. Here, she tells us about her conversion to agriculture, her love of the land and her passion for all cuisines – Japanese, French and more.

Where do your strong links to culture, land and terroir stem from? Did you inherit them?

Not at all. No one in my family owns any land or has any knowledge of agriculture. My family has lived in Tokyo for several generations, so I didn't even have a grandmother in the countryside who might have tended a vegetable garden. It was something entirely unknown to me. I discovered farming when I went to work in Algeria, as part of a small group of Japanese visitors tending a market garden. I really enjoyed my work and I loved this connection with, and closeness to, the land so much that I wanted to change my career and start over. And so I began to look for land to cultivate.

Why did you choose to start your market gardening in France?

I grew up in Tokyo where I went to a French-Japanese school. My family was quite Europeanized – my father managed several Italian restaurants, my mother ran a porcelain decorating school, which drew its inspiration from Danish, German and French models. We often went to Europe and we even lived in Denmark for two years. My path in life was laid out somewhere between Japan and Europe, but particularly in France.

I chose to settle here because I already knew a little bit about the country, and because I knew that the quality of the land is considered as important in France as in Japan.

Since 2015, you have been based in the Touraine province where you grow Japanese vegetables on 2 hectares (5 acres) of land.

Absolutely. In the beginning, I had intended to settle in the south because I had done part of my

studies there. I knew many people in that part of France, it was nice and warm, and I thought it would be good for my vegetables. But when I studied the landscape in a little more detail, I realized that the earth in the south was very dry and mostly limestone. Of course, lots of vegetables grow very well there, but I found the conditions too different from the land and water I knew in Japan. This is when people told me about the Touraine area, known as 'the garden of France', and that's how I ended up at this farm. I was looking for a small piece of land but in France farms tend to be very large – they easily comprise 10, 20 or even 100 hectares (24, 48 or 96 acres), whereas I just wanted one hectare. If I could find this plot of land, there would be nothing. I would have to start from scratch, set up greenhouses and dig a well.

Yet I ended up finding exactly what I was looking for, with all the greenhouses, irrigation, electricity and pumps already in place – the previous owner was leaving all his tools and equipment behind. This was great for someone starting out, so I bought the plot of land in Ligueil, one hour south of Tours.

Did you encounter any difficulties in growing your Japanese vegetables in the soil of Touraine, or did it work out straightaway?

It all worked fine straightaway. I started with those families of plants of which a 'French version' exists, such as cabbage, cucumbers and turnips … Although they are not exactly the same varieties as their Japanese cousins, these vegetables already grow here, so I could see no reason why the Japanese versions wouldn't also do well.

What had to be adapted, however, was our gardening practice. The ways of growing and harvesting vegetables, and the timing of the harvests, differ between the countries. Japanese vegetables are very often eaten raw or only very lightly cooked so they need to be tender and crunchy. They should be juicy and taste good as they are, without being prepared in any way.

In Ligueil, you cultivate your produce, which is mainly intended for chefs, without using pesticides.

Absolutely. I don't use any chemicals, not even those that are permitted and widely used by organic farmers. Yet, I do not have the 'organic' label because not all my seeds are organic; most of them are, but I cannot divide my field between organic and non-organic. So only a part of my production is labelled organic, all the plants for which I do not need seeds, such as lotus roots and ginger rhizomes. But what matters most to me personally is not the label, it is not using any chemicals on my crops.

Do you notice a difference between France and Japan in the way people cook vegetables?

In Japan, vegetables are mostly eaten raw. In France, they are usually eaten raw in salads, roasted or in stews like ratatouille, and they are generally considered an accompaniment to meat or fish. Vegetables are still considered a side dish here.

In Japan, vegetables are valuable ingredients in their own right. You can have an entire meal consisting only of vegetables, without having to be vegetarian. The term vegetarian may in fact scare some people because it creates the impression of having to restrict or constrain your diet when, in fact, this is not at all the case! The main-course vegetables are sufficient in themselves, without making the dish seem bland. So in Japan, we are more demanding in terms of flavour and texture. When you make a stew, you cook the vegetables for a very long time; they have to be flavoursome, of course, but it's still different. And then, in Japan, we try to eat vegetables in their entirety, with their tops, leaves, roots and skins … This is why they must be harvested at the right time – neither too ripe nor too under ripe.

What, in your opinion, are the characteristics of the Japanese terroir?

In Japan, the word terroir mostly describes the ingredients which are very specific to a city or a region, and there are great differences between the north and the south of the country. The climate, which also varies greatly, creates these terroirs, which are vary greatly and are very locally specific.

And then the terroir is also the way in which the people who live there ensure the preservation of local specialities and know-how, how they safeguard culinary specificities, which can often be ascribed to constraints linked to the climate. For example, in the north of Japan, in Akita, we find *takuwan*, a dried yellow radish, a bit like a crunchy pickle. Normally, radishes are dried before brining them, but in the north it is so cold that they cannot be left to dry because they are susceptible to frost. The locals therefore found a way of smoking them dry. This produces radishes with a deliciously smoky flavour, which are then fermented. It is the combination of geography, topography and climate which makes the terroir so specific, and which results in a local know-how which needs to be passed on.

Do you see any differences or similarities between French and Japanese terroirs?

There are many similarities because France is rich in different terroirs, with lots of nuances. For example, in the cheese category, we can use the same cow's milk base to obtain entirely different results in terms of taste or texture depending on the region where the cheese is produced. Regional bacteria are different; they create subtle differences. Perhaps that's what we don't have in Japan, this sort of nuance. Each region is very different in its tastes. Many dishes are associated with one particular city, which also means that gastronomy is an inherent part of each journey. The Japanese love to eat (at least I do!) and, when we travel, we immediately associate a city with a particular food, an ingredient or a dish, and so we plan the culinary stops of our journey accordingly before we even leave. They are obvious.

There is perhaps also a difference in the way these *terroirs* are protected. In France, we have AOPs, AOCs (Appellation d'origine protégée/contrôlée) ... In Japan, foods are less well protected; there are very few appellations. Instead, it's all about tradition and culture. They are the main vectors of transmission and preservation.

Your cultivation is local, but you grow Japanese vegetables. This poses the question as to what is local. Obviously, 'local' does not necessarily imply 'national'.

Absolutely. It is true that I grow Japanese vegetables in the Touraine province, but my production is local. If someone asks me what I grow in my little corner of the Touraine, the answer may seem somewhat surprising: Japanese vegetables. However, that is what I grow.

What I cultivate is a mix of local and Japanese vegetables. In my opinion, it is always better if we can produce locally, rather than importing it. Shiso and Japanese vegetables grow very well here in France and this avoids having to import them by ship or plane. Being local, even when it includes the cultivation of foreign vegetables, is connected with the preservation of the environment, which is an imperative. Who knows, maybe in 30 or 50 years, my vegetable production will be considered 'local' by everyone!

Would you say there is something like a 'Japanese taste'?

Yes, there is a Japanese taste. That of dashi, umami, the salty sweetness of mirin and soy sauce. In French restaurants, they sometimes add a little *kombu* or dashi. This gives the dish a slightly Japanese note, which reminds us of what the dishes we used to eat, and that feels good. The taste of Japan is the taste of our country. It immerses itself into our dishes so they will always remind us of Japan.

What do you think are the challenges that Japanese agriculture will have to face in the future?

In Japan, we are so happy with local production, that something is 'made in Japan', that people don't worry too much if it's organic or doesn't contain too many pesticides. Yet Japan is one of the largest consumers of pesticides in the world, even if things are starting to change.

The main thing we look for in fruit and vegetables are taste and appearance. Fruit and vegetables are sold singly, each one packaged separately ... In order to eat something tasty and beautiful, the Japanese ignore the environmental aspect. Yet my grandparents' generation did not think like that at all. For things to evolve quickly I sincerely believe that it would help if the Japanese were better informed on environmental aspects. We just don't make them think enough. We have not properly explained to them what the risks are of the methods currently employed in agriculture.

We should also move away from a culture where everything is calibrated to the nth degree. For example, cucumbers must be straight and all of the same size for logistical reasons; otherwise they will not fit into the boxes. On the producers' side, this entails enormous losses, which then have a repercussion on prices.

In Laval-en-Brie, you also co-created Mura, a Japanese ecovillage where Japanese cuisine plays a vital part. Can you tell us a little more about it?

Mura was created by women and for women, but men are, of course, also welcome! Four Japanese women - Maki Maruyama, Terumi Yoshimura, Hiromi Kobayashi and me - set up the project with the intention of creating a place where working women and mothers could come together to relax, a place where you can feel the richness of nature and what it supplies, and where you can sense the passage of the seasons. All this is firmly connected with food.

All the activities we propose are linked to Japanese culinary culture. The idea is to pick vegetables in the vegetable garden or herbs in the woods and then cook them together; to learn pottery to create our own tableware; to find out how to dye fabric to make aprons ... At Mura, we learn that we can do a lot with our hands and to appreciate what nature offers us if we respect seasonality and if we take care of what surrounds us. We want to raise awareness among our visitors through discovery, learning and sharing, but also and above all through eating well. To be honest, we were really four foodies who set up this project! ▬

Basic ingredients

Here are some ingredients you should have in your cupboard before starting to prepare a Japanese recipe. This list is a suggestion and certainly not exhaustive. It's up to you to add to it according to your tastes and preferences.

① **Anko** – If you don't want to prepare it yourself, you can buy this slightly sweetened red bean paste ready-made. It is most often sold tinned (canned), either with a smooth texture or puréed with small pieces of bean. Anko is used to make many different desserts, including *dorayaki* (a pan-cake-like patty).

② **Dashi** – This stock is considered the basis of Japanese cooking, an essential ingredient in most soups and stews. It is mainly sold in powdered form, but you can also find it in bottles. You can easily prepare your own dashi at home, using *katsuobushi* (simmered, smoked and fermented skipjack tuna) and *kombu* seaweed.

③ **Katsuobushi** – These flakes of dried, smoked and fermented bonito tuna are used to prepare dashi as well as other dishes such as *okonomiyaki* (savoury pancakes), on which the flakes seem to dance under the effect of the heat.

④ **Miso** – Miso is a paste made from soya beans (soybeans) and fermented rice or barley. There are several kinds, with their colour depending on the degree of fermentation. The most commonly used types are white and red miso paste.

⑤ **Shoyu** – This Japanese soy sauce is the equivalent of our salt and an essential ingredient in Japanese cuisine. It consists of soya beans (soybeans), wheat, salt and water. Soy sauce is used as a seasoning for meat and fish as well as in marinades. It only takes a few drops to spice up a vinaigrette and to give it a special little umami twist.

⑥ **Sake** – This rice wine is mainly used to dilute sauces. Like some wines in France, there are sakes that are used for cooking. Particularly renowned for its strong umami flavour, it gives dishes a slight malty and earthy, yet rounded, taste.

⑦ **Sansho** – Sansho is also known as 'Japanese pepper' and while it is used like pepper, it actually isn't a pepper at all. Instead, sansho belongs to the Rutaceae family of citrus fruits. This is why, in addition to its spicy, peppery flavours, we find lemony notes when we taste it.

⑧ **Wasabi** – Belonging to the same family as mustard and horseradish, wasabi rhizomes are grated before being transformed into a pungent paste. It is used to spice up and accompany sushi and sashimi as well as cold soba noodles.

⑨ **Yuzu kosho** – Yuzu kosho is a paste condiment prepared from yuzu, a Japanese lemon and chillies (chili peppers). This paste can be stirred into miso soup or into a *nabe*, a winter hotpot that resembles a fondue. Yuzu kosho can also accompany sashimi.

⑩ **Rice vinegar** – Essential in vegetable marinades, to season salads and, above all, for making sushi rice, adding just a few drops of rice vinegar gives a malty flavour to any recipe.

⑪ **Tamari** – Tamari sauce is the equivalent of soy sauce, except that it is made exclusively from soya, without any trace of wheat. It is therefore ideally suited for people with a gluten intolerance.

⑫ **Mirin** – Mirin is a sweetened rice wine that is only used for cooking. It is used in particular to prepare sauces, to which it gives a little sweet and salty taste. It must be stored in a cool place and protected from the light.

⑬ **Tempurako** – Tempurako is a mixture of potato starch and wheat flour, used for cooking tempura. It is a highly rated companion for crunchy fries and air-fried foods.

1

2

3

4

5

6

7

8

9

10

11

12

東京

TOKYO

The *konbini* – a mirror of Japanese society

Konbini mini supermarkets are emblematic of the Japanese archipelago. Here you will find absolutely everything you might need on a daily basis – and much more. When you look at it closely, you'll realize that these shops offer a perfect snapshot of Japanese society in real time.

'Irasshaimase!' As soon as you walk through the door of a *konbini*, the staff there will address you with their famous 'welcome to my shop!,' a greeting that has become emblematic of these local convenience stores. The shops are open every day, and some even 24/7. Whether you are in Tokyo, Kyoto, Osaka or in the middle of the countryside it's impossible to miss them. And for good reason: in 2020 there were 50,000 *konbinis* operating throughout Japan - that's one for every 2,500 inhabitants!

The concept was originally imported from the United States and then perfected in local fashion when the first shops arrived in Japan in 1974. The first *konbini* - a Japanese translation of 'convenience store' - first opened its doors in the Toyosu district, in Tokyo Bay. The concept is simple: here you can find everything you need on a daily basis, from food to hygiene and cleaning products. During the period of strong economic growth in the 1970s, the *konbini* became the essential go-to address for another emblematic figure, who also emerged during these prosperous years: the so-called 'salary-man', a salaried, white-collar employee. It was this model employee of Japan Inc., always dressed in a black suit and white shirt and carrying a briefcase, who made the convenience store an extension of his home. It's where he grabbed a cup of coffee in the morning, went to buy a *bento* or *onigiris* for his lunch break and, if he missed the last evening train home, he could even find a shirt, a pair of socks and underwear here, to start a new day in the office in clean clothes.

THE ART OF MAKING ONESELF INDISPENSABLE

Building on their success, the *konbinis* pounced on the smallest vacant plot to install their perfectly stocked and neatly arranged shelves. They invested in residential areas and business districts, making inroads into metro and train stations, taking over university campuses and supplying travellers at motorway (interstate) service stations. There are three chains of these stores which together make up 80 per cent of the sector's turnover: Seven Eleven is in the lead, followed by Family Mart and then Lawson. It's difficult, especially in Tokyo which has

2,100 Seven Eleven stores alone, to walk more than 200 metres (220 yards) without coming across one of these three brands. In some places, you can even happen across two *konbinis* from the same group facing each other, on either side of a road, for example. This is not a mistake but a carefully considered strategy, as Minoru Matsumoto, one of the communication managers at Seven & I Holdings Co., explained to the press: 'We apply the strategy of dominance – even if we already have a Seven Eleven at a particular junction, the presence of a second one is justified since it means that the potential customer does not have to cross the road.'

Konbinis are masters in the art of making themselves indispensable. During the 1970s, these convenience stores mainly offered food, drinks, hygiene and cleaning products, plus a few magazines. Over the years, the range they offer has grown and been extended to include multiple services. At a *konbini* you can now buy concert tickets, drop off your laundry to be washed and ironed, pay your local and road taxes, withdraw money, send a fax (still common in Japan), print a document and post your letters and parcels. No large-scale supermarket or local grocery store can boast of offering such a great range of personalized services, all in a store that doesn't take up more than 100 square metres (1,000 square feet).

THE RACE FOR REAL-TIME DATA

It's with foodstuffs that *konbinis* achieve most of their turnover, three-quarters to be precise, half of which involves immediate consumption. To further satisfy their customers, these convenience stores rely on a 'just-in-time' supply chain to their shelves, thanks to a continuous real-time data analysis. Before the

Faced with the ageing of Japanese society, the latest trend is the adaptation of konbinis to an increasingly elderly customer base. Inside, everything is designed to make life easier for seniors.

cashiers even scan your first item, they will pass on two pieces of information to the registration machine: your gender and your approximate age. This allows them to know the store's typical customer base in order to refine what they have on sale. In addition to knowing with what to stock on the shelves, this real-time data analysis helps to prevent empty shelves. In fact, the basic principle for a *konbini* is to have no stock in the back room. Thanks to barcodes, the brands' centralized distribution platforms are instantly informed of a sale, and therefore of the stock status of the product on the shelves. Restocking orders are immediately initiated, the information is transmitted to the storage centre which straightaway sends a delivery truck. This way, customers will always be able to find their freshly prepared *onigiris* or a *tamago sando*, the ultra-popular egg sandwich, on the shelves, at any time of the day or night, even in the middle of the midday rush hour.

Observing the trends and changes in these pocket-sized supermarkets also allows us to understand the mechanisms at work in Japanese society. Thus, we could observe that hygiene products took up more and more space on the shelves from the moment that women had an easier access to employment in the archipelago. Certain other items have perhaps disappeared, such as the erotic magazines which might give the stores a bad image at the time of major international competitions such as the Rugby World Cup or the Olympic

Games. The most recent trend, however, is the *konbinis'* effort to adapt to an increasingly elderly clientele. In 2021, over-65-year-olds made up 30 per cent of the Japanese population. Will single men and adolescents, who today remain the largest section of *konbini* clients, soon be replaced by seniors? This could well be the case if we are to believe the latest innovations proposed by the local retail giants. Seven Eleven recently launched a food delivery service for the elderly. The Lawson chain of shops went one step further - in 2006, it opened its first boutique entirely dedicated to seniors in Awaji, a few miles from Kobe. Inside, everything has been designed to make the lives of older customers easier - wider aisles, lower shelves, larger price labels, doors that open automatically and dining areas with tables and chairs where customers can sit and meet friends over a meal. And this is only the beginning, as the brand plans to dedicate 20 per cent of its stores to its elderly consumers by 2025.

HAS THE MODEL REACHED ITS LIMITS?

Despite their unstoppably efficient management, the *konbini* did not foresee the grain of sand that has been slowing down the machine for some time: the difficulty in recruiting staff. Each store is a franchise, and the retailers are responsible for recruiting their teams, which are mainly made up of students, housewives who want to work part-time or workers of foreign origin, mainly from South-East Asia. These *arubaito* - meaning 'small jobs', precarious and poorly paid - no longer find takers, particularly for the night shifts. Faced with the lack of candidates to make up the night shifts, some stores have started to reduce their opening hours, which does not necessarily please their parent companies. A franchisee in the Osaka region paid the price. After closing his *konbini* between 1 a.m. and 6 a.m., he incurred the wrath of Seven Eleven, who threatened him with a penalty of 17 million yen, or 94,000 GBP (119,000 USD) for violating contractual clauses. He eventually lost the franchise for his store. This highly publicized affair led to an investigation followed by a report from the Japanese Fair Trade Commission in October 2020, which called into question the commercial practices of the main chains in the sector and requested a plan of collective measures. Some brands have since given in to pressure and agreed to review the amount of income retained by franchisees. They have started to allow certain stores to reduce their opening hours, a movement accelerated by the Covid-19 pandemic. The *konbini* model, which is the manifestation of an era of strong economic growth, is undoubtedly undergoing its greatest change yet. ▬

Difficulty ●●○

Makes 4 onigiris (serves 2)

Preparation: 24 hours
Cooking: 45 mins

onigiri

1 salmon steak, about 100–120 g (3½–4½ oz)

1 tsp salt, plus extra for salting the fish

300 g (1½ cup) sushi rice

360 ml (1½ cups) filtered water

2 sheets nori seaweed

½ tsp sesame seeds

Preparation

The day before cooking, cover the salmon steak with salt, but do not salt the skin side. Leave it on a plate in the fridge for at least one night – two or three, if possible.

Cook the rice. Gently rinse the rice in clean water without breaking the grains. Repeat two or three times, then drain the rice in a colander. Place the cleaned rice in a saucepan with the filtered water. Cover and leave to rest for at least 30 minutes before cooking. Cook over a high heat for 5 minutes, then reduce to low and cook for 10 minutes. Turn off the heat and leave to rest for another 10 minutes without removing the lid.

Cook the salmon. Using kitchen paper (paper towels), remove any excess salt and water from the surface of the salmon. Place the salmon skin-side down into a hot frying pan, cover, leaving a gap if possible, and cook for 25–30 minutes over very low heat. Once cooked, cut the salmon into four pieces. If you like the skin, you can keep it on to make your *onigiri*; otherwise, remove it now.

In a bowl, combine 100 ml (scant ½ cup) of water and 1 tablespoon of salt. Use to moisten your hands to prevent the rice from sticking to them. Next, put one-quarter (one-fourth) of the rice into your hand; flatten it slightly and make a small hollow in the centre. Place a piece of the prepared salmon into the hollow and form a pyramid without pressing too hard, but enough to hold the shape. Wrap in a seaweed sheet cut into thirds or quarters. Enjoy hot.

If you are preparing the onigri in advance, wrap them in the nori just before serving to keep it crisp.

Difficulty ●○○

Makes 2 tonkatsu (serves 2)

Preparation: 5 mins
Cooking: 15 mins

tonkatsu

100 g (¾ cup) plain (all-purpose) flour

1 egg, beaten with 2 tbsp water

100 g (1 cup) panko breadcrumbs

2 slices pork loin, 1–1.5 cm (⅜–½ in) thick

1 pinch each of salt and black pepper

500 ml (2⅛ cups) oil for frying

¼ cabbage, shredded

4 tbsp tonkatsu sauce

Preparation

Prepare three plates or flat dishes – one for the flour, one for the egg and one for the panko breadcrumbs.

Season the pork loin with the salt and pepper, then cover it completely with flour.

Now dip the floured pork into the beaten egg, then turn it in the breadcrumbs to coat.

Heat the oil in a deep saucepan to 170–180°C (340–230°F), then fry the pork until the breadcrumbs are golden brown. Remove the pork from the oil and drain the excess oil.

Serve with the shredded cabbage and the tonkatsu sauce.

Difficulty ●●○

Makes 18 gyozas
(serves 2–3)

Preparation: 40 mins
Cooking: 12 mins

gyoza

Gyoza dough

125 g (generous 1 cup) plain (all-purpose) flour

2 pinches of salt

85 ml (⅓ cup) boiling water

2 handfuls of potato starch

For the filling

150 g (5¼ oz) cabbage

50 g (1¾ oz) young leeks

50 g (1¾ oz) spring onions (scallions)

¾ tsp salt

150 g (5¼ oz) minced (ground) pork or chicken

1 tsp grated garlic

1 tsp grated ginger

1 tsp sesame oil

1 tsp mirin

1 tsp sake

1 tsp soy sauce

1 pinch finely ground black pepper

Preparation

Making the dough

In a bowl, combine the flour and the salt. Add the hot water and mix with chopsticks or a fork. The dough will not come together at this stage. Knead for a good 5 minutes to form a smooth ball, without any creases or cracks.

Cover the dough with cling film (plastic wrap) or an inverted bowl, and leave to rest for 15–30 minutes at room temperature.

Now cut the dough ball in half and form two logs by rolling it with your hands. Cut each of the logs into nine equal pieces (eighteen in total), then shape them into small balls.

Sprinkle the work surface and one of the balls with potato starch. Flatten the ball with the palm of your hand, then roll it out using a rolling pin. Form a circle about 10 cm (4 in) in diameter, making the edge slightly thinner than the centre. Repeat to make a total of eighteen discs.

Watch out! The dough dries very quickly, so cover it and the balls with a clean cloth while you are not working them to prevent them from hardening.

Making the filling

Finely chop all the vegetables for the stuffing (cabbage, leek and spring onions [scallions]). Add the salt, mix lightly and leave to rest for 10 minutes to allow them to drain.

Put all the other filling ingredients into a bowl and stir to combine well.

Drain the vegetables well, then add the other ingredients. Mix again.

The filling is now ready. Leave it to rest in the refrigerator for 15 minutes.

HOW TO FOLD YOUR GYOZAS CORRECTLY

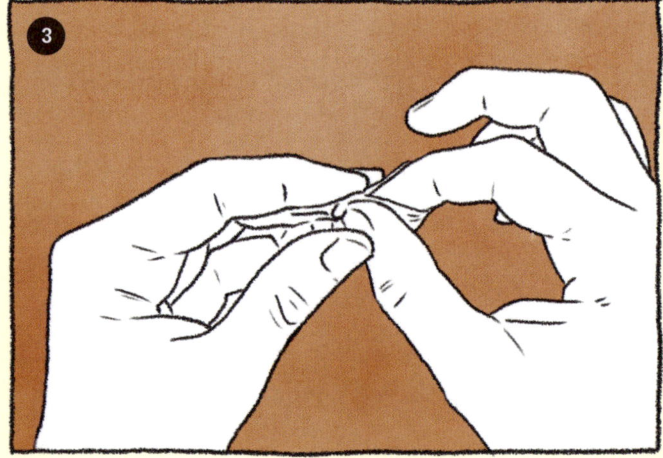

Cooking

1 tbsp vegetable oil

1 tbsp sesame oil (optional)

For the dipping sauce

1 tbsp soy sauce

1 tbsp rice vinegar

a few drops of chilli oil (optional)

Making the gyozas

Sprinkle a large plate with potato starch. Place a bowl of water and a small spoon or butter knife next to it. Take a small disc of dough in your hand, and place 2 tablespoons of the filling on top. Wet the edge of the dough with your fingers, fold it in half and stick the edges together, pinching them to seal. Close the dough tightly to prevent any of the juices from escaping during cooking. Place the gyozas on the plate.

Cooking

Pour the vegetable oil into a frying pan and heat over a high heat, then place the gyozas in the pan next to each other, closed side facing up. Leave to brown for 1–2 minutes. Pour in a glass of water to halfway up the gyozas, cover and cook over a medium heat for 5–10 minutes.

After 5 minutes, lift the lid to let the remaining water evaporate, add the sesame oil, if using, for a crisper finish and cook for another 1–2 minutes. Check that the gyozas are not stuck to the pan. Turn them cooked side up and serve.

Stir all the ingredients for the dipping sauce together to combine.

Enjoy the gyozas hot, dipped into the sauce.

The fish market, a Tokyo institution

Tokyo's new central marketplace for food professionals, the Toyosu market, opened in 2018. Its soul, however, remained in Tsukiji, the historic market where fish were traded in the past.

The clock shows it is a little after five in the morning and the excitement has already peaked inside the large auction hall of the Toyosu market, while the rest of Tokyo is still (mostly) fast asleep. The dark green floor is covered with tuna, all perfectly aligned. The auctioneer, his cap fitted tightly over his head, wearing a striped shirt and his microphone in place, orchestrates this morning's ceremony. Next to him, buyers assess the merchandise and communicate with him via a frantic and clever game of finger movements called *teyari*, their hands wave, draw circles, indicate numbers and, in less than an hour, all the merchandise is sold. Then another kind of ballet begins, that of the forklift trucks which carry the purchased lots to the fishmongers' or restaurateurs' vans. Some have to drive hundreds of miles to get fresh supplies of fish and seafood.
In a matter of minutes, the auction room is emptied; only the still-soaked ground and the polystyrene thermal boxes piled up in a corner bear witness to the recent hive of activity.

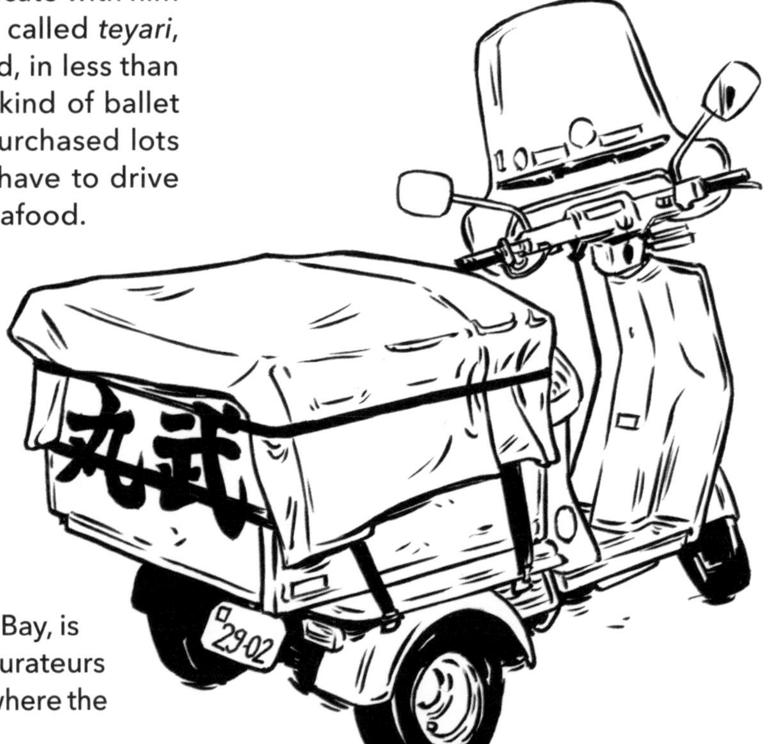

THE LARGEST FISH MARKET IN THE WORLD

Toyosu Market, located in the Odaiba district of Tokyo Bay, is the largest fish market in the world. Traders and restaurateurs flock there from Monday to Saturday. This is, of course, where the

DID YOU KNOW?

Why is the floor of the auction room green while the floors of the other rooms are white? Buyers focus on the bright red colour of the tuna flesh, and that colour stands out more on a green than on a white background.

world-famous tuna auctions are held, but professionals also buy salted and dried fish, sea urchin, live fish, shrimp, octopus, shellfish and simply fresh fish here. Here Tokyo's tables are also supplied with fruit and vegetables, both from the Japanese archipelago and from abroad.

Despite the quality of the products on sale, however, the shiny new Toyosu market never managed to win all the votes, either from the professionals or from the visitors. Opened in 2018, it succeeded the iconic Tsukiji Market, whose pulse had been beating since 1936. Deemed too small for the volume of business, decaying and no longer meeting the latest building standards to ensure it could withstand an earthquake, the market closed its doors. All the activity moved to Toyosu, less than 3 km (2 miles) away, but in a much less accessible area. Less easy to find but also – and above all – heavily polluted. Indeed, during the first environmental controls, the levels of arsenic, cyanide, mercury and benzene, among others, far exceeded the maximum levels authorized by the current legislation – the soil and the groundwater still bore the scars of the old gas plant which previously occupied the site. The opening of the market was therefore postponed to allow for the decontamination of the area, and it was not until October 2018 that the first tuna auction took place under the gaze of cameras from around the world.

Toyosu is a gigantic complex made up of three buildings, dedicated respectively to auctions, wholesale sales and the fruit and vegetable market, all connected by walkways. The routes are signposted and visitors are now asked to watch the auctions and wholesale sales from special observation decks, perched several metres (yards) above the ground and separated from the activity by a large window. 'Although a small gap has been left open between the glass and the ceiling so that visitors can hear a little of what is happening and smell some of the odours, the impression is more that of being in a museum than in a fish market,' regrets Akiko, who came to watch the auction with her son Sota. 'The building where you can most easily soak up the atmosphere is the one dedicated to fruit and vegetable sales, which is somewhat surprising for a market that is famous for its fish!' The excitement is perhaps what is missing from this market where sushi and other seafood products are now enjoyed in restaurants and no longer standing right in front of the fishmongers' stalls, where visitors would have bought their purchases. 'It's as if the soul of Tokyo, which has lived in these markets for centuries, has died a little,' laments Sota.

THE MARKETS, A CENTURY-OLD STORY

In Japan, the wholesale of fish dates back to the barter trade of the Edo period (1603–1867). Fishmongers who supplied the Tokugawa Shogunate were then allowed to sell the remainder of their catch to locals near the Nihonbashi Bridge. The latter, which now connects the Ginza district with Tokyo Station, was the starting point of Japan's five major routes. During the Taishō era (1868–1926), markets played an important role in securing supplies for the population, but World War I caused prices to sky-rocket so that in 1918, rice riots broke out. The Market Act of 1923 entitled the city to prioritize the creation of a central wholesale market which made it possible to stabilize the prices of foodstuffs. Then in 1923 the Great Kanto earthquake struck and devastated the Japanese capital. It was finally in the year 1935 that the Tsukiji Market was created, following the creation of a wholesale public procurement system by the metropolitan government of Tokyo.

Although the main building closed its doors in 2018, the outdoor market still remains open to this day, and food shops, kitchen utensil stands and restaurants continue their activity in the maze of lanes that surround the old building.

Even when the rain descends on Tokyo, nothing seems to stop the gourmets who open their transparent umbrellas as they head to the next culinary stop. 'I didn't want to move to the new market because I didn't really have the means to do so,' explains fishmonger Yukio Okiguchi. 'I mainly sell to individuals and since this is not possible in Toyosu, I would have lost some of my income. So I decided to stay here instead, and judging by the results I think I made the right decision,' he confides with a smile, before serving one of the many customers waiting in front of his stand.

TSUKIJI, 'A PIECE OF JAPANESE CULINARY HISTORY'

Next to the fishmonger, Takashi and Yasuko Shioda are putting their shop in order. There are no empty spaces on the shelves. Every small area is occupied by bags of seeds, spices and condiments essential in the preparation of delicious Japanese specialities. Yasuko has been running this store since 1954, today supported by her son. They did not have the means to move to the new market either, and the uncertainty of hanging on to their customers was too great. 'Here, people can come on foot from their homes. The restaurateurs with whom we work can get here without getting stuck in traffic jams – which is not at all the case at the new market. It was too risky for us, so we stayed.'

Tomoko was born and raised in Tokyo. Today, she is showing one of her English friends around the market. Leaning on the high table set up a stone's throw from the stalls of the Saito Suisan fish market, they are getting ready to sample the sea urchins, plucked fresh out of the water. 'Tsukiji saw me grow up. I came with my grandmother, my mother and today I am taking my friends here, even though the main building is now closed. It is much more than a fish market, Tsukiji is a gigantic part of the culinary history of Japan.'

面白い

TOYOSU IN NUMBERS

- 500: The number of different types of fish that are sold at the Toyosu market.
- 270: The number of different kinds of fruits and vegetables found on Toyosu's stalls.
- 42,000: The number of people who work at Toyosu Market every day.
- 2.5 GBP (3.2 USD): The total market turnover recorded for the year 2020.

山鰹節
けづり
秋山
加盟店
14-16
築地 東通り
Refund IN CASH
築地 土産
1,200円

築地
四丁目
12-8
中央区
築地四丁目
12
Chuo-ku
Tsukiji
4-chome

Difficulty ●●○ | Serves 4 | Preparation: 30 mins | Cooking: 30 mins

kaisendon

For the sushi rice

450 g (2¼ cups) sushi rice

560 ml (2⅓ cups) filtered water

110 ml (scant ½ cup) rice or cider vinegar

40 g (scant 3 tbsp) sugar

12 g (2½ tsp) salt

For the Japanese omelette

3 eggs

1 tbsp sugar

½ tsp soy sauce

1 pinch of salt

oil for cooking

shiso leaves (optional)

nori sheets (optional)

For the garnish

about 15 thin slices of raw fish of your choice (salmon, tuna, sea bream, prawn [shrimp], etc. or salmon roe)

For the dipping sauce

a slice of lemon

shiso or nori sheet (optional)

soy sauce

wasabi (optional)

Preparation

Cooking the rice

Gently rinse the rice in two of three changes of water taking care not to break up the grains, then drain it in a colander.

Put the washed rice and filtered water into a saucepan, cover and leave to stand for at least 30 minutes before cooking.

Cover and cook over a high heat for 5 minutes. Once it has come to the boil, reduce the heat and simmer for 10 minutes. Turn off the heat and leave to stand, covered, for 10 minutes.

In a small bowl, combine the rice or cider vinegar, sugar and salt.

Spread the cooked rice over the surface of a large flat tray.

Add the vinegar mixture and stir gently while cooling the rice with a fan.

Making the Japanese omelette

Beat the eggs with the sugar, soy sauce and salt.

Heat the oil in a frying pan, then pour in a small quantity of the beaten egg to form a thin omelette.

As soon as the omelette is cooked, roll it up like a crepe and place on one side of the pan.

If necessary, grease the pan with a piece of oiled paper (kitchen) towel, then pour in another small amount of the egg mixture, lifting up the rolled-up omelette slightly so that a little of the egg mixture goes underneath it.

Roll up the new omelette together with the existing omelette and place on one side of the pan. Repeat this operation until you no longer have any of the egg mixture left.

Presentation

Place the sushi rice in a bowl and arrange slices of raw fish and omelette on top. Garnish with lemon, finely sliced shiso or nori sheet and serve with soy sauce and wasabi, if desired.

Difficulty ●○○ Serves 4 Preparation: 35 mins Cooking: 20 mins

fukagawa meshi

450 g (2¼ cups) sushi rice
50 g (1¾ oz) carrots
20 g (¾ oz) ginger
800 g (1¾ lb) mussels

For the broth

520 ml (2⅛ cups) dashi stock (or 520 ml/ 2⅛ cups water + 8 g/ 2 tsp freeze-dried dashi)
50 ml (generous 3 tbsp) sake
½ tbsp soy sauce
1 tsp salt

Preparation

Gently rinse the rice in two or three changes of water taking care not to break up the grains. Place the rice in a pan of fresh water and leave to stand for 30 minutes.

Cut the carrots into small cubes.

Finely chop the ginger.

In a saucepan, combine the dashi stock or the water and the freeze-dried dashi, with the sake, soy sauce and salt. Add the mussels and cook until they open.

Drain the mussels, reserving the broth. Remove the mussels from their shells and discard the shells.

Drain the rice in a colander. Put it into a saucepan together with the broth from the mussels, the carrots and the ginger. Cover and bring to a boil, then lower the heat and simmer for about 12 minutes. Turn off the heat, add the mussels, cover and leave to stand for 10 minutes.

Difficulty ●○○

Makes 8 temakis (serves 3 or 4)

Preparation: 40 mins
Cooking: 30 mins

salted salmon temaki

For the sushi rice

450 g (2¼ cups) sushi rice

560 ml (2⅓ cups) filtered water

110 ml (scant ½ cup) rice or cider vinegar

40 g (scant 3 tbsp) sugar

12 g (2½ tsp) salt

For the variations (A to D)

A. 1 slice of smoked salmon

A. ½ avocado

B. 2 cooked prawns (shrimp)

B. ½ avocado

C. ¼ onion

C. 1 pinch of salt

C. 1 small tin (can) tuna

C. 1 tsp mayonnaise

D. ½ cucumber

D. 2 shiso leaves

4 nori sheets

wasabi (optional)

shiso leaves, chopped (optional)

soy sauce, for dipping

Preparation

Cooking the rice

Gently rinse the rice in two of three changes of water taking care not to break up the grains, then drain it in a colander.

Put the washed rice and filtered water into a saucepan, cover and leave to stand for at least 30 minutes before cooking.

Cover and cook over a high heat for 5 minutes. Once it has come to the boil, reduce the heat and simmer for 10 minutes. Turn off the heat and leave to stand, covered, for 10 minutes.

In a small bowl, combine the rice or cider vinegar, sugar and salt.

Spread the cooked rice over the surface of a large flat tray.

Add the vinegar mixture and stir gently while cooling the rice with a fan.

Preparing the 4 variations:

A. Cut the slice of smoked salmon in half. Cut the avocado into four or five equal wedges.

B. Peel the prawns (shrimp) and make three or four small cuts into the belly of each to straighten them. Cut the avocado lengthways into four to five equal wedges.

C. Finely chop the onion and combine with the salt. Add the tuna and mayonnaise. Mix well.

D. Cut the cucumber into julienne strips. Wash the shiso leaves.

Presentation

Cut the nori sheets in half. Place half a nori sheet in one hand. Gently spread 3 tablespoons sushi rice on top, then place the topping of your choice (A to D) in the centre of the rice. And add some wasabi and chopped shiso, if desired.

Roll up the nori sheet with the ingredients inside. Dip in the soy sauce and enjoy.

A walk through the Kappabashi-dori, the street of food lovers

Ceramic tableware, kitchen utensils, pans, knives and even ovens ... You can find everything and the kitchen sink in this 800-metre-long (875-yard-long) Tokyo street entirely dedicated to kitchenware and cooking.

Just look at him! With his white hat, a little sky-blue scarf tied around his neck and his well-brushed black moustache, the chef perched on the top of the building marks the start of Kappabashi-dori. This Tokyo street, also known as Kitchen Town, is legendary to cooks and food lovers. There's plenty of everything - in just over 800 metres (875 yards) there are no fewer than 160 stores dedicated to the culinary arts - except that no fresh products line the shelves here. Instead, Kappabashi-dori is a temple to utensils, tableware and household appliances. It was at the beginning of the 20th century, in around 1910, that this street, located between the Ueno and Asakusa districts in the northeast of the capital, first saw its arcades occupied by specialist (specialty) businesses. Initially reserved for wholesale companies selling to professionals, the stores gradually opened up to retail, and eventually to all types of customers.

Here, you'll find everything, from the absolutely essential to the most deliciously improbable. It was obvious that some shops were destined to become iconic institutions, for example Kama-Asa. You will find iron pans, cast-iron products and even handmade saucepans here. But in fact, it is mostly for its knives that all the chefs from Tokyo and elsewhere flock here. Since 1908, Kama-Asa has developed an unparalleled expertise in Japanese blades. The store sells numerous different types of knives, mainly manufactured in the Sakai region, the cradle of Japanese cutlery, which is only a stone's throw from Osaka.

A CUTTING HISTORY OF JAPAN

By focusing on the blades, their shapes and their lengths, we can learn much more about the history and practices of Japanese cuisine than from any type of culinary handbook. Until the middle of the 20th century, Japanese blades were all single-edged – the blades are bevelled and only cut on one side. It is important to understand that the advantage of this is that a single-edged knife cuts through the fibres of the food without damaging them. Within this category there are, however, a multitude of different knives dedicated to specific types of cuts.

Thus, we find knives with long, thin blades like the *fuguhiki* or the *yanagiba*, which are used to slice fish. The blade is longer than normal and allows the fish to be sliced in a single cut, without damaging the fibres of the flesh. A discerning eye will even be able to tell you if the blade comes from Kansai (in the Kyoto and Osaka region) or Kanto (Tokyo). There are also knives with thicker blades, such as *deba* and *ajikiri*, which are ideal for filleting fish. And finally, there are knives, such as the *kamagata usuba* and the *azumagata usuba,* exclusively designed for chopping vegetables.

During the Meiji era (1868-1912), Japan opened its borders and Western cultures swept across the archipelago. This is when the first double-edged blades appeared in Japanese kitchens. Local blacksmiths and knife sharpeners also began manufacturing these knives, and today they are among the bestselling

knives on the planet. Japanese cutlery is booming – according to Japanese customs declarations, exports reached a record 77 million GBP (99 million USD) in 2021, twice as much as 20 years ago.

FROM THE ESSENTIAL TO THE SUPERFLUOUS

A few metres (yards) along we find Kanaya, a paradise of brushes entirely made in Japan, from the handles to the bristles, since 1914. Entering this store means discovering that there are many more types of brushes than you could have imagined. You can brush your pets, the smallest folds and recesses in your clothes and shoes, your floor coverings or car seats – using the correct tool every time.

In the middle of the shop is a space dedicated to cookery. Before your very eyes, there is a multitude of sauce brushes, with bristles of different types and densities depending on the sauce that you intend to make to enhance your food. There are also condiment brushes, vegetable brushes and even specific brushes for cleaning frying pans, saucepans and other items ... It has to be said that, without the detailed explanations from the salesperson or the small instruction labels, the uninitiated eye would not be able to play the 'find the difference' game. It's all in the details. The materials used for their manufacture varies: the pan brush must not damage the surface, a brush for glasses needs to reach the bottom of the glass easily and, above all, without leaving any scratches.

On the same stretch of the road, a little further along under the arcades, Katsutoshi Arai is busy with his cookie cutters, while his wife carefully wraps an enormous stainless-steel cake pan. Their shop, Arai, was established on the street in 1949. In this bric-a-brac store, no larger than a pocket handkerchief, you will find neat stacks of everything you need for baking. Whisks, spoons, piping bags, waffle irons, cake pans and cookie cutters in all sizes, from the tiniest to the most ambitious. 'I don't think you can leave here empty-handed,' says Katsutoshi Arai with a broad grin on his face. For several decades already, chefs and home cooks have paraded through his store. He has watched pastry fashions evolve through their purchases. 'We sell fewer and fewer wooden moulds for *wagashi*. On the other hand, for some time now, there has been an increase in demand for individual cake pans, and the same goes for Japanese cheesecake pans,' explains the vendor, who makes a point of offering pans almost exclusively made from stainless steel. 'They are the best on the market. This doesn't necessarily suit me because we keep them for a very long time, and this is why I offer lots of different sizes and shapes. When you love cooking, you always want to try new things, right?'

It was at the beginning of the 20th century, in around 1910, that this street, located between the Ueno and Asakusa districts in the northeast of the capital, first saw its arcades occupied by specialist (specialty) businesses.

TOKYO GA

Sampuru fascinate the world beyond the borders of Japan. The German filmmaker Wim Wenders visited the manufacturing workshops and filmed the meticulous stages of their production at a time when the food displays were still mainly made from wax. To find out more about it, watch *Tokyo Ga*, a documentary released in 1985.

JAPAN, HOME OF THE *SAMPURU*

Finally, the Kappabashi-dori also hosts a special shop, where the ice creams never melt, whatever the temperature, where the skewers of chicken seem to have been taken off the charcoal at that very moment and where the broth has only just been added to the bowl of ramen. Everything makes you salivate and yet, when you open the door, your nostrils will not detect the slightest aroma. Ganso Shokuhin Sample-ya sells *sampuru*, an adaptation from the English word 'sample'. These larger-than-life food figurines are moulded from silicone and meticulously hand-painted by specialist artisans.

Sampuru adorn many restaurant windows to present the dishes that are prepared in the kitchen to their potential customers. The custom dates back to the 1940s, when these artificial food models were still made of wax. The origins of the sampuru are unclear. Some explain their popularity with the growing number of - non-Japanese speaking - foreigners visiting the archipelago during this period. Others believe that they allowed the Japanese to familiarize themselves with the new dishes that Japanese restaurateurs were starting to offer.

More than half a century later, *sampuru* are still quintessential to the country. Although most are now made in China, Japan remains the master of this meticulous art, and the most beautiful pieces, mostly made by artisans from the town of Gujo in the Japanese Alps, are now worth a small fortune. With the arrival of silicone, which replaced the wax, the *sampuru* became more hardwearing. The production methods have also been adapted. While the restaurateurs of today buy far fewer models, the needs of the foreign tourists now seem to dominate the scene - today, the artisan workshops produce sushi, *gyozas* and tempura as key chains, magnets and even earrings - lasting culinary memories to take back home in your luggage. ▬

shio ramen

<u>For the noodles</u>

160 ml (generous ⅔ cup) filtered water (40% of the weight of the flour)

4 g (⅔ tsp) salt (1% of the weight of the flour)

2 g (½ tsp) bicarbonate of soda (baking soda) (0.5% of the weight of the flour)

400 g (3¼ cups) plain (all-purpose) flour (preferably with a protein content of about 12%)

2 g (½ tsp) potassium bicarbonate (0.5% of the weight of the flour) (if you can't find potassium bicarbonate, replace it with bicarbonate of soda [baking soda])

4–5 handfuls of potato starch

Preparation

<u>Making the noodles</u>

Weigh all ingredients accurately. In a small bowl, combine the water, salt, bicarbonate of soda (baking soda) and potassium bicarbonate. Stir well to dissolve.

Sift the flour into a large bowl. Gradually pour the water mixture onto the flour, using a circular movement, until you have added all of it.

Using chopsticks, mix the flour and water to distribute the liquid evenly, until small crumbs form. Make sure that no flour remains stuck to the sides of the bowl. At this point, the dough will resemble breadcrumbs rather than being a homogenous mixture. Place the dough in a large resealable plastic food (zip lock) bag and seal it carefully so that the dough does not dry out. Leave to rest for 1 hour until the water has been absorbed by the flour.

After 1 hour, start kneading the dough. The easiest way is to do this is with your feet. Open the bag a little to let the air out. Place a sheet or towel on a clean floor, place the bag with the dough on the towel, and flatten the dough by taking small steps on the bag. When the dough is flat and has filled the bag, open the bag and fold the dough towards the centre in thirds.

Return the dough to the bag, seal it and repeat the operation three more times.

Leave the flattened dough in the bag, seal it and leave to rest for at least 2 hours or a whole day, if possible.

After this, cut the dough into 4 equal pieces and flatten them using a rolling pin to form strips.

A. If you have a pasta machine, put the dough in the machine, start at level 0 (the thickest) then gradually thin it by moving from one level to another, until the desired thickness has been achieved (the recommended thickness is about 1–1.2 mm/about 1⁄25 in, level 5 on my Marcato Atlas 150 machine).

Next, sprinkle both sides of the dough with potato starch, and cut the noodles to the desired width. The width of standard spaghetti is ideal.

For the soup

500 g (18 oz pork bone (preferably thigh) (if you can't find bones or carcasses, use 1 kg/ 2¼ lb chicken wings and 300 g/10½ oz minced [ground] pork)

1 chicken carcass

2 chicken drumsticks

2.2 l (9⅓ cups) water

1 leek (green parts only)

1 slice of ginger

For the chashu

300 g (10½ oz) pork loin or belly, in one piece

150 ml (⅔ cup) soy sauce

50 ml (generous 3 tbsp) mirin

B. If you don't have a pasta machine, flatten each strip of dough to about 1–1.5 mm (about 1/25 in) thickness using a rolling pin. Sprinkle both sides with potato starch, fold them in half and cut the noodles to the desired width.

Once the noodles are cut, sprinkle on some more potato starch to prevent them from sticking together, turn them two or three times so that they are completely covered with the starch, then leave to rest in a large food container for 1 or 2 days. The noodles can be eaten immediately after making, but they are always better 1 or 2 days later.

To get slightly curly noodles, simply take a portion of noodles in your hands and gently but firmly squeeze them into shape.

Making the soup

The day before, clean and soak the pork bones in water to remove the blood. Leave to soak overnight in the refrigerator or in a cool place. After soaking, discard the water.

Break up the bones and carcass using a hammer, or chop them so that they will fit inside your pressure cooker. (This step is not necessary if you are using chicken wings and minced [ground] meat.)

Put the bones and the carcass (or the chicken wings and the minced [ground] pork), drumsticks and water into the pressure cooker.

Bring to a boil over a high heat, uncovered. Once the liquid comes to a boil and a brown foam appears, reduce the heat to medium and begin to skim. It is important to remove the foam for 15–20 minutes to obtain a clear soup.

Cover and close the pressure cooker. Cook over a medium heat. Wait for the pressure to build, then cook for 1 hour over a low heat.

After 1 hour, turn off the heat and let the temperature reduce so you can open the lid.

Open the lid, remove the layer of fat on the surface and set aside. (It will be used as an oil to flavour the ramen.)

Now add the pork for the chashu, the leek greens and the ginger.

Cook for 1½ hours over a medium to low heat, uncovered. Adjust the heat so that the water boils, forming large bubbles.

After 1½ hours, remove the pork and strain the soup. The soup is now ready. You can keep it in the freezer and use it as a base soup for several preparations such as *tantan men, shoyu ramen …*

Making the chashu

Put the cooked pork into a small resealable (zip lock) bag, together with the soy sauce and the mirin. Remove the air from the bag so that the entire surface of the meat is in contact with the marinade. Leave to marinate for at least 1 hour.

For the *shio tare*

10 g (⅓ oz) dried scallops

3 dried shiitake mushrooms

20 g (¾ oz) katsuobushi (bonito flakes) (thick shavings if possible)

10 g (⅓ oz) kombu seaweed

250 ml (generous 1 cup) filtered water

1 tbsp mirin

50 ml (generous 3 tbsp) sake

1 tsp soy sauce

2 tbsp salt

For the *ajitsuke tamago*

40 ml (scant 3 tbsp) soy sauce

30 ml (2 tbsp) water

20 ml (generous 1 tbsp) mirin

8 g (scant 2 tsp) sugar

4 eggs

Garnishes (of your choice)

2 or 3 spring onions (scallions)

flavouring oil

finely ground black pepper (optional)

cooked beansprouts (optional)

marinated bamboo shoots (optional)

Making the *shio tare*

Place all the dry ingredients (scallops, shiitake, *katsuobushi* and kombu) into a saucepan, add the filtered water to cover everything. and leave to soak overnight.

The next day, cook everything in the pan over a low heat, letting it simmer gently so that the ingredients dance lightly in the pan. One minute after the boiling point has been reached, remove the kombu, then continue to cook for 40 minutes. Now remove all other ingredients, leaving only the sauce.

Add the mirin, sake, soy sauce and salt; boil for 1 minute before turning off the heat and leaving to cool. The *shio tare* is now ready.

Making the *ajitsuke tamago*

In a small saucepan, combine all the liquid ingredients (soy sauce, water and mirin) and the sugar for the *ajitsuke tamago*, then bring everything to a boil. Turn off the heat and leave to cool.

In another saucepan, bring some water to the boil and carefully lower in the eggs (use them straight from the refrigerator). Cook for 7–8 minutes, then remove them from the pan and cool in cold water. Remove the shells, then place the cooked eggs into a small resealable (zip lock) bag together the *ajitsuke tamago* sauce. Remove the air from the bag so that the eggs are in direct contact with the marinade. Leave to marinate for 3 hours.

Preparing the garnishes

Chop the spring onions (scallions), halve the *ajitsuke tamago* lengthways, slice the *chashu* and prepare your chosen garnishes.

Presentation

Heat the soup, using approximately 300 ml (1¼ cups) per person.

Cook 140 g (5 oz) of noodles per person in plenty of boiling water for about 2 minutes. If you are cooking a lot of noodles, choose a saucepan that is large enough to hold them all. Drain carefully.

Just before the noodles are cooked, put 2 tablespoons *shio tare*, 1 tablespoon flavouring oil and a little finely ground black pepper into the bottom of a bowl, then add the heated soup (adjust the amount of *tare* according to your taste).

Carefully put the cooked noodles into the bowl of soup, then add the *chashu*, *ajitsuke tamago*, spring onions (scallions), beansprouts and bamboo shoots, if desired. Enjoy hot.

Difficulty ●●● Serves 4 Preparation: 2 days
Cooking: 4 hours

shoyu ramen

For the noodles

160 ml (⅔ cup) filtered water (40% of the weight of the flour)

4 g (⅔ tsp) salt (1% of the weight of the flour)

2 g (½ tsp) bicarbonate of soda (baking soda) (0.5% of the weight of the flour)

400 g (3¼ cups) plain (all-purpose) flour (preferably with a protein content of about 12%)

2 g (½ tsp) potassium bicarbonate (0.5% of the weight of the flour) (if you can't find potassium bicarbonate, replace it with bicarbonate of soda [baking soda])

4–5 handfuls of potato starch

Preparation

Making the noodles

Weigh all ingredients accurately. In a small bowl, combine the water, salt, bicarbonate of soda (baking soda) and potassium bicarbonate. Stir well to dissolve.

Sift the flour into a large bowl. Gradually pour the water mixture onto the flour, using a circular movement, until you have added all of it.

Using chopsticks, mix the flour and water to distribute the liquid evenly, until small crumbs form. Make sure that no flour remains stuck to the sides of the bowl. At this point, the dough will resemble breadcrumbs rather than being a homogenous mixture. Place the dough in a large resealable plastic food (zip lock) bag and seal it carefully so that the dough does not dry out. Leave to rest for 1 hour until the water has been absorbed by the flour.

After 1 hour, start kneading the dough. The easiest way is to do this is with your feet. Open the bag a little to let the air out. Place a sheet or towel on a clean floor, place the bag with the dough on the towel, and flatten the dough by taking small steps on the bag. When the dough is flat and has filled the bag, open the bag and fold the dough towards the centre in thirds.

Return the dough to the bag, seal it, and repeat the operation three more times.

Leave the flattened dough in the bag, seal it and leave to rest for at least 2 hours or a whole day, if possible.

After this, cut the dough into 4 equal pieces and flatten them using a rolling pin to form strips.

A. If you have a pasta machine, put the dough in the machine, start at level 0 (the thickest) then gradually thin it by moving from one level to another, until the desired thickness has been achieved (the recommended thickness is about 1–1.2 mm (about 1⁄25 in), level 5 on my Marcato Atlas 150 machine).

Next, sprinkle both sides of the dough with potato starch and cut the noodles of the desired width. The width of standard spaghetti is ideal.

For the soup

500 g (18 oz pork bone (preferably thigh) (if you can't find bones or carcasses, use 1 kg/2¼ lb chicken wings and 300 g/10½ oz minced [ground] pork)

1 chicken carcass

2 chicken drumsticks

2.2 l (10 cups) water

1 leek (green parts only)

1 slice ginger

B. If you don't have a pasta machine, flatten each strip of dough to about 1–1.5 mm (about 1⁄25 in) thickness using a rolling pin. Sprinkle both sides with potato starch, fold them in half and cut the noodles to the desired width.

Once the noodles are cut, sprinkle some more potato starch to prevent them from sticking together, turn them two or three times so that they are completely covered with the starch, then leave to rest in a large food container for 1 or 2 days. The noodles can be eaten immediately after making, but they are always better 1 or 2 days later.

To get slightly curly noodles, simply take a portion of noodles in your hands and gently but firmly squeeze them into shape.

Making the soup

The day before, clean and soak the pork bones in water to remove the blood. Leave to soak overnight in the refrigerator or in a cool place. After soaking, discard the water.

Break up the bones and carcass using a hammer, or chop them so that they will fit inside your pressure cooker. (This step is not necessary if you are using chicken wings and minced [ground] meat.)

Put the bones and the carcass, drumsticks and water into the pressure cooker.

Bring to a boil over a high heat, uncovered. Once the liquid comes to a boil and a brown foam appears, reduce the heat to medium and begin to skim. It is important to remove the foam for 15–20 minutes to obtain a clear soup.

Cover and close the pressure cooker. Cook over a medium heat. Wait for the pressure to build, then cook for 1 hour over a low heat.

After 1 hour, turn off the heat and let the temperature go down so you can open the lid.

Open the lid, remove the layer of fat on the surface and set aside. (It will be used as an oil to flavour the ramen.)

Now add the pork for the chashu, the leek and the ginger.

Cook for 1½ hours over a medium to low heat, uncovered. Adjust the heat so that the water boils, forming large bubbles.

After 1½ hours, remove the pork and strain the soup. The soup is now ready. You can keep it in the freezer and use it as a base soup for other preparations, such as *tantan men, shoyu ramen …*

For the *chashu*

300 g (10½ oz) pork loin or belly, in one piece

150 ml (⅔ cup) soy sauce

50 ml (generous 3 tbsp) mirin

For the *shoyu tare*

8 g (2 tsp) dried scallops

2 dried shiitake mushrooms

8 g (2 tsp) katsuobushi (bonito flakes), thick shavings if possible)

200 ml (generous ¾ cup) filtered water

1 tbsp mirin

1 tbsp rice vinegar

150 ml (⅔ cup) soy sauce

For the *ajitsuke tamago*

40 ml (scant 3 tbsp) soy sauce

2 tbsp water

20 ml (1½ tbsp) mirin

8 g (2 tsp) sugar

4 eggs

Garnishes (optional)

2 or 3 spring onions (scallions), chopped

flavouring oil

cooked soya beans (optional)

finely ground black pepper (optional)

marinated bamboo shoots (optional)

Making the *chashu*

Put the cooked pork into a small resealable (zip lock) bag, together with the soy sauce and the mirin. Remove the air from the bag so that the entire surface of the meat is in contact with the flavourings. Leave to marinate for at least 1 hour.

Making the *shoyu tare*

Place all the dry ingredients (scallops, shiitake, *katsuobushi*) into a saucepan; add the filtered water and leave to soak overnight.

The next day, cook everything in the pan over a low heat, letting it simmer gently so that the ingredients dance lightly in the pan. Add the mirin and the vinegar, then cook for another 10 minutes. Now remove all the other ingredients, leaving only the sauce.

Turn off the heat, add the soy sauce and leave to cool. The *tare* is now ready.

Making the *ajitsuke tamago*

In a small saucepan, combine the soy sauce, water, mirin and sugar. Bring to the boil, then turn off the heat and leave to cool.

In another saucepan, bring some water to the boil, then carefully add the eggs (use them straight from the refrigerator). Cook for 7–8 minutes, then remove them from the pan. Cool in cold water. Remove the shells, then place the cooked eggs into a small resealable (zip lock) bag together with the *ajitsuke tamago* marinade. Remove the air from the bag so that the eggs are in direct contact with the marinade. Leave to marinate for 3 hours.

Preparing the garnishes

Chop the spring onions (scallions), halve the *ajitsuke tamago* lengthways, slice the *chashu* and prepare your chosen garnishes.

Presentation

Heat the soup, using about 300 ml (1¼ cups) per person.

Cook 140 g (5 oz) noodles per person in plenty of boiling water for about 2 minutes. if you are cooking a lot of noodles, use a saucepan that is large enough to hold them all. Drain well.

Just before the noodles are cooked, add 2 tablespoons *shoyu tare*, 1 tablespoon flavouring oil (reserved pork fat) and a little ground black pepper to the bottom of a bowl, then pour the heated soup on top (adjust the amount of *tare* according to your taste).

Gently put the cooked noodles into the bowl, then add the *chashu*, *ajitsuke tamago* and garnishes of your choice. Enjoy hot.

Difficulty ●●○

Makes 8 tenmusus (serves 2)

Preparation: 2 hours
Cooking: 15 mins

tenmusu

300 g (1½ cups) sushi rice

360 ml (1½ cups) filtered water

1 tbsp salt

For the tempura

8 raw prawns (shrimp) (or a vegetable or meat of your choice)

1 tbsp soy sauce

1 tsp grated garlic

1 tbsp potato starch

60 g (scant ½ cup) plain (all-purpose) flour

60 ml (¼ cup) chilled sparkling water (you can use still water but sparkling water will give you a crispier batter)

1 tsp salt

500 ml (2 cups) oil for deep frying

2 sheets nori

Preparation

Cooking the rice

Gently rinse the rice in cold water without breaking the grains. Repeat two or three times and drain in a colander.

Transfer the washed rice to a saucepan, add the filtered water, cover and leave to soak for at least 30 minutes before cooking.

Cook covered over a high heat for 5 minutes. When it comes to the boil, reduce the heat and simmer, covered, for 10 minutes. Turn off the heat and leave to rest, covered, for 10 minutes.

Preparing the tempura

Shell and devein the prawns (shrimp). If they are very large, cut them in half lengthways.

Put the prawns (shrimp) into a bowl, add the soy sauce, garlic and potato starch and stir to combine. Leave to marinate for 1 hour.

In a small bowl, combine the flour, chilled sparkling water and salt to make a batter. Dip the marinated prawns (shrimp) in the batter to coat them all over.

In a small saucepan, heat the oil to 180°C (360°F), add the prawns (shrimp) and cook them, turning them from time to time. Remove the prawns (shrimp) from the oil before they get too brown and place on a rack to drain.

Assembling the *tenmusu*

In a bowl, combine 100 ml (scant ½ cup) water and 1 tablespoon salt. Stir well. Dip your hands in this saltwater to prevent the rice from sticking to them.

Take one-eighth of the cooked rice in one hand and shape into a ball. Make a small hollow in the centre of the ball of rice and place a prawn (shrimp) inside, then shape into a pyramid using both hands and without pressing too hard. Leave some of the prawn (shrimp) sticking out from the top of the pyramid. Quarter a sheet of nori lengthways, then wrap one piece around the rice pyramid. Enjoy hot or cold.

Ryōko Sekiguchi: 'As there is no farmland here, Tokyo makes use of all that is available.'

Ryōko Sekiguchi is a writer and translator. She writes mostly about culture – whether Japanese, French, Lebanese or Italian – and its connection to food. But what happens when she takes a closer look, both sharp and poetic, at the city of her birth, to which she returns every year? This is Tokyo, as seen through the eyes of Ryōko Sekiguchi.

You grew up in Shinjuku, then you left for France where you settled in 1997. But you frequently return to Japan. Have you noticed any changes in the culinary world of Tokyo between your childhood and today?

Where to begin? I've been in this world for more than 50 years, so, yes, of course there have been changes! The most striking thing is that there are now fewer and fewer, if not almost none, of the traditional specialist stores, such as tofu shops or fishmongers ... I heard that each year, nearly 100 fish stores close in Japan. When I was young, I lived quite close to a tofu store. My task was to go there with our box and bring back the tofu. Each customer used to bring their own container. In a way, this was quite eco-friendly before it became fashionable. I had to be careful not to spill anything, and I was very proud when I managed to avoid doing so. We also had a local butcher, who made some excellent *korokke*. And there was even someone who made sweets; we watched in anticipation while he made them!

As in France, people now tend go to the supermarket rather than the corner shop. Efforts are still being made, especially by the younger generations, to preserve the recipes of yesteryear and the unique taste of Tokyo. For example, *edo miso*, which disappeared after the war. So not everything is without hope.

Do you think that the 'taste' of Tokyo has evolved at all as the city becomes ever more densely populated and concreted over?

I think it's easy to forget that a whole range of foods were once produced, harvested, fished and cooked in the city of Tokyo itself! Tokyo is the largest city in the world, so we think it's normal that everything is concreted over and that nothing is produced here anymore, but that's not really the case. It is so today, but it was very different in the past. Without even going as far back as the Edo period, vegetables, such as *komatsuna*, were grown in Tokyo, and they were really unique to the town. Itabashi-ku, a district in the north of Tokyo, was renowned for its

many vegetable gardens and fields, as well as the daikons that were grown there.

Nori seaweed was cultivated in Tokyo Bay, and fishing played a major role here. *Tsukudani* – tiny fish that are cooked with sake, shoyu and mirin – was a side dish that Tokyoites had all the time at home. That, I think, is the typical taste of Tokyo. Today we tend to think that in Tokyo everything comes from the other regions of Japan, but no, there once existed a genuinely local cuisine here, at least it did when I was a child.

What was the tipping point?

I think it all happened in the 1980s. Most of these small artisans lived in historic districts, which became very popular on the property market. For example, in my grandparents' area, I saw real estate developers who came and 'offered' to sell people's homes because prices were increasing – they behaved almost like *yakuza* (a notorious crime syndicate). So obviously, if you threaten people and offer them a good price, they will sell and leave the area. They will move to Chiba, Ibaraki or Kanagawa, and that's how we lost a lot of our local know-how.

Are there any iconic dishes that you look forward to when you return to Japan?

Yes, there are some dishes that my mother cooks, a ritual that goes back more than half a century. She prepares a dish called *osekihan*. *Seki* means 'red' and *han* means 'rice', so *osekihan* is a red bean rice dish. We keep the cooking water from the beans and use it to steam the rice rather than cooking it in a rice steamer. It's a simple dish, typically cooked for the holidays. So members of the Sekiguchi family like to eat it when we celebrate something, a work success or when someone is coming to visit, for example.

Preparing *osekihan* takes time, but it must not become too tender or soft. Sometimes you have to start all over again; it takes some commitment. And as it was a dish that my grandmother was renowned for in the family, my mother asks me every time she makes it herself: 'Is it as good as the one your grandmother used to cook?'

I think it's easy to forget that a whole lot of foods were once produced, harvested, fished and cooked in Tokyo itself!

It's hard to say, because every time I travel to other parts of Japan, I discover completely new things. Really we should instead talk about Japanese cuisines in the plural. And obviously this regional variation also shows in the fact that we do not have a single language but many different dialects in Japan.

You could say that Japanese cuisine is the language of water, because this element really determines a lot of things in Japan. But be aware, I'm not saying that the water is better here, that's a myth. It's just that, in geographical terms, Japan is made up of many mountains which allow us to benefit from their relatively pure waters. The Japanese often think that it is the quality of the water that determines the final outcome of a dish. For the Japanese, water is not tasteless, as you do hear people say in France.

This meal is also an opportunity to think of those who are absent or no longer with us. We talk about the times my grandmother prepared it for my grandfather. In fact, we celebrate the return of the living but also the dead with *osekihan*.

I understand that you have another ritual when you return, which is to visit FARO, the restaurant of chef Kotaro Noda. FARO is a vegan Italian restaurant. Why has this cuisine also become synonymous with your visits to Japan?

Noda-san uses a lot of Japanese vegetables. In reality, what he offers is not that far removed from Japanese cuisine, because it draws a lot of its inspiration from *shojin ryori*. I think his dishes are perhaps closer to *washoku* [the traditional Japanese cuisine] than some dishes that we regularly prepare in Japan without really thinking about it.

When Noda-san makes ravioli he includes mountain or spring herbs. This means he observes the natural rhythm of nature. Through his dishes, I can sense the seasons as they pass in the mountains and in the sea, all while remaining in Tokyo. And I also like creating rituals. I met Noda-san in Rome ten years ago. Since then, going to his restaurant has become a regular habit every time I visit the Italian capital, and now that he has opened a restaurant in Tokyo, I'm continuing this tradition, I'm just changing countries!

As well as being an author, you are also a translator. If Japanese cuisine were a language, what would its characteristics be?

We often hear that we find the best-prepared foreign dishes in Tokyo. So, you can find the best pizza, the best croissants here ... How do you think this can be explained?

Everyone now thinks that Tokyo no longer has a culinary identity of its own, which is, on the one hand, regrettable. On the other hand, though, this has allowed cooks and pastry chefs to forage here and there to discover new products and techniques from other countries. As there is no farmland here, Tokyo makes use of all other possibilities, everything must be allowed here, no matter how original, or how bizarre, without doing just any old thing, of course. We therefore find vegan Italian cuisine that uses Japanese vegetables. Only in Tokyo can you find things like this. So, I don't know if this is where you find the best pizzas, but what is certain is that in Tokyo, you can find pizzas and Italian cuisine like nothing you will find anywhere else.

Tokyo is also the city where we find the greatest number of Michelin-starred restaurants in the world, whether their chefs are Japanese or not. Are the culinary standards in Tokyo different from what you can find elsewhere?

I think it's due to several factors. First of all, logistical ease. In Tokyo, everything arrives straight away, in an excellent condition, perfectly fresh. And for a cook that is wonderful. Fish, meat, vegetables and so on always arrive in an impeccable state - which is not the case everywhere else. In France, for example, when it is not the hauler who lets us down, there may be supply problems or shortages among the suppliers. This is not a minor problem, and it is directly linked to the structure of Japanese society.

I also think that many young chefs left Japan in the 1980s, 1990s and 2000s to study in Europe (for example in France). So today, if you are a French chef and you want to open a restaurant in Tokyo, you have a very well-trained workforce at your disposal, capable of adapting themselves to the French style of cuisine. It's not enough to have a great chef to produce excellent food; you need an entire kitchen team and first-class suppliers. It is the readiness to easily bring together these two elements together which explains why Japan stands out in this area.

Finally, we must also keep in mind that Japan is an island that remains very remote from anywhere, and which has been isolated for several centuries. The products found there are quite different. When I travel around the country, even I find vegetables and shellfish that I have never eaten before. So, just imagine, for a cook, it's paradise! There is always something new to discover, a novel food to work with or to combine with another to create something entirely original.

In your view, what does the future hold in store for Japanese cuisine?

Of course, the situation is not easy. But I think there is hope. Often, when we talk about globalization, we see it as an 'absolute evil', but there are also good things to come out of it.

In terms of preserving our fishery resources, for example, there may be a synergy between the actions undertaken by the younger generation, whether Japanese or foreign. In the past, we fought these battles separately and alone, but this is no longer inevitable. The same thing happens with cooks - they are, of course, in constant competition with each other, but we also observe a sort of solidarity between them. A cook from the Japanese coast may be in contact with their counterpart from the French coast. In my opinion, the traditional conception of terroir is outdated; we must think of our world globally, in constant movement, as if it were made up of national terroirs linked in a constellation.

Finally, if you had to choose one dish that represents Tokyo, what would it be?

That would most definitely be *asari gohan*. *Gohan* means rice and *asari* means shellfish. It's a simple dish - you just have to cook the rice with the shellfish, adding a little ginger water. It is a family dish that may also be served in *kaiseki* restaurants (*kaiseki ryōri* is a traditional type of meal, consisting of several small dishes all served together). It's a very traditional dish, dating back to the Edo period. I think every Tokyoite must have eaten this dish at least once in their life. It's a typical spring recipe. Contrary to popular belief - which is that we see the start of spring with the arrival of certain vegetables on the shelves - in Tokyo, it is when you see *wakame* and shellfish return that we know a new year has begun. Obviously, today, *asari* no longer come from Tokyo Bay, but this dish remains, in my opinion, utterly emblematic of the city. ▬

Difficulty ●○○ Serves 2 Preparation: 5 mins
Cooking: 10 mins

monjayaki

500 ml (2⅛ cups) katsuobushi dashi stock (or 500 ml/2⅛ cups water + 2 tsp freeze-dried dashi)

2 tbsp Worcestershire sauce (+ 2 tbsp tomato ketchup if the Worcestershire sauce is not Japanese)

3–5 scallops

50 g (scant ¼ cup) plain (all-purpose) flour

1 handful of tempura flakes *(tenkasu)* (optional)

1 tbsp pickled ginger (optional)

1 tbsp dried squid *(kiriika)* (optional)

1 tbsp vegetable oil

200 g (2¼ cups) thinly sliced cabbage

Preparation

In a bowl, combine the dashi stock and the Worcestershire sauce. Adjust the amount of Worcestershire sauce to taste.

Quarter the scallops, then add them to the bowl with the flour. Add the tempura flakes, ginger and dried squid, if desired, and stir to combine.

Heat the oil in a saucepan, then add the scallops (reserving the sauce mixture) and the cabbage and fry until cooked.

Add the sauce mixture to the pan and cook over a medium heat until reduced to a smooth paste. Enjoy hot.

Be sure to scrape off and eat any bits that get stuck to the base of the pan – they taste delicious!

curried udon

1 tbsp vegetable oil

200 g (7 oz) thinly sliced pork (or other meat or mushrooms)

1 onion, chopped

2 tbsp curry powder

2 tbsp sake

1 generous tbsp mirin

900 ml (3¾ cups) katsuobushi dashi stock

1 leek

generous 3 tbsp soy sauce

2 servings of udon noodles

4 tbsp potato starch

Preparation

In a saucepan, heat the oil and sauté the meat. Add the onion and continue cooking. Stir in the curry powder and cook for another 2–3 minutes.

Add the sake and the mirin. Continue to cook for 1–2 minutes.

Add the dashi stock and wait for it to come to a boil.

Slice the leek diagonally so that all the slices are the same length and thickness.

When the stock is hot, add the sliced leek. When the leeks are cooked, add the soy sauce.

In another pan, cook the udon noodles according to the packet instructions.

Stir the potato starch into 4 tablespoons of water, then add this mixture to the stock and stir until it has a smooth, silky texture. Turn off the heat.

Transfer the udon noodles to a bowl, pour over the dashi stock and serve hot.

Difficulty ●○○

Makes 4 sandos (serves 2)

Preparation: 10 mins
Cooking: 10 mins

tamago sando

3 eggs

½ small cucumber

1–2 tbsp mayonnaise

1 pinch of salt

butter

4 slices of soft white bread

Preparation

Hard-boil the eggs (cook for 9–10 minutes). Leave to cool, then shell them.

Wash the cucumber, then slice it diagonally.

Place the hard-boiled eggs in a bowl and mash them with a knife or the back of a fork.

Add the mayonnaise and the salt. Stir to combine.

Butter the bread. Top 2 slices of the bread with the sliced cucumber, then add the egg mayonnaise on top. Cover with the remaining bread to make two sandwiches.

Stack the sandwiches, remove the crusts, then cut the sandwiches into triangles.

Bento, the Japanese art of the lunch box

Meals in small boxes, bentos are emblematic of the archipelago. Their invention dates as far back as the 5th century, and they reveal a lot about Japanese society.

Rice, vegetables, some meat or fish, tofu, marinated vegetables ... all perfectly arranged in a small airtight box that you can easily carry around. The bento box – a Japanese meal in a box for one person – is omnipresent, from the shelves of convenience stores and supermarkets to Instagram feeds. They boast all the ingredients they need for success: they are filled with food with a high nutritional value, are neatly presented and the designs feature the most *kawaii*[1] characters in Japanese pop culture.

Bentos are far from being a takeaway snack, rather they are a whole meal in their own right. To understand where these very special meals come from we have to go back in time.

1 'cute' in Japanese.

Leave the slick Instagram posts and plastic bento boxes behind and return to the 5th century. At the time, a bento was basically a ball of rice resembling an *onigiri*. But history is always on the move. Bentos were first mentioned in the *Kojiki*, 'a chronicle of ancient facts'. This collection of the founding myths of the archipelago, dating from 712, is the oldest text written in the Japanese language. It describes a dish made of rice that melts in the mouth. During the feudal era, the bento took on the shape we know today. In addition to the rice, savoury foods were included with a very specific purpose: to invigorate the fighters. However, it was not until the end of the Sengoku period (1477–1573) that the word bento first appeared in its current written form (弁当). Oda Nobunaga was a leading warlord who, together with Toyotomi Hideyoshi and Tokugawa Ieyasu, founded the Japanese state. He had complete and substantial meals, featuring a delicate mixture of rice, meat products and vegetables, served to the workers who built his castle. By the Edo period (1603–1867), bentos had become even more popular. They were no longer reserved for blue-collar workers or artisans, but became commonplace with all classes of Japanese people, from busy salaried office workers to ever-hungry children.

SHOW ME YOUR BENTO, I'LL TELL YOU WHO YOU ARE

A lot of symbolism is hidden inside these little gourmet boxes. We can even use it to decode the

I YOU

Ekiben is the must-have bento box to take on a train journey. It allows you to eat but also to discover local culinary specialities.

social status of the family that prepared it. Social inequalities grew at the beginning of the 20th century. In 1918, rice riots broke out following a sudden steep increase in the price of goods. All these social disparities were reflected in the composition of the bentos that mothers gave their children for lunch. To remedy the situation, canteens were established across Japan in the mid-1950s. Goodbye bentos - now the menu was the same for everyone. It was not until the 1980s, the prosperous years when consumerism reigned supreme, that the bento box regained its popularity. The secret of its newfound success was notably thanks to the so-called *kyaraben*, bentos in which the flagship characters of Japanese popular culture, such as Doraemon and Hello Kitty, appeared. An unstoppable parade of these figures was used to incite children to eat all the foods that they would normally categorically refuse to have if they hadn't been transformed into the clothes or accessories of their favourite heroes! The bento is also the apogee of *ofukuro no aji*, the taste of mum's cooking. After all it is mainly, if not exclusively, women - usually wives or mothers - who are in charge of preparing the bentos. Their preparation takes time and can even become a source of competition between mothers. You have to know how to satisfy your husband, pamper your child, live up to other people's bento boxes ... Bento therefore says a lot more about the place of women in Japanese society than it may initially seem.

EKIBEN, THE ART OF EATING ON A TRAIN

Bentos don't just give us an insight into a person's home life, they are also an excellent way to discover different Japanese culinary cultures. Although it is

frowned upon in Japan to eat on the tram, metro or in the street, there is an almost essential ritual when travelling longer distances: you need to take along and eat an *ekiben*, a contraction of *eki uri bento*, meaning 'meal tray sold at the station'. This tasty bento usually contains culinary specialties from the city or prefecture where you begin your trip. Although *ekiben* are mostly eaten cold, some innovative prefectures have provided ingenious systems which also allow you to enjoy a hot lunch or dinner. This is the case, for example, with the Miyagi Prefecture and its *Tan To* bento: you pull a string and a chemical reaction is unleashed in the small pocket placed underneath the dish. Just five minutes later, the dish is reheated, ready to be devoured.

Ekiben were invented at the end of the 19th century, at a time when railway lines were being built all over Japan. Sellers of nutritious lunch parcels bustled along the station platforms, their arms laden with wooden boxes, allowing these early rail travellers to enjoy a proper meal during their journey. Since then, kiosks specializing in bentos have set up directly on the platforms of the busiest railway lines. For those who would like to taste the delights of places they are not likely to visit during their journey, one address is worth remembering: Ekibenya Matsuri, a shop located on the first floor of Tokyo Station, which offers 170 kinds of different *ekiben* from all over the country.

TAKE aways

EACH BENTO HAS ITS OWN NAME

- Aisai bento: A wife prepares this so-called 'love' bento for her husband; the food is sometimes cut into the shape of a heart, and a romantic message may be added with characters cut out of dried seaweed ...

- Hinomaru bento: This bento is reminiscent of the Japanese flag. Its design is very simple: it features a bed of rice with a salted red plum called *umeboshi* placed in the middle.

- Koraku bento: This bento is intended to be enjoyed by several people eating together, especially during the Hanami period in springtime, when the Japanese traditionally gather for a picnic under the cherry tree blossoms. The boxes therefore contain more than their everyday counterparts.

- Kyaraben bento: A wide variety of different foods in the shape of popular characters, particularly from manga comics, is contained in this bento, meant to entice children to eat more vegetables.

- Makunouchi bento: The name of this bento translates as 'curtain closing bento'. Initially enjoyed during the interval of particularly long performances at kabuki and nō theatres, it dates back to the Edo period (1603–1867).

- Shikaeshi bento: The so-called 'revenge bento.' Its intention or, at least that of the person who prepares it, is quite clear: to convey a message through food. Inside you would find badly cooked rice, raw eggs or, once again, a few words written with seaweed or ketchup, but this time not with the friendly messages found in an aisai bento ...

- Shokado bento: Most often served during the end-of-year holidays, this bento comprises black beans, sweet potatoes, marinated condiments and perhaps sautéed prawns (shrimp).

KANSAI

・ソースマヨ＆塩
10個~800円
十八番

Osaka, street food paradise

Osaka, the capital of the Kansai region, is famous for its street food – small dishes that can be enjoyed on the go, at any time of the day or night. Let's take a look at some of the must-trys during a culinary stroll through the city which, a few centuries ago, was called 'the granary of the nation'.

It's only 11 a.m. and yet Nori is already busy and there is a large number of small hemispherical moulds in front of him. His movements are precise, mechanical, and one follows another at lightning speed: he greases the moulds one by one, then fills them with pastry before adding pieces of octopus; he lets them brown then, with a perfectly controlled movement, turns them over to allow them to cook evenly. This hypnotizing process only takes a few seconds, and there are never any mistakes. Now it's time to place the moulds onto a tray for those eagerly awaiting them - customers whose mouths are watering and who have not missed a crumb of the preparation - then to cover them with a sauce, mayonnaise and dried flakes of bonito tuna.

'I've been making *takoyaki* all day every day for almost four years. At the beginning, it was difficult, because you mustn't go at it too hard or everything will end up on the floor, nor too gently or the dough will not stick together,' says the 27-year-old man during a well-deserved break. '*Takoyakis* are Osaka's street food par excellence. You can eat them wherever you want, whenever you want and, unlike in Tokyo, you can be sure that they will be delicious!' With a smile, he launches this gentle dig at the Japanese capital which, according to him, too often looks at this great megacity in Kansai with a little disdain. It's true that you can read everywhere that Osaka, Japan's third largest city in terms of population, is a world apart. People's behaviour there, it is said, is generally less polite,

'Takoyakis are Osaka's street food par excellence. You can eat them wherever you want, whenever you want and, unlike in Tokyo, you can be certain that they will be delicious!'

'In Osaka, there is no set time for eating,' says Souhonten-san, a chef who specializes in kushikatsu.

and the inhabitants supposedly lack good manners. It's noisier, even a little raucous – that's true enough. 'I don't know if we're more this or less that, but I know one thing for sure: I won't leave here, I love this city and, above all, its cuisine. In Osaka, we don't eat like anywhere else,' Nori says proudly and emphatically.

'OSAKA NO KUIDAORE'

It's certain that the city of Osaka is inextricably linked to food. During the Edo period (1603–1867), it earned the nickname *tenka no daidokoro*, which can be translated as 'the nation's kitchen'. Indeed, the city plays a leading role in the rice trade. Osaka is prosperous, its traders are wealthy, there is no shortage of money and, in the restaurants, ever-new specialties are created by the chefs as they wield their chopsticks. There is even a saying, *'Osaka no kuidaore,'* which means that, 'in Osaka, we eat until we run out of money!'

But what exactly is so special about eating in this city? Before going into detail, we need to set the scene. Our culinary journey begins at Dotonbori, a wide street, which runs parallel to a canal. It's a different sort of place, and your tastebuds, ears and eyes will certainly be challenged here. All day long, you can hear the cries of shopkeepers, who want to attract hungry onlookers to their tables or stands, all mixed with loud background music. Above all, however, Dotonbori is known for the gigantic culinary decorations that adorn the restaurants. Raise your eyes, and you'll discover a giant spider crab with animated legs, a hand proffering a gigantic piece of sushi or giant gyozas, neatly arranged in a bowl. Dotonbori is the ultimate realm of *takoyakis*, those small balls of dough with pieces of octopus nestled inside. They are best enjoyed hot, when the slivers of seafood seem to dance on the surface under the effect of the heat. It's very simple, you can't even walk a few

TAKE aways

It was in Osaka that instant noodles and sushi bars first saw the light of day.

Don't hesitate to go inside the tiny restaurants even if you cannot see what is happening and can only guess at what is going on inside.

metres before coming across yet another stand. The octopus, which also appears in a multitude of souvenir gadgets sold along the street, is the undisputed star of the city.

A PASSION FOR GRILLED FOOD

Another local specialty is the *okonomiyaki*, a sort of savoury pancake, the dough of which is composed of finely chopped cabbage, eggs, flour and a touch of dashi. You add whatever you fancy: pork, octopus, prawn (shrimp), seaweed or spring onions (scallions) ... Once grilled, you cover it with a sauce, mayonnaise and dried bonito tuna flakes. In Kansai, people enjoy it with *tororo,* a kind of Japanese yam which gives it a more glutinous texture. A few miles away in Hiroshima, the method of preparation is quite different: here, the ingredients are not cooked together, but separately. No matter where you are, this filling pancake can be enjoyed straight at the counter, while watching the cooks at work.

Another grilled specialty are the *ikayaki.* Throughout the whole of Japan, *ikayaki* are skewers of grilled squid, which are topped with soy sauce and eaten on the go. Osaka, however, invented its own version. Here, the squid is nestled within a soft pancake and cooked in an iron grid, a bit like a waffle. Once cooked, it is covered with Worcestershire sauce, which has a sweet and sour and slightly spicy taste.

AWAY FROM THE CITY'S MAIN ARTERIES

Dotonbori Street is not the only place where you can savour the typical dishes of Osaka. Head towards the Shinsekai district, where the city's emblem, the Tsutenkaku Tower, is located. A large number of small restaurants fight for space at its feet. Until September 2020, it was here that you could find the famous Zuboraya restaurant, which specialized in *fugu*, the Japanese pufferfish which, if prepared incorrectly, could cost you your life. With the restaurant's closure, an emblem of the neighbourhood, 5 metres long and 3 metres high and wide (5.5. x 3.2 x 3.2 yards) – the enormous *fugu* that was suspended above the entrance breathed its last breath – has been taken down.

Don't hesitate to go inside the tiny restaurants in these narrow alleyways, even if you cannot see what is happening and can only guess at what is going on inside. At Souhonten-san's, for example, you'll encounter a chef who prepares *kushikatsu,* or breaded skewers, and he does this in a room which only has a counter

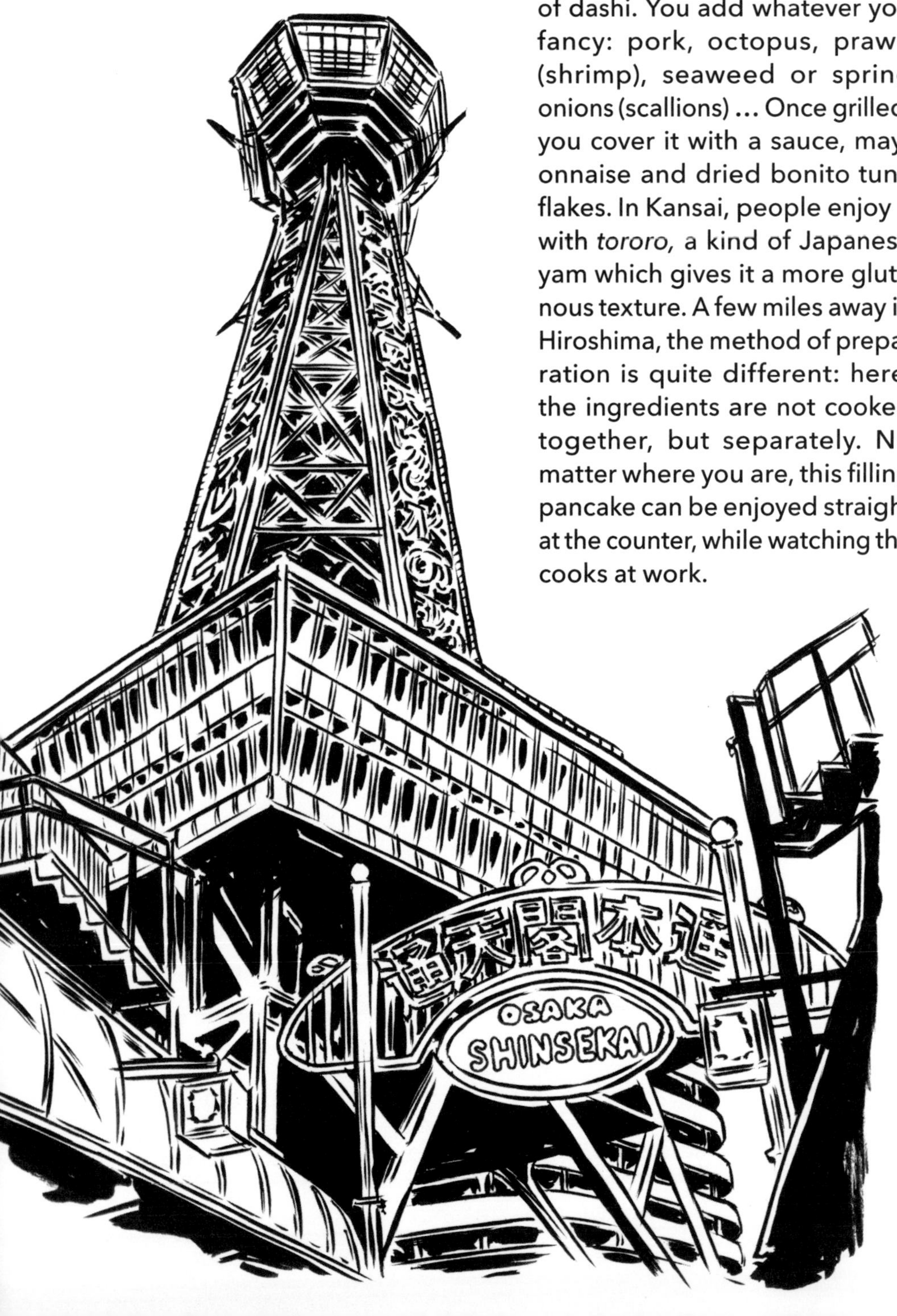

and a dozen chairs at most. His speciality? A beef skewer, flavoured with finely chopped herbs and coated in breadcrumbs, to be enjoyed hot, dipped into a sauce. There are manifold variations: with pork or prawns, and there are, of course, vegetarian versions, since sweet potato, asparagus, lotus roots and even pumpkin are very good bases for a tasty *kushikatsu*. 'The success lies entirely in the quality of the breading. It must be freshly prepared every day with the greatest care. The oil has to be changed several times a day, otherwise you lose the flavour of the ingredients,' explains Souhonten-san, who has been in charge of the kitchen here for 30 years. 'It's a challenge to live up to because it was here, in our neighbourhood, that *kushikatsus* were invented in the late 1920s.'

When he is asked if he knows a good place to visit to discover another culinary side of the city, without any hesitation he mentions the Kuromon Ichiba Market, a popular place thanks to its daily arrivals of fresh fish. 'You have to come early in the morning because the market fills up quickly. It's a place where you find very good foods to cook with. And there are also a whole lot of stalls that invite you to taste their products, or even to prepare them,' adds the chef. 'Eating raw fish at 8 a.m. might be a little early for you, but in Osaka any time is the right time to eat!' ▬

TAIKO MANJU, A SWEET SNACK

Many savoury dishes are emblematic of Osaka, but we must not forget to mention sweet delights like *taiko manju* and *imagawayaki*, a larger version of the *taiyaki*. This sponge cake is filled with *azuki* (the ubiquitous red bean paste), but you can usually also find some cakes that are filled with cream. This pastry is generally eaten on the go. It was invented in the city of Osaka during the 18th century.

Difficulty ●○○

Makes 1 okonomiyaki (serves 2)

Preparation: 10 mins
Cooking: 10 mins

okonomiyaki

100 g (generous ¾ cup) plain (all-purpose) flour

180 ml (¾ cup) *katsuobushi* dashi stock (or 180 ml/ ¾ cup water + 3 g/scant 1 tsp freeze-dried dashi of your choice)

2 eggs

300 g (3⅓ cups) finely chopped green cabbage

50 g (½ cup) finely chopped spring onions (scallions) or chives

2 tbsp cooking oil

3 thin slices of pork belly (or 3 prawns [shrimp] or another meat or fish of your choice)

2 tbsp *okonomiyaki* sauce

mayonnaise (optional)

pickled ginger (optional)

bonito flakes (optional)

Preparation

Mix together the flour, dashi stock and eggs until you have a smooth mixture. Stir in the cabbage and onions until they are combined.

Heat the oil in a frying pan, then add the mixture, spreading it out to create a thick pancake. Cook the *okonomiyaki* over a medium heat without pressing down so that it remains soft.

Once the underside is cooked, cover the pancake with your chosen ingredients (pork, prawns [shrimp] or other topping).

Turn the pancake over.

Once it is golden on both sides, transfer the pancake to a plate. Top with the *okonomiyaki* sauce, mayonnaise and ginger and sprinkle with bonito flakes, if using. Cut the pancake into eight wedges and enjoy hot.

Difficulty ●○○

Makes 16 takoyakis (Serves 2)

Preparation: 10 mins
Cooking: 6 mins

takoyaki

(Adapt to suit your takoyaki *machine)*

90 g (2/3 cup) plain (all-purpose) flour

1 egg

330 ml (1⅓ cups) *katsuobushi* dashi stock (or 330ml/1⅓ cups water + 5 g/generous 1 tsp freeze-dried dashi of your choice)

1 pinch of salt

½ tsp soy sauce

50–60 g (1¾–2¼ oz) cooked octopus (or 4 prawns or 4 scallops)

2 tbsp vegetable oil

pickled ginger, finely chopped (optional)

50 g (½ cup) finely chopped spring onions (scallions)

2 tbsp *okonomiyaki* sauce

mayonnaise (optional)

bonito flakes (optional)

Preparation

Mix the flour, egg, dashi stock, salt and soy sauce to make a thick batter.

Cut the octopus into 16 pieces, approximately 1 cm (⅜ in) thick.

Using absorbent paper, grease each cell of the *takoyaki* machine with the oil and then turn it on to a medium heat.

① Place a piece of octopus in each cell.

② Cover with some of the batter and sprinkle with the ginger and spring onions (scallions). Cook for 2–3 minutes.

③ Once one side is golden, turn the balls over one by one, using a toothpick or a thin chopstick to make them roll over.

Once the *takoyakis* are cooked, serve them with the *okonomiyaki* sauce and mayonnaise. Sprinkle with bonito flakes, if using.

1

2

3

Difficulty ●○○

Makes 8 skewers
(Serves 2)

Preparation: 10 mins
Cooking: 10 mins

kushikatsu

For the *kushikatsu* dipping sauce

5 tbsp *tonkatsu* (or *okonomiyaki*) sauce

1 tbsp ketchup

100 ml (scant ½ cup) sake

1 tsp sugar

For the coating

100 g (¾ cup) plain (all-purpose) flour

100 ml (scant ½ cup) milk (or water)

1 egg

100 g (2⅔ cups) fine fresh breadcrumbs

200–400 ml (1–1⅔ cup) oil for deep frying

Possible ingredients for the skewers

2 whole shiitake mushrooms

2 slices of lotus root *(renkon)* about 1 cm (⅜ in) thick

2 whole okra (tops trimmed)

2 whole green asparagus spears (ends trimmed)

6 hard-boiled quails' eggs (cooked for 4 minutes and shelled)

2 x 50 g (1¾ oz) meat of your choice, cut into bite-sized pieces

1 onion ring, cut in half

2 portions of Camembert (each one-sixth of a whole cheese)

Preparation

Making the dipping sauce

Place all the sauce ingredients in a small saucepan and stir. Bring to the boil, then leave to cool.

Making the coating

In a bowl, mix the flour with the milk (or water). Add the egg and mix again.

Spear your preferred ingredients onto thin bamboo skewers. If you have chosen meat, it is best to separate the pieces with half an onion ring to prevent them from falling or turning on the skewer.

Dip the skewers into the egg mixture, then into the breadcrumbs to coat them.

Pour the oil into a saucepan and heat it to 200°C (400°F), then deep-fry each skewer.

Once they are golden brown, take them out and leave them to drain.

Enjoy hot with the sauce.

Kissaten, or café culture 'made in Japan'

Once upon a time, particularly after the war, the kissaten cafés, offering coffee and a selection of dishes borrowed from Western culture, were very successful. Although the economic crisis caused their decline, for some time now they have regained in popularity among the younger generations.

A chaos of wooden furniture and soft leatherette benches, with porcelain cups hanging behind the counter, little plastic flowers and a cosy atmosphere enlivened by some jazz tunes or classical music – there's no doubt that you are in a *kissaten*. Ki-ssa-ten, three syllables, three *kanji* or characters (喫茶店), three steps which encourage us to take a leap back in time to the wonderful Shōwa era (1926–1989), a period of fast economic growth which today seems to be no more than a distant memory. To open the door of a *kissaten* is to travel back in time, to the mid-20th century, into a place which does not seem to have changed one iota.

But what exactly is a *kissaten*? The etymology of the term provides us with some clues. If you read the characters that make up the word one at a time, you'll get this: 'consume' (喫), 'tea' (茶) and 'shop' (店). Therefore a *kissaten* should be a tearoom. Yet it was another drink that made it successful and famous: coffee.

To understand all this, we need to go back in time. The first coffee beans arrived in Japan with the Portuguese missionaries in the 1500s, but it was not until the end of the 19th century that this drink carved out its place as a favourite everyday drink in Japan. The archipelago was just beginning to open its borders to the world during the Meiji era (1868–1912). Brazilian coffee traders visited the archipelago ever more frequently and, supported by their government, in 1900 they created the world's first chain of coffee shops – among them was the Café Paulista in Japan.

AN INDISPUTABLE SUCCESS

And where were the *kissaten* in all this? The very first one opened in 1888, in the Taito district, northeast of Tokyo. Each one has to serve tea, of course, a sacrosanct

In 1981, when the Japanese economic miracle was in full flow, the country was home to more than 150,000 kissaten.

Japanese drink if ever there was one, as well as pastries and light snacks. The most sophisticated Japanese taste buds, however, wanted to sip the dark beverage from abroad. Served at times filtered through a fabric, at times discharged from a siphon, precisely and accurately measured by the owners of the premises, it was this drink that made the *kissaten* so successful – a success that was interrupted by World War II, when coffee exports were suspended. It was not until the post-war period that customers returned to the *kissaten*, and they did so in increasing numbers.

Not a single district in Japan's cities can do without them, and for good reason – *kissaten*, or at least their owners, know how to adapt to their surroundings. There's a university nearby? The *kissaten* will supply the right ambience for students to revise. Is it a neighbourhood of chic boutiques? The *kissaten's* decor will be elegant, in order to attract window-shoppers. The cafés also became popular meeting places for neighbours and stay-at-home mums who visit them to read the newspaper or to have lunch together. *Kissaten* can also be political. At the dawn of the uprisings in the 1960s, they warmly welcomed students and freethinkers as well as anti-system rebels and anti-militarist reformers. It was a success: in the midst of the Japanese economic miracle in 1981 there were more than 150,000 *kissatens* across the country. The majority of these places did not survive after the speculation bubble burst during the years 1985–1991 and the subsequent recession. Yet some establishments remain in use today, with exactly the same organization, the same decor, the same menu and, very often, the same owner as in the 1980s.

FOREIGN FLAVOURS

On the wooden tables of a typical *kissaten*, you will find coffee as well as a whole lot of dishes characteristic of these establishments. It serves so-called *yoshoku* recipes, a Western-inspired cuisine adapted to Japanese tastes, the origins of which date back to the beginning of the Meiji era, when Westerners and their way of life crossed the borders of the archipelago. Examples of these dishes include the famous breakfast, featuring toast, eggs, bacon and black coffee, gobbled up in the morning by busy employees or students who want a quick snack on their way to college. They also serve the famous *omurice*, a contraction of omelette and rice, which is an omelette with fried rice, part-covered with ketchup. Another example of *yoshoku* is the *naporitan*, very soft spaghetti, dressed with oil, ham, onion and tomato ketchup - an American influence if ever there was one, since the USA sold its wheat surplus to Japan after the war, ensuring that spaghetti, hamburgers, pizzas and bread arrived on Japanese plates.

Kissaten are also famous for their desserts. These can be one of the great classics, such as *purin*, a custard cream or crème caramel, traditionally made in tall aluminium moulds. You will also come across sweets bordering on kitsch, such as cream soda: these little sugar bombs are large glasses of a fizzy drink (soda), most often melon-flavoured and lagoon blue in colour (a very artificial lagoon ...), in which floats a scoop of vanilla ice cream. We also mustn't forget the *kakigori*, a dessert made from shaved ice, flavoured with green tea and a sesame or fruit syrup - and in fact this may often be a melange of syrup, condensed milk and Japanese azuki beans or even small *mochi*, Japanese rice cakes, which give this dessert a touch of class.

RETRO NOSTALGIA

The 1990s and 2000s undermined the fortunes of the *kissaten*, as the Japanese began to prefer Japanese coffee chains like Doutor and Tully's, as well as the American chain Starbucks. Some owners have gone out of business, due to a lack of customers and insufficient income, yet a handful of these establishments are actually experiencing a new lease of life. Perhaps, at a time when growth prospects are weak and economic life is becoming more precarious, a certain nostalgia for the famous Shōwa era can be detected. More and more young people are now coming through the doors of these old-fashioned cafés, fascinated by their kitsch interiors where time seems to have stood still. Photographs of cream soda, *naporitan* (a pasta dish), even large candy-pink landline phones abound on social networks like Instagram, accompanied by eloquent hashtags, such as #retrocool or #showanostalgia ... And this trend is spreading - it is now not uncommon for new *kissaten*-style cafés to open up. Their owners are often in their thirties, the walls of the cafés are completely new, but the decoration and the menu resemble those of their predecessors in every detail. We have not seen the end of the *kissaten* yet.

THREE MUST-VISIT ADDRESSES

• OTAFUKU COFFEE

Wedged between a lingerie store and an estate agent (realtor), this *kissaten* is located in the very heart of the Teramachi shopping arcade in central Kyoto. You go down a few steps, the bustle subsides and you discover Noda-san and his regular clientele to whom he serves a must-have filter coffee like no other.
B1F, 609 Teianmaenocho, Shimogyo Ward, Kyoto, 600-8031, Japan

• KAYABA COFFEE

Hidden in the Yanaka district, this wooden building housed a *kissaten* from 1938 until 2006, when its owner died. The premises were saved from demolition by a local not-for-profit organization which, along with the owners of the neighbouring gallery, reopened the café, keeping the original sign and façade intact.
6 Chome-1-29 Yanaka, Taito City, Tokyo 110-0001, Japan

• HIRAOKA COFFEE

Entering this *kissaten* is almost like stepping back in Japanese history. Hiraoka was, in fact, the very first *kissaten* to open in Osaka! Here, the menu has been narrowed down to a few dishes, notably doughnuts freshly prepared by hand every day by the owner, and accompanied by one of a wide range of coffees.
3 Chome-6-11 Kawaramachi, Chuo Ward, Osaka, 541-0048, Japan

Difficulty ●○○

Serves 2

Preparation: 5 mins
Cooking: 10 mins

naporitan

200 g (7 oz) spaghetti

1 tbsp vegetable oil

½ onion, chopped

2 small (or 1 large) red peppers (bell peppers), chopped

100 g (¾ cup) mushrooms (or 1 pork sausage, about 50–80 g/1¾–2¾ oz), sliced

1 pinch each of salt and ground black pepper

2–3 tbsp tomato ketchup

2 tbsp red wine

grated Parmesan cheese (optional)

Tabasco (optional)

Preparation

Cook the spaghetti according to the packet instructions. Drain well.

Heat the oil in a saucepan, add the onion, peppers and mushrooms or sausage and sauté over a medium heat until cooked. Season with salt and pepper.

Push the ingredients to the side of the pan to make space at the front. Add the ketchup in the space you have created and simmer until you have a thick sauce. Deglaze the pan with the red wine.

Stir the contents of the pan well to combine, then stir in the cooked spaghetti.

Add the Parmesan and the Tabasco, if using, and enjoy hot.

omurice

1 tbsp butter

½ onion, roughly chopped

½ carrot, roughly chopped

2–3 mushrooms, thinly sliced

1 pinch each of salt and ground black pepper

200 g (7 oz) chicken thighs, cut into 1 cm (⅜ in) cubes

1 tbsp white wine

330 g (2¼ cups) cooked sushi rice

1–2 tbsp tomato ketchup, plus more to serve, (optional)

4 eggs

Preparation

Cooking the chicken and rice

Melt half the butter in a frying pan. Add the onion, carrot and mushrooms and sauté over a medium heat. Season with salt and pepper.

Add the chicken and fry until cooked. Stir in the white wine.

Add the rice and the ketchup, and continue to cook, stirring gently so as not to break up the rice grains.

Transfer to a plate.

Cooking the omelette

Beat the eggs. Heat the remaining butter in a clean frying pan over a medium heat. Pour in the beaten eggs and mix gently. When the mixture starts to set, gently roll it up to make an omelette so that the inside remains soft. Shape into an oval, and carefully place it on top of the rice.

Make a lengthways cut in the centre of the omelette to open it out and add a little ketchup if you wish. Enjoy hot.

Difficulty ●●○ Serves 4 Preparation: 15 mins Cooking: 1 hour

curry with rice

300 g (10½ oz) chicken thighs, pork leg or mushrooms, cut into bite-sized pieces

1 pinch each of salt and ground black pepper

1 tbsp curry powder

2 tbsp vegetable oil

3 onions, chopped

1 tbsp grated garlic

1 tbsp grated ginger

2 potatoes, diced

2 carrots, diced

1 tomato, diced

750 ml (scant 3¼ cups) water

1 bay leaf

1 tbsp Worcestershire sauce

1 pot yoghurt (150 g/⅔ cup)

For the curry sauce

3 tbsp butter

3 tbsp plain (all-purpose) flour

1 tbsp curry powder

1 tbsp brown sugar or honey

660 g (4½ cups) cooked sushi rice, to serve

4 hard-boiled eggs (optional)

Preparation

Season the meat or mushrooms with salt and pepper. Add the curry powder. Stir well and leave to marinate.

In a deep saucepan, heat the oil over low heat. Add the onions and sauté until golden brown.

Add the grated garlic and ginger and continue cooking. Add the potatoes, carrots and meat. Cook for another 20 minutes, until all the ingredients are cooked and tender.

Once all these ingredients are cooked, add the diced tomatoes, water, bay leaf, Worcestershire sauce and yoghurt. Simmer for 30–40 minutes, skimming any foam off the top if necessary.

Making the curry sauce

In a saucepan, heat the butter to melt, then add the flour, stirring constantly so that it does not stick to the bottom of the pan. Once you have a smooth mixture and it has taken on a little colour, add the curry powder. Turn off the heat and stir vigorously.

Add the curry paste to the meat and vegetables a little at a time, mixing well. Add the sugar or honey, then adjust the seasoning. Serve hot with the rice, adding one hard-boiled egg per person if desired.

講堂

Shojin ryori, the cuisine of the Buddhist temples

With an emphasis on fresh, local and seasonal ingredients, the values of *shojin* cuisine are in tune with the times. However this style of cookery, which has its origins in the Zen Buddhist tradition, is in danger of disappearing.

'Some shojin dishes are still served in temples and restaurants, but most are now aimed at tourists, and the spirituality of shojin has vanished.'
Toshio Tanahashi

'*Shojin* cuisine is followed by very few around the world, but it has a universal value, especially since it meets the imperatives of preserving health and the environment, but also of sustainability and mindfulness.' When it comes to *shojin ryori*, literally the 'cuisine of devotion' from the Zen Buddhist tradition, chef Toshio Tanahashi, a specialist in the genre, is full of praise.

It is notable that this cuisine's governing principles resonate well with current concerns: to always favour seasonal and local products; to avoid all waste as much as possible by using all parts of the vegetables, even the less popular ones, as ingredients in a broth or as a garnish; and to celebrate the natural flavours, shapes, textures and colours of foods by altering them as little as possible.

The focus on cooking locally grown and sustainable food has its roots in the beliefs of the Buddhist religion, which originated in China and arrived in Japan in the 6th century. It was not until 1237, however, that it began to be properly regulated, notably thanks to the *Kyōkun* – in English, *Instructions for the Cook* – which was written by Dōgen Zenji, one of the great thinkers of medieval Japan and the founder of Zen Buddhism.

HIGHLIGHTING PRODUCTS AND FLAVOURS

With meals limited to three vegetarian dishes, accompanied by a bowl of rice and broth, *shojin* cuisine is sometimes considered to be ascetic. However, this is not the case at all. It simply highlights the products that are used, which offer up all their flavours thanks to the way that they are cooked or prepared. This range of dishes gives pride of place to whole grains, pulses, vegetables, seaweed, wild herbs and dried or fermented foods. On the other hand, *shojin ryori* is entirely vegetarian, or actually even vegan. There is no trace of any dairy product, meat or any other animal product. Foods with very strong flavours, such as garlic, leeks and onions, are also excluded from the dishes because *shojin* cuisine is, above all, about harmony. Throughout the meal, the five tastes must follow one another: sour, bitter, salty, sweet and umami. A similar emphasis is placed on the five main colours that stand out when you look at one of the small bowls or plates on which the food is served: white, green, red, yellow and finally black - or, let's say, dark colours.

This culinary ballet is mainly prepared in the temples by Zen Buddhist monks. *Shojin ryori* is considered a spiritual and meditative practice. In recent years, however, a handful of chefs, including Toshio Tanahashi, have been trying to promote this type of cuisine outside religious establishments. After graduating in agricultural economics, the 27-year-old decided to leave everything behind and spend three years at the Gesshin-ji Temple in the town of Otsu, located between Kyoto, the former imperial capital, and Lake Biwa. Alongside Myodoni Mirase, a nun and cook, he learned the basics of *shojin ryori* and immersed himself in its philosophy. 'For three years I was the only man in a world of women. I got up every day at 4 a.m. and that's how I discovered *shojin* cuisine. The two characters *shō* ('purify') and *jin* ('move forward') essentially evoke the journey of the pure heart through food towards peace and light,' explains Toshio, who decided to leave the monastery and open his own restaurant in Tokyo, the highly acclaimed Gesshinkyo. It became a key place to visit and drew international attention to Zen cuisine. 'I tried to free myself from the religious ties and to generalize and to universalize *shojin* cuisine, to prevent it from disappearing,' the chef explains.

A CULINARY TRADITION UNDER THREAT

Vegetarian *shojin* cuisine, which uses fresh, seasonal ingredients, struggles to appeal to the Japanese for their everyday meals. 'Japan and the Japanese cuisine attract worldwide attention but, in fact, the precious *shojin* way of cooking is on the verge of disappearing,' laments Toshio Tanahashi. 'Some *shojin* dishes are still served in temples and restaurants, but most are now aimed at tourists, and the spirituality of *shojin* has vanished.'

In 2007, the chef closed his Tokyo restaurant and made it his mission to share the principles of *shojin ryori* with the rest of the world. He became a travelling chef, gave lectures, taught about the relationship between the culinary arts and philosophy at the Kyoto University of Art and Design and opened the Zecoow Culinary Institute, a Kyoto school where he trained the next generation in *shojin ryori*. Here again, though, foreigners tend to make up the majority of those who enrol for the classes. 'My student with the greatest potential is a 28-year-old Italian. This shows how far *shojin* cuisine is now removed from Japanese cooking ... Now in his sixties, Toshio Tanahashi continues his mission however, whatever the cost: 'I now strive to promote the excellence of *shojin* cuisine and Japanese food culture abroad, in the hope of reviving it in Japan.'

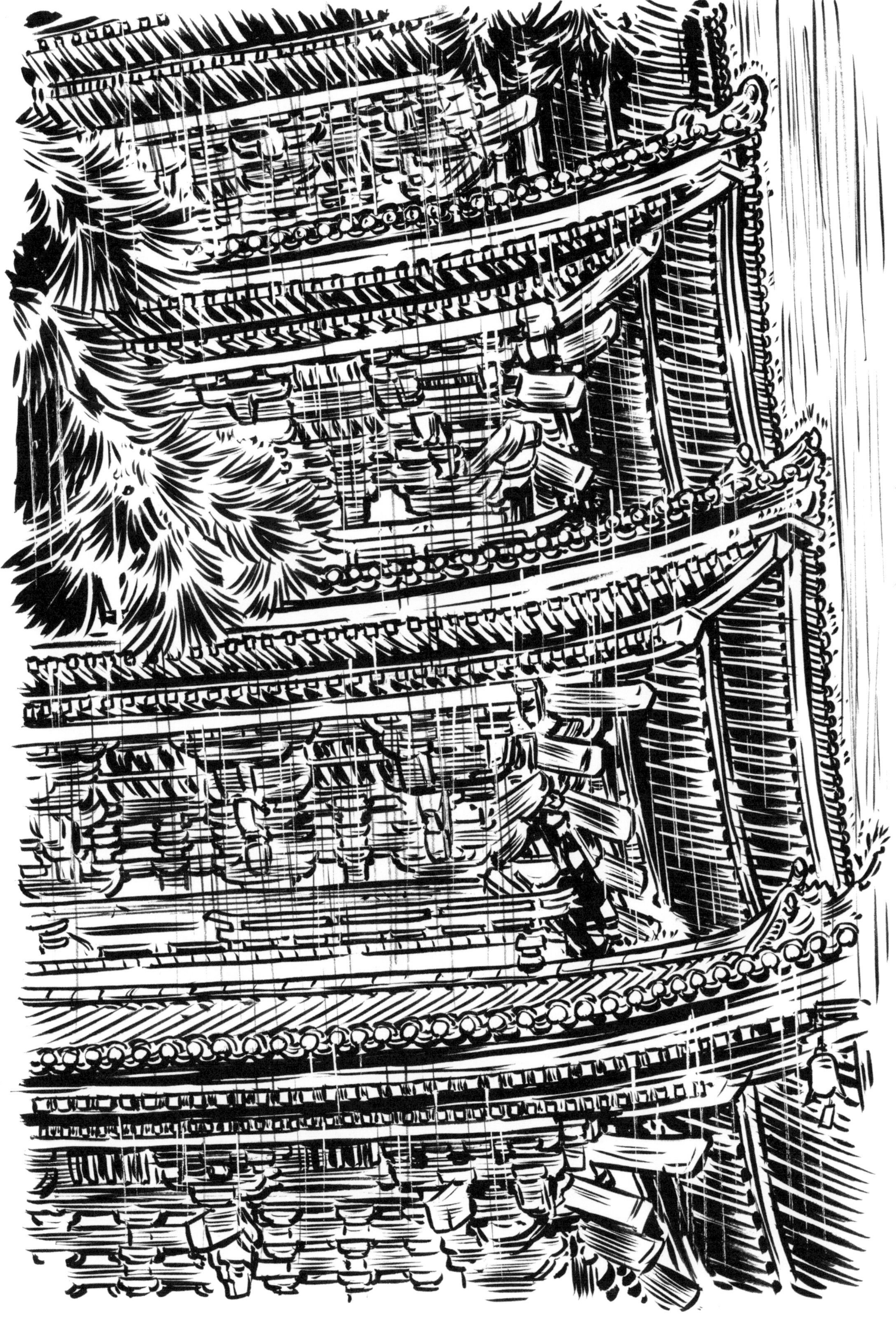

Difficulty ●○○

Makes 2 nasu dengaku (serves 2)

Preparation: 10 mins
Cooking: 20 mins

nasu dengaku

For the *dengaku* miso sauce

3 tbsp miso paste

2 tbsp brown sugar

1 tbsp mirin

1 tbsp sake

1 tbsp dashi powder

For the aubergine (eggplant)

1 large aubergine (eggplant)

3 tbsp water

1 pinch of salt

1 tbsp vegetable oil

For the garnish

1 pinch white sesame seeds

1 tsp grated ginger

1 pinch of finely chopped shiso (or spring onion [scallion] greens)

Preparation

In a small saucepan, combine all the ingredients for the *dengaku* miso sauce and cook for 5 minutes over a low heat, stirring frequently to stop the mixture from sticking. The finished sauce should be glossy and smooth.

Wash the aubergine (eggplant) and cut it in half lengthways. Using a knife, make a few slashes in the skin to make it easier to cook.

Heat the water with the salt in a frying pan, add the oil and place the aubergine (eggplant) pieces in it flesh-side down. Cook gently over a medium-to-low heat for about 10 minutes, until the aubergine (eggplant) is golden and tender. The cooking time depends on the size of the aubergine (eggplant).

Turn the aubergine (eggplant) over, cover and continue cooking for a further 5 minutes.

Serve the aubergine (eggplant) with the *dengaku* miso sauce and sprinkled with the sesame seeds, ginger and shiso (or spring onion/scallion greens).

Difficulty ●●○

Serves 2
(6-7 tempura per person)

Preparation: 15 mins
Cooking: 10 mins

vegetable tempura

For the tempura sauce

350 ml (scant 1½ cups) dashi stock (if you have *katsuobushi* [bonito flakes], prepare a *katsuobushi* dashi stock with 500 ml/2⅛ cups filtered water and 5 g/generous 1 tsp katsuobushi)

½ tbsp sugar

1 tbsp mirin

1½ tbsp sake

generous 3 tbsp soy sauce

Vegetables in season, for example:

1 small aubergine (eggplant)

2 spears green asparagus

2 okra

¼ sweet potato

⅛ lotus root

⅛ kabocha pumpkin

½ carrot

½ onion

2 fresh whole shiitake mushrooms

2 green shiso leaves

Preparation

Making the tempura sauce

If you are makign a fresh *katsuobushi* dashi stock, bring the filtered water to a boil. Pour the bonito flakes into the boiling water and cook over a low heat for 2-3 minutes. Turn off the heat and leave the bonito flakes to steep for another 2 minutes, then strain. Reserve 350 ml (scant 1½ cups) of the stock.

Reheat the reserved dashi stock over a medium heat, then add all the other tempura sauce ingredients. Once the mixture has come to the boil, turn off the heat. The sauce is now ready.

Preparing the vegetables

If the aubergine (eggplant) is small, cut it lengthways into quarters (if it is large, cut it into eighths), leaving the skin on.

Remove the ends from the asparagus spears by breaking them off with your fingers.

If the okra are not smooth, place them on a board and rub them with salt using the palms of your hands on the board, then rinse. If the okra are young and smooth, this step is unnecessary. Remove the stem ends of the okra without cutting into the pod.

Slice the sweet potato and lotus root. Slice the pumpkin. Cut the carrot into julienne strips, thinly slice the onion.

Combine the onions and carrots in a bowl.

For the tempura batter

30 g (1 oz) egg (equivalent to ½ large egg)

200 ml (generous ¾ cup) iced water (water + ice cubes)

100 g (¾ cup) plain (all-purpose) flour, sifted

400–600 ml (1⅔–2½ cups) oil for deep frying

salt, matcha or wasabi powder (optional)

Making the tempura batter

In a bowl, beat the egg, add the iced water and stir well. Now add the flour and carefully stir again. It doesn't matter if there are any lumps; the important thing is not to stir too much so that the batter becomes sticky.

Pour at least 2.5 cm (1 in) oil into a saucepan approximately 20 cm (8 in) in diameter and heat the oil to 170–180°C (340–360°F).

Making the carrot and onion tempura

In a ladle, take a portion of about 60 g (2 oz) of the carrot and onion mixture. Add 1 tablespoon of the batter, stir and gently let everything float on the surface of the oil, lightly spreading out the ingredients. Push the pieces back together again if they come apart.

Cooking the other vegetables

Dip the vegetables in the tempura batter to coat them all over, then carefully place them in the oil, one after the other. Turn them occasionally, checking them all the time.

Adjust the temperature of the oil depending on the size and the consistency of the ingredients. For example, for meat, you would need to lower it to 170°C (340°F) to cook it through.

Once the tempura are cooked, remove them from the oil and leave to drain.

Enjoy the tempura hot, dipping them in the tempura sauce or sprinkling them with salt. You can also season them with a mixture of salt and matcha or wasabi powder.

soy
in all its forms

レシピブック

Difficulty ●○○

Serves 2 or 3

Preparation: 50 mins
Cooking: 30 mins

250 g (2½ cups) dry yellow soya beans (soybeans)

1.2 l (5 cups) filtered water

2-6 tsp *nigari* (magnesium chloride), depending on the concentration (or 2 g/¾ oz diluted in 1 tbsp of water if the *nigari* is solid)

tofu

Preparation

Sort the soya beans (soybeans) to remove any damaged or blackened beans. Wash and then drain them.

Pour half the filtered water into a large bowl, add the soya beans and leave them to soak for 24 hours.

Once the soya beans have swollen, transfer them and the soaking water to a blender. Process for at least one minute until you have a smooth mixture. You can do this in 3 or 4 batches if you have a small blender.

Pour the mixture into a large saucepan, then add the remaining water. Heat over a medium heat, stirring continuously with a wooden spoon. Once the mixture begins to simmer, reduce the heat and cook for another 10 minutes, stirring frequently so that it does not stick to the bottom of the pan.

Place a colander covered with a large square of muslin on top of a large bowl. Pour the hot mixture through the muslin to filter it.

The bowl now contains a soy drink; the solid residues that remain in the cloth are known as *okara*.

Making the tofu

Pour the soy drink into a saucepan and heat it to 70-75°C (158-167°F), then turn off the heat. Slowly pour in the *nigari* solution by carefully running it over the back of a wooden spoon while moving it in a circular pattern.

Stir twice, no more, using the wooden spoon, then cover with a tea (kitchen) towel and a lid. Leave to rest for 30–60 minutes. The tofu will firm up as it cools.

Place the muslin over a tofu or cheese mould, or over a colander.

Remove the lid to see if the tofu has become firm. Once the tofu holds its shape, use a ladle to gently place it into the mould.

Weight the tofu down by placing a saucer or plate on top. Leave to rest for another 10–30 minutes, depending on the firmness of tofu you desire. The more you press it, the firmer it will become. Tofu can be eaten fresh with soy sauce and grated ginger, or with sesame oil and salt.

To prepare the tofu for use in a *yudofu*, press it for 30 minutes or longer. If you want to use it for a *ganmodoki*, press it for longer, at least 4 hours.

yudofu ①

300–400 ml (1¼–1¾ cups) filtered water, depending on the size of your saucepan

1 sheet dried kombu (5 x 5 cm/2 x 2 in)

1 block of tofu (bought or home-made, about 300–400 g/10½–14 oz)

½ tsp salt

soy sauce (or ponzu) for dipping

chives (optional)

white sesame seeds (optional)

grated ginger (optional)

Pour the filtered water into a small saucepan, add the kombu. Leave to rest for 30 minutes without heating. Dice the tofu.

After 30 minutes, add the tofu and the salt to the pan. Turn on the heat and bring to a boil.

When the water boils, reduce the heat and cook for 1 minute.

Cover the pan, turn off the heat and leave to rest for 10 minutes before serving.

Prepare the soy or ponzu sauce and the seasonings, and enjoy hot or lukewarm.

Difficulty ●○○

Serves 2 to 3

Preparation: 30 mins
Cooking: 15 mins

500 ml (2⅛ cups) homemade soy drink

soy sauce for dipping

wasabi or grated ginger (optional)

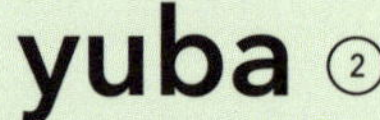

yuba ②

Preparation

In a small saucepan, heat the 400 ml (1⅔ cups) of the homemade soy drink over a medium heat.

Once the liquid starts to simmer, lower the heat and simmer for 2–3 minutes until a solid film forms on the surface – this is the *yuba*.

Pour the remaining soy drink into a container or glass jar.

When the film on the heated soy drink has thickened, dip a long chopstick into the pan and carefully lift it out, trying not to break the solid film.

Transfer the film to the container of soy drink.

Repeat the process until there is no drink left in the pan.

Enjoy the *yuba* hot or cold, dipping it in soy sauce with wasabi or grated ginger.

2
3
4
1

okara ③

2 tbsp sesame oil

¼ gobo (burdock root), cut into julienne strips

½ carrot, cut into julienne strips

2 fresh shiitake mushrooms, chopped

150 g (5¼ oz) *okara* (soy pulp)

1 spring onion (scallion), roughly chopped

½ bunch chives, roughly chopped

1 tbsp sake

1 tsp dashi powder

2 tbsp soy sauce

200 ml (generous ¾ cup) water

Rich in fibre and proteins, you can use *okara* to make hamburgers or *korokke*. The most traditional way to enjoy it, however, remains *unohana*, the recipe which I am offering you here.

In a frying pan, heat the oil, add the greater gobo (burdock), then the carrot and finally the shiitake mushrooms. Sauté all the ingredients until browned.

Add the *okara* and cook until the water has evaporated. Once all the water has evaporated, add the spring onion (scallion) and chives.

Finally, add the sake, dashi powder, soy sauce and water. Continue cooking for 5–10 minutes. Enjoy hot or cold.

300 g (10½ oz) solid (extra-firm) tofu

30 g (¼ cup) chopped carrot

30 g (¼ cup) gobo (burdock root), chopped

5 dried black mushrooms

2 fresh shiitake mushrooms, chopped

2 tbsp finely grated yam *(yamaimo)*

1 egg

1 pinch of salt

1 pinch of sugar

400–500 ml (1⅔–2 cups) oil for deep frying

soy sauce for dipping

grated ginger (optional)

ganmodoki ④

Firmly press the tofu for 4–5 hours under a weight of 500–600 g (1–1½ lb), in order to remove all the water. Once ready, pat it dry to remove any remaining water.

Blanch the carrot and gobo (burdock) in boiling water.

Soak the black mushrooms in hot water for 10 minutes, then slice them.

Place the tofu in a blender and process until you have a smooth paste.

Combine the blended tofu with the carrot, gobo (burdock), black mushrooms, shiitake mushrooms and yam.

Beat the egg, then mix it little by little with the tofu and vegetable mixture until you have a smooth paste.

Season with the salt and the sugar. Form the mixture into 4 or 5 balls, slightly flattening the tops. You may need to oil your hands to make the balls easier to handle.

Heat the oil to 160–170°C (320–340°F), add the balls and deep-fry them until golden brown.

Serve hot with soy sauce and grated ginger, if liked; or cold in dashi stock or *oden*.

The unmissable Nishiki Market in Kyoto

The Nishiki Market, known as the 'kitchen of Kyoto', supplies the chefs and cooks of the former imperial capital. And although locals also regularly shop here, it is particularly busy with shoppers from the city around the New Year celebrations.

It's nearly 10 a.m. and Sachiko Hatanaka is ready to start her day. Wearing her denim apron, an embroidered white fabric mask pulled up over her nose and mouth, her round glasses firmly on her nose, the septuagenarian keeps an eye on her son as he raises the iron grille in front of their fishmonger's stand. The first customers are already arriving. The sun shines through the market's stained-glass roof, its red, green and yellow colours imbuing the place with a friendly ambience. 'The light is always beautiful here. As you walk around to do your shopping, it's not like anywhere else – this place has a soul,' confides the fishmonger. The 'here' that she is referring to is Nishiki Market, located in the heart of Kyoto, a few metres from the Gion district and not far from the former imperial palace. Nicknamed the 'kitchen of Kyoto', it accommodates fishmongers, butchers, people selling fruit, vegetables and soya beans (soybeans), as well as a whole host of stands featuring local specialities.

This market has its own rhythm, a score cleverly orchestrated by its daily visitors, for whom shopping here has become a ritual. The first businesses open at around 10 a.m. This is when you see the first few visitors arrive; they have an air of concentration, and want to weigh the vegetables and find out about the best fish of the day. While Nishiki is a landmark for locals or passing tourists, it is even more importantly the chefs' kingdom. Its products are renowned for their freshness and quality, and regularly feature on the plates of the city's best restaurants.

When both hands of the clock reach 12, the chefs return to their kitchens, and the locals who have come to do their shopping are joined by a handful of visitors who are attracted by the reputation of the place. The bright colours are now joined by a variety of strong aromas, which become more noticeable throughout the day. As you advance along this 400-metre-long (437-yard-long) thoroughfare, you can guess which shops you are passing with your eyes closed. The scent of roasted tea is mixed with the aroma of freshly ground spices. A few steps further along the street, tempura batter is being fried in oil, while opposite, scallops are roasting on the grill.

TASTING REGIONAL SPECIALTIES

In Nishiki, you really can find absolutely everything, but in particular the specialities of this city and its region. Kyoto is the city of vegetables. They even have their own name: *kyo yasai*. There are bamboo shoots, green onions called *kujo negi*, large deep purple aubergines (eggplants) known as *kamo nasu* as well as the long green chillies (chili peppers) named *manganji togarashi*. They are, of course, sold fresh at the market, but also as *tsukemono* - fermented and preserved in large wooden barrels or glass jars.

Another essential part of the Kyoto cuisine is tofu, the star of both *shojin ryori*, the Buddhist vegetarian cuisine, and *kaiseki*, traditional Japanese gastronomy. In Nishiki it is found in different forms: fresh or cooked and seasoned with spices or seaweed. You are especially advised to sample *yuba*, the thin film that forms on the surface of soy milk when it is heated. It can be eaten fresh as it is, accompanied by vegetables or dipped into a dashi stock. Finally, don't hesitate to taste a rolled omelette known as *tamagoyaki*. This sweet-and-salty snack is made fresh in a small square pan and can be enjoyed on the spot, although you can also buy it to take away.

As Kyoto is located relatively close to Uji, the Japanese tea city par excellence, where the very best essences in the entire country are produced, the Nishiki Market naturally also gives pride of place to tea. It comes in all kinds of forms: you can of course buy it loose, but you can also discover its very particular taste in green tea-flavoured ice cream or in a *warabi mochi*, which is a small square rice dough cake that is flavoured and covered in fine matcha powder.

JAKUCHU ITO'S WORKS OF ART

As you are about to enter the Nishiki Market, you just have to look up and you will see the work of Jakuchu Ito - a reproduction of one of his paintings adorns the entrance to the market, several metres above the ground. This is not a coincidence. In fact, the 18th-century painter came from a family of wholesale vegetable traders from Kyoto, who owned the Masuya shop in the market. Jakuchu Ito took over the management of the shop after his parents, before passing it on to his brother at the age of 40, when he decided to devote himself entirely to painting. He quickly became one of Japan's most prominent painters, depicting mostly real or imaginary animals, as well as plants. Just like the reproduction at the Nishiki Market, which depicts a cockerel showing off and a few fish swimming between aquatic plants.

A BIT OF HISTORY

Today this covered market houses more than 130 different businesses, but it was not always so. The beginnings of the market can be traced back to the Heian period (794-1185), although we cannot really ascertain if it was specialized back then. The Nishiki Market was first mentioned in official documents in the year 1615. At the time, it was one of the three fish markets authorized by the Edo shogunate in Kyoto. Fish was exclusively sold wholesale and only to professionals. It was only from 1770 onwards that market gardeners were allowed to come and sell their goods in this open-air market.

中 商 店
定休日
Eat now OK
Don't eat while walking Please

So, the market had two unique selling points. Firstly, its location close to the imperial palace. Kyoto was the capital of Japan, where the emperor and his family resided until 1884, and they had to be supplied with fresh food every day. Secondly, the market was built above an underground cold spring, which made it ideal for preserving perishable goods. At the time, each store had a well that provided direct access to the source of this water. In 1928, the market earned the nickname 'Kyoto cuisine' when butchers and grocers also won the right to set up their stalls there. Once you arrive at the end of this delightful gourmet thoroughfare, you will see a *torri*, a portico marking the entrance to a Shinto shrine, and a few metres along, you will come across the Nishiki Tenmangū shrine. Its entrance is decorated with lanterns on which the names of the shops and their owners are inscribed – and for good reason: Nishiki Tenmangū is renowned as the shrine that is home to Tenjin, the god of scholarship and commercial success ... ▬

The light is always beautiful here.
As you walk around to do your shopping,
it's not like anywhere else – this place
has a soul.

笹巻き 麩まんじゅう(こしあん入り)
140円
特製ひろうす
一ケ 百五十円
小ひろうす
(きくらげ入参ごぼう入)
一個 六十円

錦
NISHIKI
錦市場商店街
宇治屋
宇治茶
生菓子
ギャラリー
NiSHiKi
GALLERY
NiSHiKi
抹茶
ソフトクリーム
EGGS
FRESH EGGS

Difficulty ●○○

Makes 1 kg (2⅛ lb)

Preparation: 50 mins
Cooking: 15 mins

tsukemono and umeboshi

***Tsukemono* are marinated or fermented vegetables that accompany all traditional Japanese meals. They're usually served with a bowl of rice and (miso) soup.**

<u>For 1 kg (2⅛ lbs) turnips</u>

1 sheet dried kombu seaweed (10 x 10 cm/ 4 x 4 in)

1 l (4 cups) filtered water

1 kg (2⅛ lbs) turnips

4-5 dried red chillies (chili peppers)

110 g (generous ½ cup) sugar

30 g (2 tbsp) salt

150 ml (⅔ cup) rice vinegar

Making the turnip senmaizuke ①

Soak the kombu sheet in the filtered water for 30 minutes.

Wash and thinly slice the turnips using a knife or mandolin, cutting at right angles to the direction of the fibres. Break open the dried chillies (chili peppers) and remove the seeds.

Add the sugar, salt and vinegar to the water used to soak the seaweed. Bring to the boil, then turn off the heat. Add the dried chillies (chili peppers).

Add the sliced turnips while the water is still hot, then leave to cool.

Enjoy cold. The turnips will keep in the fridge for a week.

1
2

For 1 kg (2⅛ lbs) *umeboshi* (plums) (or apricots)

1 kg (2⅛ lbs) *umeboshi* (plums) or apricots

150 g (5¼ oz) salt for the umeboshi (plums) (15% of the weight of the fruit)

200 g (7 oz) red shiso (optional)

40 g (scant 3 tbsp) salt for salting the shiso (only if you are adding red shiso)

Making *umeboshi* (salted dried plums) ②

Choose ripe, orange-yellow *umeboshi* (plums). If they are still green, leave them in a cool place for 2–3 days until they are ripe. (If you are using apricots, choose fruits that are ripe, but not overripe.)

Gently wash and dry each *umeboshi* with a clean cloth. Remove any that are damaged.

Remove the small stalk end using a bamboo skewer.

Choose a glass, enamel or ceramic container - such as a salad bowl, saucepan or jar. Avoid plastic or metal, which may react with the salt or acid. You will also need some items to serve as weights. These should weigh twice the weight of the plums.

Use boiling water to disinfect both the container and the items which will serve as weights as they will come into contact with the plums.

Pour a layer of salt into the bottom of the container, then place a layer of plums on top; arrange them close together without leaving any spaces but do not crush them either. Pour over a layer of salt and continue alternating layers of *umeboshi* and salt, finishing with a thick layer of salt.

Place the weights on top.

After three or four days, check that the plum juice *(umezu)* has been extracted and covers the plums.

If the juice has been extracted, remove a number of the weights so that the weight on the plums is the same as the plums when you placed them in the container (1 kg/2⅛ lbs).

If the juice has not yet come out of the plums, add another 3% salt (30 g/2 tbsp) and wait two more days.

If you make the dish without using the red shiso, cover everything with a clean cloth and leave to rest in a cool, dark place for 3 weeks.

If you are using red shiso (which gives it a pleasant scent and a nice colour), you need to salt the shiso.

Remove the large stems of the red shiso, leaving only the leaves. Wash and dry. Sprinkle the shiso with half the shiso salt. Mix well, then squeeze to remove all the red juice from the shiso leaves.

Repeat with the remaining salt.

Pour 1–2 ladles of the plum juice over the drained red shiso leaves and stir thoroughly to cover the shiso leaves.

Place the soaked shiso leaves on top of the plums in the container.

Place weights equal to half the weight of the plums on top (500 g/18 oz). Cover everything with a clean cloth and leave to rest in a cool, dark place for 3 weeks.

After three weeks, check the weather: if there is likely to be a window of three consecutive days of good weather, arrange the plums and the shiso leaves in a shallow colander or a clean sieve and dry them outside in the sun all day. Turn the plums once or twice so that they dry evenly.

In the evening, return the plums to the original container with the plum juice.

Repeat the next day.

On the third day, dry the plums in the sun again for a whole day. The *umeboshi* are now ready.

Place the *umeboshi* into sterilized containers. They will keep in a cool place or at room temperature for 1 year.

kaki no ha zushi

1 or 2 mackerel fillet(s) for 12 slices

450 g (1 lb) sushi rice

560 ml (2⅓ cups) filtered water

1 sheet dried kombu seaweed (5 x 5 cm/ 2 x 2 in)

120 ml (½ cup) rice vinegar

120 g (⅔ cup) sugar

6 g (1 generous tsp) salt plus 1 pinch for the fish

1 or 2 salmon fillet(s) for 12 slices

persimmon leaves

24 shavings of pickled ginger

Warning! To avoid any risk of a parasitic diseases called anisakiasis, the mackerel must be cooked on both sides or, if consumed raw, it must be frozen for at least 48 hours at -20°C (-4°F) before preparation.

Preparation

Freeze the mackerel if you intend to eat it raw. Salt the mackerel fillet(s) and leave to drain for 10 minutes. Pat dry, then wrap in cling film (plastic wrap). Place in the freezer for at least 48 hours at -20°C (-4°F). (This step is not necessary if you will cook the mackerel.)

Defrost the mackerel fillet in the refrigerator when you are ready to eat it.

Making the sushi rice

Wash and gently rinse the rice in clean water taking care not to break up the grains. Repeat two or three times, then leave to drain in a colander.

Transfer the washed rice to a saucepan, then add the filtered water and the kombu sheet. Cover and leave to rest for at least 30 minutes before cooking.

Cook, covered, over a high heat for 5 minutes. Once it has come to the boil, reduce the heat to low and simmer for 10 minutes. Turn off the heat and leave to rest, covered, for 10 minutes.

Remove the kombu. In a small bowl, stir together half the rice vinegar, half the sugar and all of the salt.

Spread the cooked rice on a large flat-bottomed tray. Stir gently, adding the vinegar mixture and cooling the rice with a fan.

Prepare the vinegar for the fish – stir together the remaining rice vinegar and sugar and the pinch of salt.

Marinate the salmon in the mixture for 10 minutes. Now cut the fillet into 12 equal slices and place in the refrigerator.

Next marinate the mackerel in the mixture for 2 minutes. If the fillet was frozen, cut it into 12 equal slices. Otherwise pan-fry it on both sides before cutting it into 12 slices.

Preparing the *kaki no ha zushi*

Wash, then pat dry the persimmon leaves.

Place a persimmon leaf onto a board with the smooth side uppermost.

Place a strip of pickled ginger, a slice of fish and 40 g (scant 3 tablespoons) sushi rice in the centre of the leaf, in the shape of an elongated cube.

Wrap the fish and the rice in the sheet, as if you were wrapping a present in paper.

Place the parcels into a container next to each other. Once it is filled, close it and place a weight on top of the lid. Leave to rest in a cool place for half a day, then enjoy the same day. The persimmon leaves are used to preserve the sushi – they are not meant to be eaten.

Difficulty ●○○

Makes 4 slices

Preparation: 6–12 hours
Cooking: 10 mins

saikyo zuke

4 slices of black salt cod (or cod if not available)

20 g (4 tsp) salt

150 g (½ cup) miso paste

50 ml (generous 3 tbsp) sake

50 ml (generous 3 tbsp) mirin

2 tsp sugar

pickled ginger (optional)

cooked rice

Preparation

Sprinkle the fish with the salt and leave to rest in the fridge for 30 minutes. Pat it dry.

Stir together the miso, sake, mirin and sugar. Add the fish so that it is completely covered.

Leave to marinate in the fridge for 6–12 hours.

Remove the fish from the marinade and gently pat dry. Cook the fish in a frying pan over a medium heat. Once one side has caramelized, turn the fish over, lower the heat, cover and cook for another 3–4 minutes.

Serve with pickled ginger and enjoy hot with a bowl of rice.

Wagashi, Japanese delights

Taiyaki waffles filled with red bean paste, a slice of moist cheesecake or a bright pink *namagashi* shaped like a cherry blossom – immersing yourself in the world of Japanese sweet treats means evoking all five senses.

Japanese pastries guarantee that your taste buds are in for a treat, but these sweet foods will also delight your eyes and your sense of smell. Even your sense of touch will be mobilized – nothing beats the sensation as your fingertips touch a *daifuku* which has been covered in a light dusting of rice flour, or as you trace the outlines of the shapes of the sea bream scales when a *taiyaki* is fresh out of the mould. But before you indulge, you need to know what you are about to taste: the world of Japanese pastries is a universe of its own and you will best appreciate it if you understand the subtleties.

A QUESTION OF VOCABULARY

First of all, it's a matter of differentiating between *wagashi* and *yogashi*. *Gashi* means 'cake' in Japanese, and so everything therefore depends on the prefix: *wa* can be translated as 'Japanese' and *yo* as 'Western'. So *wagashi* are Japanese cakes, a category with multiple ramifications. Western *yogashi* pastries can be made by both Western and Japanese cooks.

Back to the *wagashi*. This term describes several different types of traditional pastries. First of all, there are fresh pastries called *namagashi*, which contain more than 40 per cent water. Their texture is soft, even creamy, and these little snacks should be consumed on the day they are made – or in fact instantly after purchase for those with a sweet tooth. The group of *namagashi* comprises *mochi mono,* pastries made with sticky rice, such as *daifuku* or mochi; *nerikiri*, true works of art featuring delicate shapes; and *yaki mono*, cooked pastries *(taiyaki* or *dorayaki*, for example). A second group are dry pastries known as *higashi*, which contain less than 10 per cent water. They look more like little boiled sweets (hard candies) than pastries. The best known among them are the brightly coloured *konpeito* and *kintaro ame*.

MOMENTS TO SAVOUR

Wagashi should not be eaten at just any time – the world of Japanese pastries is quite regulated. The most traditional *wagashi* – the *nerikiri* – are found in specialist establishments and are most often enjoyed straightaway. They originated as part of the tea ceremony, and this is when they are served. Other, less 'presumptuous' *wagashi*, such as the *dorayaki*, are found in bakeries as well as all the *konbinis* in Japan. Finally *taiyaki*, the famous sea bream-shaped waffles, are one of the emblems of Japanese street food. They are often sold during the local festivals, known as *matsuri*, which take place all over Japan throughout the year.

TAKE *aways*

ANKO, AN ESSENTIAL INGREDIENT

Anko, or red bean paste, is an essential ingredient for making wagashi. There are several varieties.

- *Tsubu an*: the beans are boiled, then skinned and puréed.
- *Tsubushi an*: the beans are boiled and puréed once they are soft, without removing the skin.

Anko can have two different textures: smoother or lumpier, with small pieces of bean remaining intact in the mixture.

HISTORY IN PROGRESS

So there are many different varieties of traditional pastries. However, when people speak of *wagashi*, it's mainly the pocket-sized works of art that they think of. They form a fixed part of the tea ceremony and have to meet very precise specifications. The history and evolution of these *nerikiri* is closely linked to that of the country. It all begins with sugar, because without sugar, there can be no *wagashi*. During the Nara period (710–794), sugar was imported to Japan from China, but it was expensive and therefore remained reserved for a privileged few. Tea was taken

MOCHI THROUGH THE YEAR

For New Year, people enjoy *kagami* mochi, made from two superimposed *mochi*. Hinamatsuri or Girls' Day on 3 March is celebrated with *hishi mochi* – pink, white and green diamond-shaped mochi, while on 5 May, Children's Day, it is customary to enjoy *kashiwa mochi*, which are mochi wrapped in an oak leaf.

with rice cakes, chestnuts, persimmons and seaweed. A few centuries later, during the Muromachi period (1336–1573), the volume of imported sugar increased, notably thanks to trade with the Portuguese. It was still only used in small quantities to make pastries because its price was quite high, yet sugar had become a sort of precious powder, which could be sprinkled onto the sweets served during the tea ceremony.

It is also thanks to these ceremonies, with their excessively codified process, that *wagashi* evolved in terms of their method of preparation as well as their shape. In 1683, a collection was published that compiled the many variations made by the Kikuya pastry house, listing names that are still used today, such as 'night plum tree' or 'light snowfall'. Ten years later, in 1693, another collection listed 250 different *wagashi*, this time with illustrations for each one, as well as some details concerning their ingredients and how they were made.

Wagashi are a pleasure for your sense of taste, but what is essential is that they respect the precepts of the tea ceremony: following and highlighting, with delicacy and poetry, the passage of the seasons.

REPRESENTATIONS OF NATURE

We have by now reached the 17th century, and *wagashi* are enjoyed by the cultural elite of Kyoto, but also by the lords of Edo (the old name for Tokyo). *Wagashi* bring pleasure to your sense of taste, but what is essential is that they respect the rules of the tea ceremony: following and highlighting, with delicacy and poetry, the passage of the seasons. To do so, master pastry chefs have a number of different techniques at their disposal because the ingredients used in the making of these edible jewels are always more or less identical: water, sugar and anko (red bean paste).

From nature, *wagashi* first of all borrow the colours: light pink is used to recall the vibrant spring hues of cherry and plum blossoms; red represents the incandescence of leaves in the autumn; and white reminds us of snowflakes in the winter. But the pastries also adopt nature's forms: *wagashi* live and evolve in the plant world. They are made to represent some of the most beautiful seasonal flowers, and you can also enjoy these sweet delicacies in the shape of fruits or leaves, although all pastry chefs are of course free to come up with their own creations as proof of their limitless imagination and poetry.

EXPORTING LOCAL KNOW-HOW

While *wagashi* enjoyed great popularity from the 17th century onwards, the ever-growing consumption of coffee in Japan and increasingly rare tea ceremonies meant that gradually these precious pastries were consumed less often.

At the same time, however, large houses, like Toraya, began to export their know-how beyond the borders of the archipelago. Founded in Japan in the middle of the 16th century, Toraya was one of companies that supplied the imperial family. Initially established in Kyoto, the company followed the emperor to Tokyo when the capital was transferred there in 1869. In 1980 it opened a store in France to introduce traditional Japanese pastries to French taste buds. Futoshi Yoshida, one of Toraya's master pastry chefs, learned the basics of pastry making in Tokyo. 'It may seem easy, but in fact you have to understand the techniques of making and handling anko,' he explains. 'The texture of the dough must be consistent and the taste of *azuki* must be neither too strong nor too mild.' He started his career in the kitchen, but later decided to swap his white coat for a rep's suit. 'I was interested in understanding what customers wanted, what they liked, what their tastes were,' says Futoshi Yoshida. After three years, he picked up his chef's whites again and began to make more complex *wagashi*.

At the age of 26, Futoshi took off for his first internship in Paris, and a few months later he returned there to settle in the French capital for a longer period of time. He remained in Paris for more than a decade. In 2012, the chef returned to Japan to teach the art of *wagashi* and to supervise the preparation of cakes for the imperial family. In 2021, Futoshi returned to France and to the Toraya restaurant and coffee shop on the rue Saint-Florentin. His work is a subtle blend of Japanese traditions and French culinary customs. He draws inspiration from Parisian patisseries and restaurants to make creations with typically French ingredients, such as a pear and caramel *wagashi*. At the same time, he introduces his customers' palates to typically Japanese tastes, such as *yomogi* (mugwort), a herb that introduces a vegetable and mint note, *sakura* (Japanese cherry) leaves for spring *wagashi* and white miso from Kyoto, which adds sweet and salty flavours.

Difficulty ●●○

Makes 8 pieces (Serves 4)

Preparation: 60 mins
Cooking: 10 mins

yubeshi

50 g (½ cup) walnut kernels (pieces)

150 ml (⅔ cup) filtered water

100 g (½ cup) dark muscovado sugar

1 tsp soy sauce

100 g (¾ cup) glutinous rice flour plus 1 handful for sprinkling

Preparation

Lightly roast the walnut kernels, then roughly chop them.

In a small saucepan, heat the water, then add the sugar and the soy sauce. Stir well until the sugar is completely dissolved.

Put the glutinous rice flour in a bowl, then gradually stir in the sugar mixture.

Place this batter in a saucepan and heat over a low heat, stirring vigorously, until you have a sticky paste. Add the chopped walnuts.

Sprinkle some of the handful of glutinous rice flour on to a plate, then place the cooked paste on top. Cover everything with cling film (plastic wrap) and flatten the dough evenly. Leave to cool.

Once the dough has cooled, remove the clingfilm and sprinkle the dough with the remaining glutinous rice flour. Cut into large or small pieces as desired.

Difficulty ●○○

Makes 4 mochi

Preparation: 20 mins
Cooking: 12 mins

matcha mochi

<u>For the mochi paste</u>

60 g (7 tbsp) glutinous rice flour

60 g (scant ⅓ cup) sugar

5 tbsp filtered water

1½ tsp matcha powder

100 g (⅓ cup) anko (red bean paste)

1 handful potato starch

Preparation

Place all the mochi paste ingredients except the anko and the potato starch into a bowl and stir to combine.

Transfer the mixture to a shallow container.

Steam for 12 minutes.

Shape the anko into four equally sized balls.

Once the mochi paste is cooked, place it in a bowl and stir until you have a sticky paste.

Sprinkle an empty dish with the potato starch.

Place the mochi paste on top of the potato starch, then divide it into four equal pieces.

Take a portion of the mochi paste in your hand, then place a portion of anko into the centre. Shape into a ball.

Enjoy within two days.

Difficulty ●●○

Makes 12 dorayaki (24 crêpes)

Preparation: 2 hours
Cooking: 10 mins

dorayaki

180 g (6¼ oz) egg (about 3 eggs)

1 tsp bicarbonate of soda (baking soda)

1 tsp water

1 tbsp mirin

2 tsp honey

160 g (generous ¾ cup) sugar

180 g (1¼ cups) plain (all-purpose) flour

2–3 tbsp milk

1 tbsp melted butter

300 g (1 cup) anko (red bean paste)

Preparation

Beat the eggs in a bowl.

Dissolve the bicarbonate of soda in the water, then add it to the beaten eggs, together with the mirin and the honey. Stir well to combine at each step.

Add the sugar and stir in. Add the flour and stir in. Finally, add the milk and the melted butter. Stir everything to combine well. Leave the batter to rest in the fridge for at least 1 hour.

Heat a frying pan over a low heat. Pour the equivalent of 2–3 tablespoons of batter into the hot pan to form a mini pancake about 8–10 cm (3.5–4 in) in diameter; as soon as small bubbles appear on the surface, gently turn it over.

Repeat until you have 24 pancakes. (Always use the same amount of batter so that the *dorayaki* will be the same size.)

Once the 24 pancakes are cooked, take one, cover it with about 2 teaspoons anko, then cover it with another pancake to make a sandwich. This will make twelve *dorayaki*.

KYUSHU

Yoshoku, a Japanese take on Western cuisine

Tempura, *karerice*, *tonkatsu* and *naporitan* are all omnipresent foods in Japan, served everywhere from restaurants to domestic kitchens. While they are now considered typical Japanese fare, they are actually a uniquely Japanese take on Western dishes.

As you bite into crunchy tempura, the light batter gives the food a crispy yet soft and luscious texture. It is hard to believe that these dishes are not Japanese. They are found all over the archipelago, on restaurant tables, at street-food stalls ... and even at Japanese restaurants around the world. Except that tempura is not originally from Japan. It is as Japanese as *karerice*, *tonkatsu*, *naporitan* and *korokke*. All these dishes are classified as *yoshoku* or 'Western cuisine', as opposed to *washoku* or 'Japanese cuisine'; the prefix *yo* means 'Western' and *wa* 'Japanese'.

OPENING UP TO FOREIGN CUISINES

It wasn't always this way. The distinction was first established in the 19th century, and for good reason: before that, the archipelago was a closed empire, where contact with the outside world was minimal, verging on non-existent; there was no need to know what was classified as Japanese cuisine and what was not. However, Western powers started to force the country to open it borders. The Meiji era (1868–1912) saw foreigners arrive, bringing with them their food cultures among other things. Middle-class Japanese palates began to discover new flavours, and even meat, which had largely been prohibited until then, started making its way onto dinner plates.

However, it was not until the 20th century that these dishes really grew in popularity, becoming symbols of everyday, mainstream cuisine par excellence.

And yet, *yoshoku* is not technically Western cuisine - at least not totally. There is a more subtle mechanism at play here. It is not so much a case of Japan copying Western recipes, but rather putting its own spin on them. The familiar base is there, but it has been reworked, enhanced and mastered by Japanese chefs, resulting in dishes that are so entrenched in Japanese food culture that it is almost impossible to tell whether they are Japanese or not.

Yoshoku means 'Western cuisine', the prefix yo stands for 'Western'.

THE PORTUGUESE MISSIONARIES' CULINARY CONTRIBUTION

While *yoshoku* cuisine emerged in the mid-19th century, Japan had already had a few forays into foreign food several decades earlier. In the 16th century, Portuguese Jesuit missionaries landed in the country and through them Japan discovered *peixinhos da horta*, which served as the creative inspiration for tempura, the crunchy batter used to coat anything from vegetables to prawns (shrimp).

The Jesuit missionaries introduced the Japanese archipelago to other recipes too, such as *castella*, a Genoise-style cake made using eggs, flour and sugar. As sugar was a rarity in Japan, *mizuame*, a starch syrup-based sweetener, was often used as a substitute. Today, *castella* is considered a speciality of Nagasaki, one of the main ports on the island of Kyushu.

SOME TYPICAL *YOSHOKU* DISHES

Korokke

Korokke are an adaptation of Western potato croquettes. Introduced in the late 19th century, they were initially more of an upmarket dish, served with a béchamel sauce. These days, *korokke* are everywhere, most commonly sold cheaply at grocery and butcher's shops. Perfect as a snack or bento accompaniment, depending on your appetite, they are made by combining mashed potatoes with minced (ground) meat and onions. The mixture is rolled into balls, which are then coated in panko breadcrumbs before being fried.

Kare raisu or curry rice

Kare raisu is a typical fusion dish with multiple origins. While India may be the home of curry par excellence, curry came to Japan via England. *Kare raisu* is rice with a thick curry sauce containing onions, potatoes and carrots. Initially made using curry powder, this dish grew in popularity after World War II, when the famed mass-produced curry blocks, offering various degrees of spiciness, were launched onto the market. As its name suggests, curry rice is eaten with white rice and the popular breadcrumbed pork known as *katsukare*. Recent decades have seen certain regions of Japan develop their own recipes served with, for example, game in Hokkaido or seafood and tofu in Okinawa.

Doria

Doria is a French-inspired potato gratin where the vegetable is replaced with rice. The rice is covered in a white - béchamel - sauce and cheese before being cooked in the oven. This recipe originated in the port city of Yokohama, hence the use of seafood, namely scallops, as a garnish. These days, there are variations that substitute the scallops with octopus or, more commonly, chicken.

Naporitan

As its name suggests - given that r is pronounced [l] in Japanese - *naporitan* is a *yoshoku* recipe inspired by Italian cuisine, although the dish may well send cold shivers down the spine of any chef hailing from the Bay of Naples. It consists of spaghetti in a sauce of green peppers, onions, mushrooms and ... ketchup instead of tomato sauce. The pasta is cooked until it

is very soft and topped with sliced sausages. Here's a bit of history: this dish came about as a means of feeding General Douglas MacArthur, who landed in Yokohama on 30 August 1945. He was staying at a portside hotel which offered shelter from the bombings. The hotel's head chef took inspiration from the American military rations to create his ketchup spaghetti dish (legend has it that he used tinned tomato purée (paste), not ketchup, for his recipe), leaving the pasta in the cooking water for longer than usual in order to achieve a texture akin to udon noodles, which are exceptionally popular in Japan. It proved to be a success. The recipe was adopted by numerous restaurants, which replaced the tomato purée (paste) with ketchup, the latter being less expensive and much more readily available on Japanese supermarket shelves.

Omuraisu

Omuraisu, or *omurice*, is an iconic dish of the *kissaten* coffee shops that were typical in the 1970s and where time seems to have stood still. *Omurice* is a contraction of the English words 'omelette' and 'rice', and the dish consists of rice covered in a soft, fluffy omelette. Preparing it merely requires browning the rice in a frying pan with garlic, onions, green peppers and ketchup, and then placing the mixture on top of an omelette that is then wrapped around the rice. One variation involves simply placing a circular omelette on top of the rice. And the final touch? Pictures or Japanese characters drawn with ... tomato ketchup, of course!

Difficulty ●○○ Serves 2 Preparation: 15 mins
Cooking: 10 mins

miyazaki chicken nanban

400 g (14 oz) chicken fillet (boneless chicken breast) (or 400 g/14 oz boned chicken thighs)

1 pinch each of salt and black pepper

1 handful plain (all-purpose) flour

400 ml (1⅔ cups) oil for deep-frying

1 egg, beaten

For the tartare sauce

1 hard-boiled egg, chopped

¼ onion, chopped

2 cornichons, very finely chopped

3 tbsp mayonnaise

½ tsp soy sauce

1 tsp lemon juice

1 pinch each of salt and black pepper

For the *nanban* sauce

3 tbsp soy sauce

3 tbsp vinegar

3 tbsp mirin

2 tbsp sugar

Preparation

Cut the chicken into bite-sized pieces, season with the salt and pepper and sprinkle with the flour.

Making the tartare sauce

Combine all the ingredients In a bowl and stir. Keep in a cool place.

Making the *nanban* sauce

Put all the ingredients into a small saucepan and bring to a boil.

Cooking the chicken

Heat the oil to 180°C (360°F). Dip the chicken pieces into the beaten egg, then fry them in the oil.

Dip the fried chicken pieces in the *nanban* sauce. Arrange them on a plate and serve with the tartare sauce on the side.

tonkotsu ramen

For the noodles

160 ml (generous ⅔ cup) filtered water (40% of the weight of the flour)

4 g (⅔ tsp) salt (1% of the weight of the flour)

2 g (½ tsp) bicarbonate of soda (baking soda) (0.5% of the weight of the flour)

400 g (3¼ cups) plain (all-purpose) flour (preferably with a protein content of about 12%)

2 g (½ tsp) potassium bicarbonate (0.5% of the weight of the flour) (if you can't find potassium bicarbonate, replace it with bicarbonate of soda [baking soda])

4–5 handfuls of potato starch

Preparation

Making the noodles

Weigh all ingredients accurately. In a small bowl, combine the water, salt and bicarbonate of soda (baking soda) and stir to dissolve.

Sift the flour into a large bowl.

Gradually pour the water mixture onto the flour, using a circular movement, until you have added all of it.

Using chopsticks, mix the flour and water to distribute the liquid evenly, until small crumbs form. Make sure that no flour remains stuck to the sides of the bowl. At this point, the dough will resemble breadcrumbs rather than being a homogenous mixture. Place the dough in a large resealable plastic food (zip lock) bag and seal it carefully so that the dough does not dry out. Leave to rest for 1 hour until the water has been absorbed by the flour.

After 1 hour, start kneading the dough. The easiest way is to do this is with your feet. Open the bag a little to let the air out. Place a sheet or towel on a clean floor, place the bag with the dough on the towel, and flatten the dough by taking small steps on the bag. When the dough is flat and has filled the bag, open the bag and fold the dough towards the centre in thirds.

Return the dough to the bag, seal it, and repeat the operation three more times.

Leave the flattened dough in the bag, seal it and leave to rest for at least 2 hours or a whole day, if possible.

After this, cut the dough into 4 equal pieces and flatten them using a rolling pin to form strips.

A. If you have a pasta machine, put the dough in the machine, start at level 0 (the thickest) then gradually thin it by moving from one level to another, until the desired thickness has been achieved (the recommended thickness is about 1–1.2 mm (about ¹⁄₂₅ in), level 5 on my Marcato Atlas 150 machine).

Next, sprinkle both sides of the dough with potato starch and cut the noodles to the desired width. The width of standard spaghetti is ideal.

For the soup

500 g (18 oz) pork rib bones

500 g (18 oz) pork thigh bone

300 ml (1¼ cups) water

B. If you don't have a pasta machine, flatten each strip of dough to about 1–1.5 mm (about 1/25 in) thickness using a rolling pin. Sprinkle both sides with potato starch, fold them in half and cut the noodles to the desired width.

Once the noodles are cut, sprinkle some more potato starch to prevent them from sticking together, turn them two or three times so that they are completely covered with the starch, then leave to rest in a large food container for 1 or 2 days. The noodles can be eaten immediately after making, but they are always better 1 or 2 days later.

To get slightly curly noodles, simply take a portion of noodles in your hands and gently but firmly squeeze them into shape.

Making the soup

The day before, clean and soak the pork bones in water to remove the blood. Leave to soak overnight in the refrigerator or in a cool place. After soaking, discard the water.

Break up the bones and carcass using a hammer, or chop them so that they will fit inside your pressure cooker.

Put the bones and water into a pressure cooker. If the amount of water in the ingredients list is not sufficient to cover the bones, add more. The amount of water given is only approximate, and you may need to add more water as the soup cooks.

Cook, uncovered, over a high heat to bring the mixture to the boil. Once the soup has started boiling and a brown foam starts to appear, reduce the heat to medium and begin to skim off the foam. You do not have to remove all the foam; after 20 minutes move on to the next step even if a little foam remains.

Cover and close the pressure cooker and set it to medium heat. Wait for the pressure to build, then cook for 2 hours over a low heat.

After 2 hours, turn off the heat and leave the pressure cooker to cool until you can open the lid.

Open the lid, add the pork for the chashu and cook, uncovered, over a medium heat for a further 1 hour. Increase the heat so that the water comes to a boil, forming large bubbles. At this stage, the soup is quite thick, so stir it frequently to prevent it sticking to the bottom of the pan. Add a little water if the level of the liquid drops too much.

Remove the pork and strain the soup through a colander. Press the residue well to squeeze out all the soup that has soaked up the meat fibres. You should have about 1.2 litres (5 cups) soup. Add more water if there is not enough soup. The soup is now ready.

<u>For the *chashu*</u>

300 g (10½ oz) cooked pork loin or belly, in one piece

150 ml (⅔ cup) soy sauce

50 ml (generous 3 tbsp) mirin

<u>For the *shoyu tare*</u>

10 g (⅓ oz) kombu seaweed

150 ml (⅔ cup) filtered water

120 ml (½ cup) soy sauce

50 ml (generous 3 tbsp) mirin

4 tsp crushed garlic

<u>For the *ajitsuke tamago*</u>

40 ml (scant 3 tbsp) soy sauce

2 tbsp water

20 ml (1½ tbsp) mirin

2 tsp sugar

4 eggs

<u>For the garnish (as desired)</u>

2–3 spring onions (scallions), chopped

flavouring oil

cooked black mushrooms (optional)

marinated bamboo shoots

salt (optional)

pickled ginger (optional)

***takana* (spicy pickled cabbage) (optional)**

<u>Making the *chashu*</u>

Place the cooked pork into a small resealable bag together with the soy sauce and the mirin. Remove the air from the bag so that the entire surface of the meat is in contact with the marinade. Leave to marinate for at least 1 hour.

<u>Making the shoyu tare</u>

Place the kombu and the filtered water in a saucepan and leave to soak for 30 minutes, then bring to the boil. Add the soy sauce and the mirin. Cook for 10 minutes over a low heat, then remove the kombu and leave to cool. The *tare* is now ready. Add the crushed garlic just before serving.

<u>Making the ajitsuke tamago</u>

Combine all the liquid ingredients and the sugar in a small saucepan and bring to the boil. Turn off the heat and leave to cool.

Fill another saucepan with water, bring to the boil then gently immerse the eggs straight from the fridge. Cook for 7–8 minutes, then remove them from the saucepan and place in a bowl of cold water to cool. Shell the eggs, then place them into a small resealable bag together with the sauce prepared in the previous step. Remove the air from the bag so that the eggs are in contact with the marinade. Leave to marinate for 3 hours.

<u>For the garnishes</u>

Chop the spring onions (scallions), halve the *ajitsuke tamago* lengthways, slice the *chashu* and prepare all your chosen garnishes.

<u>Presentation</u>

Heat the soup (about 300ml/1¼ cups per person).

If you are cooking a lot of noodles at once, make sure your saucepan is large enough to hold them all. Bring plenty of water to the boil, then cook 140 g (5 oz) noodles per person for about 2 minutes. Drain carefully.

While the noodles are cooking, put 2 tablespoons *shoyu tare*, 1 tablespoon flavouring oil and 1 teaspoon crushed garlic into a bowl, then pour in the hot soup (adjust the amount of *shoyu tare* to taste).

Carefully arrange the cooked noodles in the bowl with the soup, then add the *chashu, ajitsuke tamago* and garnishes to taste. Enjoy hot.

chicken karaage

400 g (14 oz) boned chicken thighs

1½ tbsp sake

2 tbsp soy sauce

10 g (2 tsp) grated ginger

10 g (2tsp) grated garlic

4 tbsp potato starch

500 ml (2 cups) oil for deep-frying

salad and lemon wedges

Preparation

Cut the chicken into bite-sized pieces and put them into a bowl.

Add the sake, soy sauce, ginger and garlic. Mix and leave to marinate for at least 15 minutes.

Transfer the chicken pieces to a bowl, shaking off any excess marinade. Sprinkle over the potato starch and stir well to coat the chicken.

Heat the oil to 160–180°C (320–360°F) – the temperature will depend on the size of the chicken pieces – and fry the chicken. Serve hot with salad and lemon wedges to squeeze over.

まんさく
オリジ
予約受付中
レッシュ
営業中
100

Kyushu, market-gardening in the shadow of volcanoes

Kyushu Island is home to two volcanoes considered to be among the most active on earth, but it makes good use of its fiery cohabitants – its soil is one of the most fertile in all of Japan.

'If you know what to look for, there are signs that will tell you if an eruption is imminent. For example, when animals refuse to go near the mountainside, you know there's one coming.' This is Shiro Watanabe's response when asked about the risks of living near an active volcano. The 55-year-old works as a market gardener right in the heart of the Aso caldera, which is home to some 15 volcanic peaks over an area spanning 25 km (16 miles) north-to-south and 17 km (11 miles) east-to-west. Aso-san is the largest of all Japan's volcanoes, and also one of the most active. 'You know, it's true that living here is risky, but the volcano really does help us. And then there's the legend, have you heard it?' the farmer asks. No, I can categorically say that no Mount Aso mythology has ever reached my ears. So he takes the time to go through the story for me: Takeiwatatsu no Mikoto, considered to be the god of Mount Aso, had been instructed by his grandfather, the mythical emperor Jimmu (8th–6th century BCE), to go to the mountain. There, he discovered a giant crater and a vast expanse of water, and is said to have deliberately sunk one edge of the caldera (the large depression formed when a volcano erupts and collapses) to empty out the water. The residual sediment and minerals in the soil turned the drained lake into arable land that attracted rice growers, market gardeners and arborists. 'Our island's land is still very rich. We grow the best fruit and vegetables in Japan,' says Shiro, not without a hint of pride.

MINERALS AND A SUBTROPICAL CLIMATE

The high concentration of volcanoes on Kyushu does indeed significantly enhance the quality of its soil, which is rich in nitrogen, organic carbon and minerals - a precious alloy that is a major factor in its abundant fertility. Almost everything grows here, because, in addition to excellent soil quality, it also enjoys a humid subtropical climate: the summer season is long, the winter season is milder than on the three other main islands of the archipelago, and there is regular rainfall.

Not far away, in the hills of Bungotakada, a small town near the Seto Inland Sea, is one of the island's richest fruit-growing regions. It is known in particular for the *kyoho budo* grape - a name which translates literally as 'giant grape of the mountains'. The owners of Izumi Nouen farm began growing this grape 50 years ago. They have since diversified their produce and now grow 14 grape varieties, supplying local markets and high-end fruit shops with their perfectly rounded, firm fruit. Sheichiro Ito grows a multitude of fruits, some ripening underground and others on meticulously aligned fruit trees that he adores walking through.

'The land gives us a lot, and we are also aided by the weather. To produce good varieties in adequate quantities, all you need to do is observe nature. Pay attention to the rhythm of the seasons, including their infinite variations,' explains the arborist, who follows an integrated, sustainable farming approach. As such, he grows strawberries from early January to mid-May, followed by blueberries starting in July, then peaches and grapes. The end of summer marks the arrival of pears, which adorn the branches of the trees from early August to late October. Delicious persimmons round off the year from mid-October onwards. 'The soil is rich in nutrients but also sandy which means that our fruit has very mild acidity while still being high in sugars. All without the aid of any pesticides, and instead simply adapting to what nature offers us,' says Ito-san, who uses flowers and aromatic plants to drive insects and pests away from his crops. While he primarily sells the fruits of his labour at markets several times a week, he also displays some of his produce at the entrance to his farm every day. The fruits are arranged on a wooden stand next to a money box, into which customers pay the cost of their purchase.

SURRENDERING TO NATURE'S WISHES

It was now time to head to the south of the island, to the region around Kagoshima, nicknamed the 'Naples of the East' for its close proximity to an imposing active volcano. The crater of Mount Sakurajima is only 8 km (5 miles) from the city and spews out greyish smoke, sometimes in rings, sometimes in plumes, almost every day - a situation that regularly forces farmers to seek refuge under the concrete shelters that protect them from the ash in times of more intense volcanic activity. This is the land of the daikon, a radish with a large white root that grows in sizes unlike any other of its kind; the heftiest can weigh as much as 30 kg (66 lbs), which earns them the title of *shimadekon*. 'Living with the smoke and ash of the volcano is not always easy, but we reap the benefits of Sakurajima in what we produce,' explains Mr Nakamura, one of the local market gardeners. 'Our daikon have a flavour you won't find anywhere else: smoky notes, yet still a sweet and strong taste. Firm-bodied with a soft texture.' However, Kagoshima and, more broadly, the entire southern tip of Kyushu, which is home to more volcanoes such as Mount Kaimon, whose pyramidal shape is reminiscent of the famous Mount Fuji, is the perfect place to grow citrus fruits like yuzu and *mikan*, a variety of sugary-sweet mandarin that is the Japanese winter fruit par excellence. 'The volcanoes empower the island's inhabitants through the food they are able to grow,' Nakamura-san says, before concluding that 'this cohabitation is unpredictable, even though we know the volcanoes are ultimately in control. All we can do is surrender to nature's wishes.'

KYUSHU, LAND OF VOLCANOES

Japan is home to 10 per cent of the earth's volcanic activity. Much of the island of Kyushu was formed through a volcanic eruption, specifically the subduction (when one tectonic plate collides with another) of the Philippine Sea Plate under the Eurasian Plate. Today, it spans nine active volcanic systems, two of which - Mount Aso and Sakurajima volcano - are considered to be the most active on earth.

Difficulty ●○○

Serves 4

Preparation: 5 min
Cooking: 120 min

yakiimo

4 Japanese sweet potatoes

This is a very popular snack in Japan. For this recipe, the quality and type of sweet potato you choose is extremely important. If possible, choose a Japanese variety that is firm but tender and sweet, even honeyed.

Preparation

Wash the sweet potatoes and trim the ends. Do not pat them dry, but keep them damp.

Wrap each one in slightly crumpled aluminium foil. Don't wrap them too tightly – the potatoes will cook better if you leave a little air around them.

Bake at 140°C (285°F) for 1½ to 2 hours, depending on the size of the potatoes.

The potatoes are cooked when you can easily insert a bamboo toothpick into them.

Enjoy hot or cold, with the skin on, if possible.

karashi renkon

1 lotus root *(renkon)* (about 700 g/1 lb 8½ oz)

100 ml (scant ½ cup) water

2 tsp rice vinegar

80 g (2 cups) fresh breadcrumbs

80 ml (⅓ cup) mirin

160 g (generous ½ cup) miso paste

1 tbsp Japanese mustard

100 g (¾ cup) plain (all-purpose) flour plus more for dusting

1 tbsp ground turmeric

300–500 ml (1¼–2 cups) oil for deep-frying

soy sauce or mayonnaise, to serve

Preparation

Wash and peel the lotus root; trim the ends.

Put the water and the vinegar into a saucepan and bring to the boil. Add the lotus root and cook for 4–5 minutes. Take out of the water and drain.

Mix the breadcrumbs, mirin, miso and mustard together and fill the holes in the lotus root with the mixture.

Wrap in cling film (plastic wrap) and set aside for 5–6 hours.

Remove the excess mustard mixture and dust the lotus root with the flour.

Mix the 100 g (¾ cup) flour, turmeric and water. Dip the flour-dusted lotus root in this mixture and fry at 170°C (340°F), turning occasionally, until golden brown.

Cut into slices about 1 cm (⅜ in) thick. Serve cold, with soy sauce or mayonnaise.

Difficulty ●○○

Serves 2

Preparation: 10 mins
Cooking: 10 mins

kimpira gobo

300 g (10½ oz) gobo (burdock root)

2 tbsp sesame oil

⅓ dried red chilli (chili pepper), sliced

1 tbsp sake

½ tbsp brown sugar

1 tbsp soy sauce

Preparation

Wash the gobo (burdock root) and cut it into fine julienne strips. Place them into a bowl of water for 10 minutes to remove any bitterness, then drain.

Heat the sesame oil in a frying pan, add the dried red chilli (chili pepper) and the greater gobo (burdock) and fry until browned.

When the greater gobo (burdock) is tender, add the sake, brown sugar and soy sauce. Stir-fry for another 5 minutes. Serve hot or cold as a starter, with rice or as a snack.

Yatais, a Fukuoka institution

Yatai street food stalls, where you can buy food to eat on the go, are dotted around some neighbourhoods of the metropolis of Kyushu Island. Once commonplace throughout the archipelago, Fukuoka is now their last stronghold.

It's just before 5 p.m. in Fukuoka. If you stand still for a few moments near the exit of Tenjin metro station, in the west of the city, a skilfully orchestrated choreography will unfold before your very eyes. Observant passers-by will see strange piles of odds and ends of wood arrive, pulled by bicycles, scooters or miniature vans. At 5 p.m. sharp, each of these astonishing vehicles will take its place on the pavement, in a very specific spot. In reality, what you took for a tangle of boards turns out to be a magic box, and it contains an entire portable restaurant.

Masami Ataka has been repeating the same procedure from Monday to Saturday every week since 1987 without fail. After just a quarter of an hour, his stand is completely unfolded and perfectly set up: you can now see before your eyes a scale model kitchen, with a gas bottle, water point and miniature refrigerator; as well as a wooden counter surrounded by stools with sufficient room for eight to ten customers to sit and enjoy their meal.

'Very quickly, the yatai becomes almost the story of extended family.'

The entire set-up is surrounded by a transparent tarpaulin which protects guests from rain and wind. And we mustn't forget to mention the garland of lights which gives the ephemeral establishment its finishing touch. These space-saving restaurants do not allow for any deviation or change – here, everything has a precise place and every inch of space is optimized. A meticulous sense of organization prevails among each and every one of the owners of these unusual restaurants.

A VANISHING WORLD

The steadily disappearing world of the *yatai* has its own rhythm, customs and codes.

In 2020, during the last census, there were 103 *yatai* in the Fukuoka area, most of them in three districts: Tenjin, Nakasu and Nagahama. By comparison, in the mid-1960s, the golden era of these mobile restaurants, the city counted just

over 400 *yatai*. To retrace the history of these food outlets, you have to go back to the 5th or 6th century. At the time, local rulers set up stalls to feed pilgrims on their way to shrines and temples. But it was during the Edo period (1603-1867) that the first outlines of what the yatai still are today took shape. At that time, the *daimyo*, the local Japanese lords, travelled ever more frequently to and from the imperial capital. A handful of cooks always followed them so that they could savour the specialties of their own region during the trip. From the 19th century, these mobile restaurants took root in various areas and became the main meeting points for local workers, who were delighted to find somewhere for a quick meal.

The end of World War II brought the first shake-up in the small world of mobile food outlets. The Americans occupied the territory, food was rationed and *yatai* owners were told to put away their wooden structures. But they did not bank on the emergence of a parallel network.

The *yatai* became a part of the black market, which was mostly run by immigrants from territories that were occupied by Japan, such as South Korea and Taiwan. While fewer in number, these Polly Pocket restaurants survived, particularly in Fukuoka where, in 1950, the owners organized themselves into an association to try to assert their rights.

Another blow was dealt to the yatai when Japan hosted the Olympic Games in 1964. During this major sporting event, the intention was for the archipelago to demonstrate its newfound power and competitiveness to the world, and so the Tokyo government ordered a complete clean-up. The *yatai* were considered to be unrepresentative of this glamourous new Japanese identity. With their tarpaulins and wooden panels, where people spoke loudly, where alcohol flowed freely and where hygiene was possibly not impeccable, they became the victims of this clean-up. Nothing else was needed to condemn these restaurants to a certain death.

面白い

STRICT RULES

- *Yatai* are allowed to set up on the pavements of Fukuoka from 5 p.m. to 4 a.m.
- Owners are given a specific location, which must not exceed 5 sq m (54 sq feet).
- The sale of raw foodstuffs and of takeaway meals is not permitted.
- Since 1995, the business can only be passed on to the owner's descendants or spouse.
- It is forbidden to set up the *yatai* during adverse weather conditions, such as strong rain or wind.

However, resistance groups organized in Kyushu and Fukuoka, which is now the standard bearer city for this type of street food. 'You can still find a few yatai in Tokyo and in some other large cities in Japan, but they appear mostly only during the *matsuri* [local festivals which mainly take place in summer],' explains Masami Ataka, the owner of one such restaurant. 'We in Fukuoka, however, are open whether there is any special event or nothing is happening at all.'

FORGING LINKS

It's 5:30 p.m. The restaurant is set up. Masami places bottles of sake onto the counter and lights the gas stove onto which he places a large saucepan. It contains *oden*, his speciality, a comforting soup made from cabbage, tofu and fish cakes. 'I close my *yatai* around 1 a.m., sometimes a little later in the summer. The next day, at 10 a.m., I am at the market to buy the ingredients that I will use for my different dishes. Then I start preparing the broths for the ramen, but also the *oden*. That way, I only have to worry about cooking the noodles at the stand. And then at 4 p.m., I get on the road to come here,' he tells us.

On the pavement opposite, skewers of chicken are already browning on the grill, while Yoshinobu Nishida and his wife Junko are in deep discussion with their customers. The couple has been at the head of Nanshiyohtoya since 1989. 'That's what we say in the Hakata dialect [a district of Fukuoka] when we pass each other in the street!' explains Yoshinobu. The menu is written in felt-tip pen onto strips of paper which are nailed to the wooden structure.

Their specialty? Kebabs of all sorts – with offal, chicken, mushrooms, sausages or peppers. At the counter, Iro, a drummer from Tokyo, takes a seat next to his friend Oga, who runs a record store in Fukuoka. 'Yoshinobu and Junko are the parents of a childhood friend. As soon as friends come to visit from Tokyo or Osaka, we come here because it's cheap and, above all, because it's delicious,' explains the latter, with a cigarette between his lips and his arms covered in tattoos.

A couple of Japanese tourists from Hiroshima are seated next to them. They are first-time visitors to this type of restaurant. 'We had heard about this place and wanted to try it out. The food is delicious and it's a very special atmosphere, we're right in the middle of street life!', says Ibiki, who is about to tuck into his omelette with *negi*, Japanese spring onions (scallions).

The night has now arrived, and the loud laughter of Junko Shiraishi echoes through the air from an adjacent street. Junko and her husband Kouki have been running their *yatai* for 36 years. A clientele of often exhausted office employees usually flocks here, but they are quickly invigorated by a glass of sake. There are seven of them today, lined up next to each other, some deeply immersed in conversation, while others have their eyes glued to the small television screen which is broadcasting a baseball match. In the middle of all this, Junko whirls around to serve them and exchange a few words. 'After so many years, you end up knowing all their little habits and preferences,' says Kouki, a pair of long chopsticks in his hand. At the beginning, a *yatai* is the story of someone cooking alone or as a couple, but very quickly, it becomes almost the story of an extended family.'

福浴

県
会
館
芳醇日本酒
池亀
博多屋台
長兵ラーメン
新鮮貝味
みっちゃん
本格焼酎
霧島

Difficulty ●○○

Makes 6 skewers (serves 2)

Preparation: 15 mins
Cooking: 2 mins

yakitori

For the yakitori sauce

4 tbsp soy sauce

2 tbsp mirin

1 tbsp sugar

1 tbsp honey

For the chicken

3 chicken thighs (about 400 g/14 oz of meat in total)

1 pinch each of salt and ground black pepper

1 tbsp sake

2 young leeks or spring onions (scallions)

rice or soup, to serve

Preparation

Combine the yakitori sauce ingredients in a small saucepan and heat the mixture over a medium heat until reduced. The sauce is now ready to serve.

Bone the chicken thighs and cut the meat into approximately 3 cm (1¼ in) cubes.

Season with the salt and pepper, then add the sake. Stir and leave to marinate.

Cut the white part of the leeks into 3 cm (1¼ in) lengths.

Thread the marinated meat onto skewers, alternating them with the leeks or spring onions (scallions). To ensure the meat cooks evenly, place the skewer on a board and make sure the pieces of chicken are laid out flat and straight.

Place the skewers in a frying pan and cook them for 2 minutes on each side over a high heat, then lower the heat. Slowly pour the sauce over the skewers and finish cooking them, making sure that they do not burn.

Enjoy hot, accompanied by a bowl of rice or a soup.

yakisoba

4 large leaves of choudou (or white cabbage)

½ carrot

100 g (generous ½ cup) beansprouts

2 tbsp vegetable oil

100 g (3½ oz) thinly sliced pork

2 portions of yakisoba or Chinese noodles

50 ml (generous 3 tbsp) boiling water (if required)

70 ml (5 tbsp) Worcestershire sauce (+ 4 tbsp tomato ketchup if the Worcestershire sauce is not Japanese)

1 tsp soy sauce

1 pinch each of salt and ground black pepper

For the garnish

pink pickled ginger (optional)

***aonori* seaweed powder (optional)**

Yakisoba noodles are available from Asian stores and some larger stores, or you can substitute them with the Chinese noodles more often found in supermarkets. Prepare them according to the packet instructions.

Preparation

Cut the choudou roughly into squares and the carrot into thin, half-moon slices. Wash the beansprouts.

Heat a large frying pan or wok, then add the oil. Add the pork and sauté, followed by the choudou, carrot and beansprouts.

Once all the ingredients are cooked, add the noodles. Gently fry, adding the boiling water if necessary to prevent them burning. Add the Worcestershire and soy sauces. Season with salt and pepper. Serve hot with ginger and seaweed powder, if desired.

Difficulty ●●○

Serves 4

Preparation: 20 mins
Cooking: 1½ hours

oden

1 daikon (white radish)

4 eggs

300 g (10½ oz) potatoes

1 *konnyaku (konjak)*

4 Japanese fishcakes (such as *chikuwa, satsuma-age* or *hanpen*)

For the broth

1.5 l (6 cups) katsuobushi dashi stock (or 1.5 l/6 cups water + 20 g/5 tsp freeze-dried dashi of your choice)

4 tbsp soy sauce

4 tbsp mirin

1 tbsp sugar

½ tbsp salt

Japanese mustard or *yuzu kosho,* to serve

Preparation

Peel the daikon, then cut it into 3 cm (1¼ in) slices. Cook in water (preferably in the water that has been used to wash rice, otherwise add 1 tablespoon of raw rice to the cooking water) for about 20 minutes, until tender.

Hard-boil the eggs and shell them.

Peel, then cook the potatoes and cut them into large chunks.

Cut the *konnyaku* into quarters, then slice each piece diagonally to obtain triangular pieces.

Salt the *konnyaku* and set aside for 5 minutes. Blanch in boiling water for 1 minute.

Cut the fishcakes as desired and pour over some hot water to remove any excess fat.

Prepare the dashi stock and season with soy sauce, mirin, sugar and salt to taste.

Place the daikon, potatoes and eggs into the broth, followed by the *konnyaku*. Simmer over a low heat for about 50 minutes. Add the fishcake pieces and continue cooking for about 15 minutes.

After cooking, leave to cool so that the ingredients can absorb the broth.

When you are ready to eat, reheat and serve with Japanese mustard or *yuzu kosho*.

京橋千疋屋
創業1881年
SEMBIKIYA
静岡県産
マスクメロン化粧箱
¥32,400～¥43,200
(本体価格 ¥30,000～¥40,000)
静岡県産
マスクメロン化粧箱
1玉 ¥16,200～¥21,600
(本体価格 ¥15,000～¥20,000)
特選「マスクメロン」
【手塩にかけた「一茎一果」】
京橋千疋屋のマスクメロンは静岡県、遠州灘の近く、
日本屈指の明るい太陽を受ける地方で、
太陽光線の透過率が高いガラス張りの温室に抱かれて育ちます。
土は有機成分中心、育て方は「一茎一果」。
栽培床を地面と切り離し、養分と水の量を見極め、
一つの茎にたった一玉を選び残すことで、
一玉に全ての養分が集中。
水分が多く密度の高い繊細なマスクメロンが誕生します。
千疋屋
静岡県産
マスクメロン桐箱
1玉 ¥17,280～¥22,680
(本体価格 ¥16,000～¥21,000)
静岡県産
マスクメロン桐箱
2玉 ¥34,560～¥45,360
(本体価格 ¥32,000～¥42,000)
果物詰合せ
¥10,800
果物詰合せ
¥24,840

Fruit, Japan's luxury delights

Eaten relatively rarely in everyday Japanese life, fruit is primarily given as a gift. While this may be an original practice, it is also a very costly one.

They are all there, sitting in their wooden or paper crates, shielded from the touch of curious hands by immaculate glass windows. Viewed from the outside, the scene could be from a luxury leather-goods boutique or jewellery shop, except that the shelves here are not displaying handbags or diamonds, they are displaying fruit. We are at Sembikiya, an iconic upscale Japanese fruit supplier whose good reputation has been unwavering since 1834. Strawberries, cherries, grapes and melons, including watermelons, are all meticulously arranged, proudly showing off their perfect curves, just like exhibits in a gallery. Every item is plump and juicy – there's not a flaw in sight – it is as if the fruits were created from a divine mould, such is the exceptional nature of their perfection. Indeed, the melons usually look as if they had been individually wrapped in lace.

However, all this excellence comes at a price. Here, strawberries cost over 3 GBP (4 USD) each, as do cherries, and a melon will set you back about 85 GBP (107 USD). Yet the shop, which has several outlets across Tokyo, is constantly packed with people. Fruit is certainly not like any other food in Japan. You can find some priced relatively cheaply in supermarkets, but it does not form a big part of the daily Japanese diet. In this part of the world, fruit is a luxury gift given on very special occasions – a custom followed by nearly 80 per cent of Japan's population.

THE FLAVOUR OF THE FIRST FRUITS OF THE SEASON

While you might think that this trend dates back to Japan's period of rapid growth between the mid-1950s and the late 1980s, it actually started in the 8th century, when these fruity offerings were used as love tokens by courting couples, as a means of paying taxes or to establish and maintain social relationships. This usage was further cemented during feudalism. In the Edo period (1603–1867), which saw the Tokugawa clan rise to power, wealthy merchants would vie to buy the first produce of the season, known as *hashiri*. This was due to the common belief that the fruits of the first harvest had the best flavour and could even add an extra 75 years to the life expectancy of those

LUXURY FOOD GIFTS

Many events in Japan involve the giving of gifts, especially fruit. 'Gifts are a major industry in Japan. The Japanese gift *oseibo* or 'end of year' gifts in December before New Year and *chugen* during O Bon[1] in June or July, Rath adds. 'And that's not all; it is also customary to bring a *temiyage* gift when going to someone's house or returning from a trip, or *omiyage* for one's family, friends or colleagues.'

This is how the upscale fruit shops get their customers. 'Cantaloupe (musk melon) and grapes are among the most popular luxury food gifts, though there are others too. Anything luxurious will do the trick. A dozen of any old apples won't be considered a potential gift, but a dozen traditional apple varieties sourced from a small Aomori town, sold in their own artisanal wooden box, will,' the historian explains. So how does Sembikiya, the aforementioned famous fruit shop, manage to sell its customers such perfect fruit? These veritable works of art are crafted by the Oshima family, who have been running Sembikiya since 1834. At the time, Benzo Oshima opened a stall in the middle of the Nihonbashi district to sell fruits at a discount. Tokyo, which was still called Edo back then, had a vast canal network which was used to transport goods to the Japanese capital. The Oshima family soon decided to change its strategy and sell more luxury

who ate them. Everyone played the game: the samurais would offer mandarins or melons to their shogun as a token of their loyalty, and farmers would gift fruit to their neighbours in return for their help with harvesting.

For these fruits were not simply gifts; they drove an entire system that combined the joy of gifting with hope and a sense of duty. While they initially served as offerings to honour gods and to commemorate ancestors twice a year, fruit was exchanged between mere mortals for two main reasons. 'Firstly, the Japanese become attached to the idea of the monetary value of a gift, which expresses how much the gifter values the recipient or what they expect from them in return,' explains Eric Rath, a professor of Japanese history at the University of Kansas and a specialist in Japanese food culture. 'Secondly, food demonstrates an awareness of seasonality, acting as a way for the gifter to show their knowledge of important aesthetic rules for the various forms of artistic impression, particularly poetry.'

1 A Japanese Buddhist festival honouring the spirits of the ancestors.

products. It chose to work with the best fruit producers – and continues to do so to this day, nearly two centuries later. Sembikiya works with a handful of market gardeners specializing in these luxury fruits.

A RADICAL PICKING PROCESS

The picking process for the famous cantaloupes (musk melons), which incidentally have their own dedicated television programme during the initial harvest period, is a radical one: The seeds are planted in a greenhouse and the weakest flowers removed, while the others are pollinated manually by the farmers. The result is that a single melon – the best one – remains on each plant, to ensure it receives all the plant's nutrients. A short length of string is tied around the stem to prevent fatal falls that would damage the perfect round shape of the fruit, and small cone-shaped hats provide protection from the sun. Once ripe, the melons are picked and sorted according to size, shape, sweetness and fragrance. 'Fuji' melons are considered to be the crème de la crème, and only make up 3 per cent of the harvest. Melons, grapes, strawberries and persimmons are then transported from regional Japan to Tokyo's Ota Market, where intermediaries select the absolute best of the best to send off to Sembikiya every day.

In an age where so much effort goes into combatting wastage and preserving resources, one might assume such practices would be called into question – yet that does not appear to be the case. At the first auction of the year, for instance, the famous *hashiri* fruits are sold at unfathomable prices: in May 2022, a pair of melons went for 3 million yen, which is just over 17,800 GBP (22,460 USD). The future still looks bright for these little edible jewels.

Difficulty ●○○

Makes 3 sandos

Preparation: 20 mins
Resting: 1 hour

fruit sando

200 ml (generous ¾ cup) double (heavy) cream

2 kiwi fruit (or bananas, white grapes, nectarines, or a mixture of fruits)

20 g (scant 2 tbsp) sugar

6 slices of soft white bread

9 hulled strawberries

9 cubes pineapple (2 × 2 cm/¾ x ¾ in)

Preparation

Place a bowl, the whisks of your hand mixer and the cream in the freezer for 10 minutes to chill.

Peel the kiwi fruit, then quarter them lengthways. If you are using other fruit, prepare them as necessary.

Take the bowl, cream and whisks out of the freezer. Pour the cream into the bowl, add half the sugar and whisk. When the cream starts to increase in volume, add the rest of the sugar. Whisk until the whipped cream forms stiff peaks.

Divide half the whipped cream between 3 of the slices of bread, and spread it evenly, leaving a border around the edges as it may ooze out when you close the sando.

Then place the fruit on top of the cream layer, in an X shape. You can make a strawberry sando, a kiwi sando and a pineapple sando, or mix the three fruits in the same sandwich.

Cover with the rest of the cream, then place the remaining 3 slices of bread on top to make the sandos.

Wrap the sandos in cling film (plastic wrap) and leave them to chill in the fridge for 1 hour.

Cut the crusts off the bread (optional), then cut the sandos into quarters along the diagonals created by the fruit, to make four equal triangles. Enjoy cold.

Difficulty ●○○

Makes 500 ml (2⅛ cups)

Preparation: 8 hours
Cooking: 1 min

ponzu sauce

200 ml (generous ¾ cup) mirin

150 ml (⅔ cup) soy sauce

100 ml (scant ½ cup) rice vinegar

1 sheet dried kombu seaweed (10 × 10 cm/ 4 x 4 in)

100–250 ml (scant ½–1 cup) freshly squeezed yuzu (or other citrus fruit) juice

Preparation

Put the mirin, soy sauce and vinegar into a small saucepan.

Bring to the boil and cook for about 30 seconds. Turn off the heat and add the kombu. Leave to cool.

When cool, add the yuzu juice, then leave the kombu to infuse in the sauce overnight.

The next day, remove the kombu and pour the sauce into a clean bottle or container.

The ponzu sauce can be used at once, or stored in a cool place and consumed within 1 month. The kombu can be eaten.

Difficulty ●●●

Serves 2

Preparation: 20 mins
Cooking: 1 hour 10 mins

kyushu castella

6 or 7 eggs

2 egg yolks

400 g (2 cups) sugar

2 tbsp honey

1½ tbsp golden (corn) syrup

90 ml (6 tbsp) water

200 g (1⅔ cup) plain (all-purpose) flour

Preparation

Preheat the oven to 170°C (340°F).

Line a rectangular cake tin (pan) (18 x 26 x 8 cm/7 x 10 x 3 in) (or two 23-cm/9-in round cake tins [pans]) with baking parchment (parchment paper).

Combine the eggs, egg yolks, sugar, honey and golden (corn) syrup in a large bowl set over a pan of boiling water, and beat until the mixture forms ribbons. Remove from the bain-marie (water bath).

Add the water and carefully fold in, then sift in the flour and fold it in.

Pour the batter into the cake tin (pan) and place it in the oven.

After 1 minute of baking, remove from the oven and lightly press on the surface of the batter using a wooden spatula to break up the crust and the bubbles that have formed. Return to the oven.

Bake for 1 more minute, then remove the tin (pan) from the oven and make a small cut in the middle of the cake to remove any bubbles that have appeared. Insert a spatula into the batter to about 3 cm (1¼ in) deep and slowly draw an 'S' shape three times. Return to the oven.

Bake for 1 more minute, then remove the tin (pan) from the oven again. Insert the spatula, this time down to the base of the tin (pan), and draw an 'S' shape three times, taking care not to mix the batter from top to bottom. Return to the oven and bake for another 30 minutes.

Cover the tin (pan) or place a baking tray (sheet) on top to prevent it from getting too brown. Lower the oven temperature to 150°C (300°F) and bake for another 30–35 minutes.

Remove the tin (pan) from the oven, cover the cake with a sheet of baking parchment (parchment paper) to prevent it from drying out, and then turn it out onto a wire rack to cool. Cut the cake into thick slices and enjoy cold.

Difficulty ●○○

Makes a 150g (5¼-oz) jar

Preparation: 20 mins

yuzu kosho

10 green yuzus (about 500 g/18 oz)

10 fresh green chillies (chili peppers) (about 65 g/2¼ oz)

30 g (2 tbsp) coarse (kosher) salt

Yuzus are harvested when they are green in August or when they are yellow in November. It's the same for chillies (chili peppers), which are green in summer, before turning red at the end of the season. To make a very green and fresh *yuzu kosho*, you have to prepare it in summer. An autumn *yuzu kosho* will be a deeper orange in colour as well as creamier and sweeter.

Preparation

Wash the green yuzus. Wipe and grate the zest. Only grate the green zest – the white membrane underneath is bitter. Cut off any small green bits remaining on the skin with a knife, then chop them very finely.

Halve the yuzus and squeeze their juice into a glass. Strain the juice to remove any seeds and pulp. Set aside.

Now put on a pair of food preparation gloves to protect your hands. To prepare the green chillies (chili peppers), cut off and discard the stems, then chop the chillies (chili peppers) into very small pieces. There is no need to remove the seeds.

Gently grind the chillies (chili peppers) with a pestle and mortar.

Add the grated yuzu zest and the salt to the mortar. Combine using the pestle.

Grind until you have obtained the desired degree of smoothness. Add a little yuzu juice if the mixture is dry and crumbly.

This *yuzu kosho* will keep in the fridge for 3 months.

The different types of noodles

Soba, udon and ramen – this is the holy trinity of Japanese noodles. Whether swallowed *tsuru-tsuru* in one quick slurp or savoured slowly to appreciate the flavour and the *nopogoshi* meaning 'the sensation of the noodle going down the throat' – they are an essential part of Japanese cuisine.

SOBA NOODLES

Soba noodles started to appear in Japan during the Edo period. They are made from buckwheat (*soba* in Japanese) flour mixed with water. To make the mixture easier to work with, however, wheat flour can also be added. As such, there are three types of soba noodles, depending on their wheat flour content: *juwari* or *towari* for those made entirely from buckwheat flour; *sotonihashi* for those containing around 17 per cent buckwheat flour; and *nihachi*, which are 20 per cent buckwheat flour.

Soba noodles eaten cold are referred to as *zaru soba* and are accompanied by dried seaweed, small onions and a *tsuyu* sauce (a mix of soy sauce, sugar, mirin and dashi stock). They can also be served hot in a broth. A soba dish known as *toshikoshi soba* is usually enjoyed with the family on New Year's Eve, as it is believed this will ensure a long life for those who eat them. Another tradition involves offering soba noodles known as *hikkoshi soba* to new neighbours when you are moving house.

UDON NOODLES

Udon are soft noodles made from wheat flour, water and salt, generally served in a simple dashi-based broth. These noodles are between 2 mm and 4 mm (1/32 and 1/16 in) thick; they are denser and thicker than buckwheat noodles and may be flat or round in shape.

The first udon noodles were sold in speciality shops in the 17th century. They are eaten all over Japan, but are particularly popular in the country's

TAKE *aways*

INSTANT NOODLES, A CULINARY CREATION 'MADE IN JAPAN'

In 2021, some 188 billion servings of instant noodles were sold! Whether purchased in a sachet or a cup-like bowl, they continue to win over tastebuds and fill bellies all over the world. According to the World Instant Noodles Association, the top three consumer countries are China, Indonesia and Vietnam, with Japan coming in 5th, the USA 6th and the UK well down the rankings at 24. Yet it was a Japanese gentleman by the name of Ando Momofuku who actually invented these noodles, which only require a splash of hot water to be enjoyed anytime, anywhere.

It took Ando many years to develop his recipe, toiling away in a workshop in his backyard. He finally succeeded at the age of 48, having started his career selling jumpers (sweaters), subsequently spending two stints in prison and also going bankrupt. In 1958, his famous Chicken Ramen took over supermarket shelves and went from strength to strength thereafter. In 1971, he launched the first CUPNOODLES, packaged in bowl-like cups to further simplify consumption; gone were the days of needing a bowl or anything else at hand to eat lunch or dinner. The product had everything covered. Ando Momofuku's creativity and ambition were truly limitless – he even managed to send his instant noodles into ... outer space. Having developed a thicker broth to combat weightlessness, his Space Ram embarked on a space mission in American space shuttle Discovery with Japanese astronaut Noguchi Soichi in July 2005.

south, from the island of Shikoku to the island of Kyushu, including Osaka. On the other hand, soba are more popular in the country's east, namely in the Kanto region that encompasses Tokyo. Like soba noodles, udon can be eaten hot or cold.

RAMEN NOODLES

Ramen noodles are today considered the iconic Japanese dish for foreigners, yet they actually originally came from China, *ramen* being the Japanese pronunciation of the Chinese *lamian*. The wheat flour noodles arrived in the archipelago in the early 20th century, in the city of Yokohama. It was at this major commercial port that one of the first shops selling these noodles opened. Ramen noodles are served in a broth with bamboo shoots, half a hard-boiled egg and a slice of roast pork.

Ramen cemented its place in Japanese culture during the period after World War II, a time when the United States exported its surplus wheat to Japan. In just a few decades, the country managed to successfully appropriate the dish and erase all memory of the fact that it was first brought to the Japanese archipelago by Chinese immigrant workers. Now entirely adapted to the Japanese palate, ramen is enjoyed everywhere from street food stalls and budget restaurants to school canteens.

There are four main types of ramen: shio ramen, with salt; miso ramen, made from fermented soy; shoyu ramen made using soy sauce; and tonkotsu ramen, in a pork-based broth. However, each region of Japan has developed its own recipe made using local ingredients. ●

北海道

HOKKAIDO

Dashi, the most Japanese of stocks

This stock, made from kombu seaweed and dried skipjack tuna, is not just one of the essential basics of Japan's food culture, it is also one of the key ingredients in Japanese gastrodiplomacy.

WASHOKU, A ROUGH DEFINITION:

Washoku is a term used to describe much more than a specific food or cuisine. According to the Japanese government, it is a combination of four criteria:

- The use of various fresh ingredients whose natural flavours have been preserved.
- A healthy, balanced diet.
- An appreciation of nature in the way it is presented.
- A connection with annual events and festivals.

What do *okonomiyaki*, miso soup and soba noodles have in common? Each of these dishes, which are as different as they are emblematic of Japanese cuisine, contains an essential ingredient: dashi stock. Dashi is made from kombu seaweed and dried skipjack tuna, known as *katsuobushi*. The seaweed, which is high in glutamic acid, and skipjack tuna, which is high in inosinic acid, make it a veritable explosion of umami, the mouth-watering Japanese-inspired fifth taste sensation.

THE CORNERSTONE OF *WASHOKU*

An icon of Japanese flavour, this stock ranks among the holy trinity of *washoku*, a meal 'built around rice at its heart, with the addition of side dishes based on the principle of *ichijū sansai*', according to the website of Japan's Ministry of Agriculture, Forestry and Fisheries.

While it might seem like a word coined several centuries ago, the term *washoku* is actually relatively recent. It first appeared during the Meiji era (1868-1912) to oppose the new dishes, known as *yoshoku*, that were introduced in the Japanese archipelago after its forced opening to Western influences. Dashi stock, along with traditional *wagashi* confectionery, was added to the UNESCO Intangible Cultural Heritage list in 2013.

NOT JUST ONE STOCK

However, there is no hard-and-fast recipe for the preparation of dashi. While its main and most popular version is made from seaweed and skipjack tuna, some people also add dried shiitake mushrooms or little sardines known as *niboshi*. Nevertheless, there is always one constant: all dashi ingredients are dried and no fat is ever added.

Below we have compiled a list of the main variations of this popular stock recipe.

Kelp dashi

This type of stock simply involves simmering the dried kombu seaweed at 60°C (140°F) for about an hour, which produces a fairly light, vegetarian, slightly salty-tasting dashi.

Ichiban dashi

After removing the kombu from the *kelp dashi*, reheat the water, removing it from the heat just before it comes to the boil. Add the dried skipjack flakes, allowing them to gradually sink to the bottom of the pan, then strain the mixture. This produces what is known as the 'first dashi'.

Niban dashi

Simmer the kombu seaweed and dried skipjack flakes used to make the 'first dashi' in the saucepan for 15 to 20 minutes, then strain the resulting mixture. With its intense umami flavour, *niban dashi* is frequently used to make stews or when sautéing vegetables.

Iriko dashi

This type of dashi stock is made from *niboshi* - little dried anchovies that provide a distinctive fish flavour. To prepare it, first rehydrate anchovies then soak them in water. Next, heat the *iriko dashi* and allow it to simmer for 10-15 minutes.

Shojin dashi

This vegetarian dashi is made from dried shiitake mushrooms. Before cooking, allow the mushrooms to soak in a pan of water for about 5 hours, then add the kombu and the *kiriboshi daikon*, a dried white Japanese radish. Simmer at 60°C (140°F) for about 20 minutes. This highly flavoursome dashi is often used when cooking vegetables or fish.

THE EXPORTATION OF JAPANESE FLAVOUR

'In recent years, the Japanese government has become increasingly aware of the appeal of contemporary Japanese culture, and Japan has indeed become one of the most active countries in terms of utilizing cultural resources to boost its international influence,' explains Felice Farina, a researcher of Japanese history at the University of Naples 'L'Orientale'. 'Of all these resources, food is playing more and more of a central role in promoting Japanese culture abroad, and has become one of the most distinctive elements of its national identity. UNESCO's recognition of *washoku* on the Representative List of the Intangible Cultural Heritage of Humanity in 2013 is a visible outcome of this strategy.'

As such, Japanese cuisine, and the Japanese culinary lifestyle, have become the greatest benchmark of the country's 'gastrodiplomacy', a term coined and theorized by public diplomacy specialist Paul Rockower. 'It is clear that gastrodiplomacy is not about simply promoting a country's cuisine abroad,' Felice Farina adds, 'but rather a means of boosting the appeal and desirability of its culture, its people, its values and its ideals, reinforcing the notion of certain foods as being associated with that country, and thus achieving economic results such as the export of foodstuffs or increased tourism.' This strategy of promoting Japanese cuisine abroad appears to be bearing fruit, because, since the inclusion of *washoku* on UNESCO's Intangible Cultural Heritage list, Japan's exports skyrocketed to some 790 billion GBP (1 trillion USD) in 2020, compared to 390 billion GBP (½ trillion USD) in the year 2012.

A FLAVOUR AT RISK?

However, the national pride and diplomatic and commercial golden ticket that are 'Japanese flavour', cultivated primarily through dashi stock, could well be at risk. Skipjack tuna, from which dashi is made, has been growing increasingly oily in recent years, and this extra oil is affecting its flavour. Experts believe that this added oiliness is due to the rising water temperatures. In the bay of Kochi, for example, one of the main skipjack tuna fishing grounds, water temperatures have increased by 2°C (35°F) since 1970. The warmer currents also attract new prey, which end up becoming an additional source of food for the skipjack tuna.

Hiroyuki Ukeda, a professor in the Department of Bioresources and vice president of Kochi University, has studied another phenomenon that may potentially be linked to the global rise in temperatures: 'Over the longer term, this warming may prevent water that is high in minerals from returning to the surface, which would in turn reduce the quantity of plankton and small fish on which the skipjack tuna can feed. As a consequence, we would see a significant drop in skipjack tuna populations in the bay.'

元祖
さっぽろ
名所
ラーメン横丁
華龍
味の華龍
味の
華龍

Difficulty ●●●

Serves 4

Preparation: 2 days
Cooking: 4 hours

sapporo ramen

For the noodles

160 ml (generous ⅔ cup) filtered water (40% of the weight of the flour)

4 g (⅔ tsp) salt (1% of the weight of the flour)

2 g (½ tsp) bicarbonate of soda (baking soda) (0.5% of the weight of the flour)

400 g (3¼ cups) plain (all-purpose) flour (preferably with a protein content of about 12%)

2 g (½ tsp) potassium bicarbonate (0.5% of the weight of the flour) (if you can't find potassium bicarbonate, replace it with bicarbonate of soda [baking soda])

4–5 handfuls of potato starch

Preparation

Making the noodles

Weigh all ingredients accurately. In a small bowl, combine the water, salt and bicarbonate of soda (baking soda) and stir to dissolve.

Sift the flour into a large bowl.

Gradually pour the water mixture onto the flour, using a circular movement, until you have added all of it.

Using chopsticks, mix the flour and water to distribute the liquid evenly, until small crumbs form. Make sure that no flour remains stuck to the sides of the bowl. At this point, the dough will resemble breadcrumbs rather than being a homogenous mixture. Place the dough in a large resealable plastic food (zip lock) bag and seal it carefully so that the dough does not dry out. Leave to rest for 1 hour until the water has been absorbed by the flour.

After 1 hour, start kneading the dough. The easiest way is to do this is with your feet. Open the bag a little to let the air out. Place a sheet or towel on a clean floor, place the bag with the dough on the towel, and flatten the dough by taking small steps on the bag. When the dough is flat and has filled the bag, open the bag and fold the dough towards the centre in thirds.

Return the dough to the bag, seal it, and repeat the operation three more times.

Leave the flattened dough in the bag, seal it and leave to rest for at least 2 hours or a whole day, if possible.

After this, cut the dough into 4 equal pieces and flatten them using a rolling pin to form strips.

A. If you have a pasta machine, put the dough in the machine, start at level 0 (the thickest) then gradually thin it by moving from one level to another, until the desired thickness has been achieved (the recommended thickness is about 1–1.2 mm (about 1⁄25 in), level 5 on my Marcato Atlas 150 machine).

Next, sprinkle both sides of the dough with potato starch and cut the noodles of the desired width. The width of standard spaghetti is ideal.

For the tonkotsu ramen soup

500 g (18 oz) pork rib bones

500 g (18 oz) pork thigh bone

300 ml (1¼ cups) water

For the chashu

300 g (10½ oz) pork loin or belly, in one piece

150 ml (⅔ cup) soy sauce

50 ml (generous 3 tbsp) mirin

B. If you don't have a pasta machine, flatten each strip of dough to about 1–1.5 mm (about 1⁄25 in) thickness using a rolling pin. Sprinkle both sides with potato starch, fold them in half and cut the noodles to the desired width.

Once the noodles are cut, sprinkle some more potato starch to prevent them from sticking together, turn them two or three times so that they are completely covered with the starch, then leave to rest in a large food container for 1 or 2 days. The noodles can be eaten immediately after making, but they are always better 1 or 2 days later.

To get slightly curly noodles, simply take a portion of noodles in your hands and gently but firmly squeeze them into shape.

Making the soup

The day before, clean, then soak the pork bones in water to remove the blood. Leave to soak in the refrigerator or a cool place overnight. The next day, throw away the soaking water.

Break the bones using a hammer, or chop with a knife, so the bones will fit inside your pressure cooker. Umami also comes from inside the bones, so it is best to break them into small pieces.

Put the bones and the water into a pressure cooker. If the water is not sufficient to cover the bones, add more. The amount of water is only approximate, because you may need to add more water as it evaporates during cooking.

Bring to a boil, uncovered, over a high heat. Once it has come to the boil and a brown foam appears, reduce the heat to medium, and simmer for 20 minutes. Skim to remove some of the foam, but it doesn't matter if a little remains. Cover and close the pressure cooker then reduce the heat to medium; wait for the pressure to build then cook for 2 hours over a low heat.

After 2 hours, turn off the heat and leave to cool until you can open the lid.

Open the lid, add the pork for the chashu and cook for another 1 hour over a medium heat, uncovered. Adjust the heat so that the water boils, forming large bubbles. At this stage, the soup is quite thick; stir frequently so it does not stick to the bottom. Add some more water if too much has evaporated.

After 1 hour, remove the pork and strain the soup. Press the residue to recover all the soup that has soaked into the meat fibres. You should have approximately 1.2 l (5 cups) of soup; add more water if necessary. The soup is now ready.

You can leave the soup as it is if you like it quite fatty; alternatively, leave it to cool and remove the excess fat once it has solidified on the surface. If you remove the fat, set it aside – it will make a good flavouring oil for the ramen.

For the *miso tare*

2 tsp sake

2 tsp mirin

¼ onion, grated

10 g (3½ tbsp) garlic purée

10 g (3½ tbsp) ginger purée

130 g (scant ½ cup) white miso paste

130 g (scant ½ cup) red miso paste

2 tsp sesame oil

½ tsp crushed sesame seeds

½ tsp scallop powder

1 tbsp soy sauce

½ tsp oyster sauce

½ tsp salt

For the *ajitsuke tamago*

40 ml (scant 3 tbsp) soy sauce

2 tbsp water

4 tsp mirin

8 g (scant 2 tsp) sugar

4 eggs

For the garnish

2–3 spring onions (scallions)

flavouring oil

200 g (7 oz) minced (ground) pork

4 tsp crushed garlic

4 tsp ginger purée

cooked beansprouts, to taste

a little dab of butter (optional)

tinned sweetcorn (canned corn kernels) (optional)

Making the *chashu*

Place the cooked piece of pork in a small resealable plastic food (zip lock) bag, together with the soy sauce and mirin. Remove the air from the bag so that the entire surface of the meat is in contact with the marinade. Leave to marinate for at least 1 hour.

Making the *miso tare*

Pour the sake and mirin into a saucepan. Cook for 2 minutes over a low heat, then add the onion, garlic and ginger. Cook for another 2 minutes, then turn off the heat. Add both miso pastes and the sesame oil, stir. Finally, add all the other ingredients of the *miso tare*, mix everything carefully. The *miso tare* is now ready.

Making the *ajitsuke tamago*

Combine all the liquid ingredients and the sugar in a small saucepan and bring to the boil. Turn off the heat and leave to cool.

In another saucepan, boil some water and gently immerse the eggs (use them straight from the fridge). Cook for 7–8 minutes, then remove them from the pan. Cool them in cold water. Remove the shells and transfer the eggs to a small resealable plastic food (zip lock) bag together with the sauce. Remove the air from the bag so that the entire surface of the eggs is in contact with the sauce. Leave to marinate for 3 hours.

Preparing the garnishes

Chop the spring onions, cut the *ajitsuke tamago* in half lengthwise, slice the chashu, and prepare all your other chosen garnishes.

In a pan, heat 6 tablespoons of the flavouring oil from the soup. Add the minced (ground) pork and stir-fry until browned. Add the soup (300 ml/1¼ cups per person), the *tare miso* (2½ tablespoons per person), the crushed garlic and the ginger. Heat everything before dividing the soup between the serving bowls.

Presentation

If you are cooking a lot of noodles at once choose a saucepan that is large enough to hold them all. Cook 140 g (5 oz) noodles per person in a large amount of boiling water for about 2 minutes. Drain carefully.

Carefully place the cooked noodles into the bowls of soup, then add the *chashu*, *ajitsuke tamago*, beansprouts, spring onions (scallions) and any other garnishes. Enjoy hot.

hakodate ramen

<u>For the noodles</u>

160 ml (⅔ cup) filtered water (40% of the weight of the flour)

4 g (⅔ tsp) salt (1% of the weight of the flour)

2 g (½ tsp) bicarbonate of soda (baking soda) (0.5% of the weight of the flour)

400 g (3¼ cups) plain (all-purpose) flour (preferably with a protein content of about 12%)

2 g (½ tsp) potassium bicarbonate (0.5% of the weight of the flour) (if you can't find potassium bicarbonate, replace it with bicarbonate of soda [baking soda])

4-5 handfuls of potato starch

Preparation

<u>Making the noodles</u>

Weigh all ingredients accurately. In a small bowl, combine the water, salt and bicarbonate of soda (baking soda) and stir to dissolve.

Sift the flour into a large bowl.

Gradually pour the water mixture onto the flour, using a circular movement, until you have added all of it.

Using chopsticks, mix the flour and water to distribute the liquid evenly, until small crumbs form. Make sure that no flour remains stuck to the sides of the bowl. At this point, the dough will resemble breadcrumbs rather than being a homogenous mixture. Place the dough in a large resealable plastic food (zip lock) bag and seal it carefully so that the dough does not dry out. Leave to rest for 1 hour until the water has been absorbed by the flour.

After 1 hour, start kneading the dough. The easiest way is to do this is with your feet. Open the bag a little to let the air out. Place a sheet or towel on a clean floor, place the bag with the dough on the towel, and flatten the dough by taking small steps on the bag. When the dough is flat and has filled the bag, open the bag and fold the dough towards the centre in thirds.

Return the dough to the bag, seal it, and repeat the operation three more times.

Leave the flattened dough in the bag, seal it and leave to rest for at least 2 hours or a whole day, if possible.

After this, cut the dough into 4 equal pieces and flatten them using a rolling pin to form strips.

A. If you have a pasta machine, put the dough in the machine, start at level 0 (the thickest) then gradually thin it by moving from one level to another, until the desired thickness has been achieved (about 1-1.2 mm / 1⁄25 in, level 5 on my Marcato Atlas 150 machine is the recommended thickness).

Next, sprinkle both sides of the dough with potato starch and cut the noodles to the desired width. The width of standard spaghetti is ideal.

For the soup

500 g (18 oz) pork bones (preferably thigh) (if you can't find any bones or carcass, use 1 kg/2⅛ lb chicken wings and 300 g/10½ oz minced [ground] pork)

1 chicken carcass

2 chicken drumsticks

2.2 l (9⅓ cups) water

1 leek or spring onion (scallion), green part only

10 g (scant 2 tbsp) ginger

½ onion

10 g (1 thick slice) carrot

B. If you don't have a pasta machine, flatten each strip of dough to about 1–1.5 mm (about 1⁄25 in) thickness using a rolling pin. Sprinkle both sides with potato starch, fold them in half and cut the noodles to the desired width. Once the noodles are cut, sprinkle some more potato starch to prevent them from sticking together, turn them two or three times so that they are completely covered with potato starch, then leave to rest in a large food container for 1 or 2 days. The noodles can be eaten immediately after making, but they are always better 1 or 2 days later.

To get slightly curly noodles, simply take a portion of noodles in your hands and gently but firmly squeeze them into shape.

Making the soup

The day before, clean and soak the pork bones in water to remove the blood. Leave to soak overnight in the refrigerator or in a cool place. After soaking, discard the water.

Break up the bones and carcass using a hammer, or chop them with a knife so that they will fit inside your pressure cooker. (This step is not necessary if you are using chicken wings and minced meat.)

Put the bones and the carcass (or the chicken wings and the minced pork), the drumsticks and the water into the pressure cooker.

Bring to a boil over a high heat, uncovered. When the liquid comes to a boil and a brown foam appears, reduce the heat to medium and begin to skim. It is important to remove the foam for 15–20 minutes to obtain a clear soup.

Cover and close the pressure cooker. Cook over a medium heat. Wait for the pressure to build, then cook for 1 hour over a low heat.

After 1 hour, turn off the heat and let the temperature go down so you can open the lid.

Now add the pork for the chashu, the leek greens, ginger, onion and carrot.

Cook for 1 hour 30 minutes over a medium-to-low heat, uncovered. Adjust the heat so that the water starts to boil, forming large bubbles.

After 1 hour 30 minutes, remove the pork and strain the soup. The soup is now ready. You can freeze it and use it as a base soup for several preparations such as *tantan men*, *shoyu ramen* …

Use the fat from the soup as a flavouring oil for the ramen.

<u>For the *chashu*</u>

300 g (10½ oz) pork loin or belly, in one piece

150 ml (⅔ cup) soy sauce

50 ml (generous 3 tbsp) mirin

<u>For the *shio tare*</u>

10 g (1 tbsp) dried scallops

3 dried shiitake mushrooms

20 g (¾ oz) *katsuobushi* (thick shavings if possible)

8 g (1 tbsp) dried sardine

10 g (1 tbsp) kombu seaweed

300 ml (1¼ cups) filtered water

50 ml (generous 3 tbsp) mirin

30 ml (2 tbsp) sake

35 ml (generous 2 tbsp) salt

<u>For the *ajitsuke tamago*</u>

40 ml (scant 3 tbsp) soy sauce

2 tbsp water

20 ml (generous 1 tbsp) mirin

8 g (2 tsp) sugar

4 eggs

<u>For the garnish</u>

2–3 spring onions (scallions)

flavouring oil

cooked beansprouts, to taste

marinated bamboo shoots, to taste

finely ground black pepper, to taste

<u>Making the *chashu*</u>

Put the cooked pork into a small resealable (zip lock) bag, together with the soy sauce and the mirin. Remove the air from the bag so that the entire surface of the meat is in contact with the flavourings. Leave to marinate for at least 1 hour.

<u>Making the *shio tare*</u>

Put all the dry ingredients (scallops, shiitake, katsuobushi, dried sardine and kombu) and the filtered water into a saucepan and leave to rest overnight.

The next day, cook everything over a low heat, letting it come to a boil gently so that the ingredients dance lightly in the pan. One minute after it starts to boil, remove the kombu, then continue to simmer the rest for 40 minutes. Remove all other solid ingredients, leaving only the liquid, before straining it.

Add all the other ingredients for the *shio tare*, boil for 1 minute before turning off the heat and leaving to cool. The *shio tare* is now ready.

<u>Making the *ajitsuke tamago*</u>

In a small saucepan, combine all the liquid ingredients and the sugar for the ajitsuke tamago. Bring to the boil, then turn off the heat and leave to cool.

In another saucepan, bring some water to the boil, then carefully add the eggs (use them straight from the refrigerator). Cook for 7–8 minutes, then remove them from the pan. Cool in cold water. Remove the shells, then place the cooked eggs into a small resealable (zip lock) bag together with the ajitsuke tamago sauce. Remove the air from the bag so that the eggs are in direct contact with the sauce. Leave to marinate for 3 hours.

<u>Preparing the garnishes and presentation</u>

Chop the spring onions (scallions), halve the *ajitsuke tamago* lengthways, slice the *chashu* and prepare your chosen garnishes.

Heat the soup (about 300 ml/1¼ cups per person).

Cook 140 g (5 oz) noodles per person in plenty of boiling water for about 2 minutes. if you are cooking a lot of noodles, use a saucepan that is large enough to hold them all. Drain well.

Just before the noodles are cooked, add 2 tablespoons *shio tare*, 1 tablespoon flavouring oil (reserved pork fat) and a little ground black pepper to the bottom of a bowl, then pour the heated soup on top (adjust the amount of *tare* according to your taste).

Difficulty ●○○

Serves 2

Preparation: 10 mins
Cooking: 10 mins

butadon

- 2 tbsp vegetable oil
- 250 g (9 oz) pork belly, thinly sliced
- 3 tbsp sake
- 3 tbsp sugar
- 5 tbsp soy sauce
- 330 g (2¼ cups) cooked sushi rice
- 3-4 iceberg lettuce leaves (or chopped choudou leaves)
- chives, chopped (optional)
- Japanese mustard. to serve

Preparation

In a frying pan, heat the oil and brown the pork slices.

Add the sake, sugar and soy sauce.

Cook over a low heat until the sauce has thickened.

Arrange the rice, a few lettuce leaves and the cooked pork slices in a bowl. Sprinkle with chopped chives and serve with the mustard on the side. Enjoy hot.

新栄丸
長福丸

Hokkaido: is Japanese fishing in danger?

The waters off Japan's northernmost island are the source of much of the country's fish and seafood. Like the rest of Japan's waters, however, the sea fish populations there are dwindling.

Bordered by the Sea of Japan, the Pacific Ocean and the Sea of Okhotsk, Hokkaido, which literally means 'Northern Sea Circuit', is the second largest island in the Japanese archipelago. Although 70 per cent of it is forest, it is particularly renowned for its fishing industry. Indeed, this is where a quarter of all of Japan's fish are caught. Various species live in its surrounding waters: saury, wild salmon, squid, herring, crab and *shishamo*, a fish native to Japan and found along the Pacific coast in the island's south ... And yet, the last few decades have seen the local fishing industry experience the same decline in fish populations as the rest of the archipelago. The reason? Overfishing, coupled with – more recently – global warming, triggering a hellish spiral: diminished volumes of fish, lowered wages for the fishermen and a decrease in job vacancies and new recruits, resulting in increasingly deserted fishing villages. Japan's Fisheries Agency is endeavouring to combat this depopulation through tourism.

How did we end up here? Japan has always been one of the heavyweights of the fishing industry. Indeed, from the 1970s to the 1990s it was the world's biggest producer in this sector. In 1992, however,

'These days, Japan is only able to meet about 60 per cent of domestic demand for fish products.'

面白い

CHEFS FOR THE BLUE: WHEN CHEFS RALLY TOGETHER

In 2017, a team of Japanese chefs from Tokyo and Kyoto established the Chefs for the Blue association. The group aims to raise public awareness about overfishing in Japan, advocates for more sustainable fishing and champions the idea that chefs who are in contact with both fishermen and consumers have a key role to play in preserving fish resources.

the volumes of wild catches began to plummet and, to this day, have never recovered.

After World War II, the Japanese government began to focus on developing the fishing sector in a bid to end the food shortages that were plaguing the country. The fishermen, of whom there were very many at the time, fished absolutely everywhere – and in vast quantities. Eventually, there were no longer enough fish for them to catch in their nets along Japan's coasts. So what happened next? Japanese ships set off for other, often far-away, destinations, such as Alaska, New Zealand and Latin America; no marine territory was off-limits for the Japanese. The notion of sustainable resources and preserving the underwater ecosystem did not even figure at the time. And this period of tremendous growth was not solely confined to Japan's land territory; there was profit to be had in both its own and in foreign waters.

FROM OVERFISHING TO IMPORTING

Things got complicated once Exclusive Economic Zones (EEZ) were introduced. In 1977, Japanese ships found themselves facing administrative limitations: it was no longer possible to simply go and fish anywhere and everywhere. Whereas, in the early 1970s, half of Japan's catches had come from foreign EEZs, its fishermen were now only allowed to operate within 200 nautical miles of the archipelago's coasts. Despite being the world's eighth largest EEZ in terms of area, Japan was struggling to haul in enough fish. Yet, according to a 2022 white paper published by the Japan Fisheries Agency, the Japanese are on average still consuming more than 23 kg (50 lb) of fish per person per year. While this figure is a far cry from the 40 kg (88 lb) of 2001, the country remains one of the planet's largest consumers of fish to this day.

As such, it now imports fish in order to feed its people. The year 2022 saw it become the world's third-largest importer of marine produce, with expenditure totalling an equivalent of 12 billion GBP (15.25 billion USD). Self-sufficient in the 1960s (peaking at 113 per cent in 1964), Japan is now only able to meet about 60 per cent of domestic demand for fish products. At its fish markets today, Japanese amberjack rubs shoulders with Norwegian mackerel, and Atlantic scallops sit alongside Chilean salmon. In a bid to halt this development, the Japanese government made amendments to its fishing legislation in 2018, with the new provisions taking effect in December 2020. Among them are the expansion of fishing quotas to include new species – there had previously only been eight – and the establishment of individual quotas for each fishing

ground, with the aim of regulating the competition between players in the sector.

THE IMPACT OF GLOBAL WARMING

Overfishing is, however, not the only reason for the decline in fish populations. Like all of the coast off Japan, the Hokkaido coast has been battered by global warming. According to the sixth evaluation report published by the Intergovernmental Panel on Climate Change (IPCC), the pH of the world's surface waters has dropped from 8.2 to 8.1 since the pre-industrial era – a drop attributed to the increased carbon dioxide in the atmosphere. 'While a decrease of 0.1 pH unit may seem negligible, it actually means acidity has increased by 30 per cent,' explains Haruko Kurihara, a professor in the Department of Chemistry, Biology and Marine Science at the University of the Ryukyus in Nishihara, Okinawa Prefecture. Researchers are not sugar-coating it: acidification of the oceans is a threat to the fishing and aquaculture sectors. A study in 2018 found that, by 2100, the cumulative economic loss in these sectors in Japan could reach 2,000 billion yen (10.9 billion GBP/13.8 billion USD).

The waters of the seas and oceans are growing warmer and more acidic all the time, forcing fish to migrate – when they are not endangered by the emergence of new, similarly displaced predators. What can be done to offset the effects of overfishing and global warming? Does the solution lie in developing aquaculture, which is often cited as the best line of defence? Not necessarily. 'Overcrowded aquaculture conditions may trigger a build-up of organic matter, which is what causes acidification of the oceans. So excessive aquaculture is not good either,' concludes Haruko Kurihara.

CHEFS ON A MISSION

At the other end of the chain, restaurant chefs also have a responsibility to preserve marine resources. French chef Olivier Roellinger, the recipient of three Michelin stars in 2006 for his Le Bricourt restaurant, has long been aware of this need. In 2011, he launched a contest to help preserve marine resources. Its aim? To raise awareness among new and future generations of chefs about the issues associated with seafood. Roellinger believes chefs are also responsible for the sustainability of fishing, particularly by ensuring that the fish they serve at their tables adhere to the required catch sizes and are not an endangered species, and by giving preference to sustainable, often lesser known, marine species. In 2022, his contest was held in Hokkaido and was won by Taiga Chiba, a young student who created a dish accompanied by a dashi stock made with a white-spotted eel notorious for being difficult to work with because of its many bones.

chan-chan yaki

4 fresh salmon steaks

1 pinch each of salt and pepper

½ choudou (or green cabbage)

1 onion

½ carrot

150 g (1½ cups) mushrooms

2 tbsp salted butter

For the sauce

100 g (⅓ cup) miso paste

60 ml (4 tbsp) sake

2 tbsp mirin

2 tbsp sugar

Preparation

Season the salmon steaks with the salt and the pepper.

Roughly chop the choudou; chop the onion; cut the carrot into thick slices; remove the stems from the mushrooms, then halve the caps.

In a large saucepan, heat the butter over a medium heat and cook the salmon, starting with the flesh side.

Arrange the prepared vegetables and mushrooms around the salmon.

Add all the sauce ingredients. Cover and continue to simmer.

Once the salmon is cooked, enjoy it hot with the vegetables and the sauce.

ikameshi

70 g (generous ⅓ cup) sticky rice

10 g (scant 2 tbsp) sliced ginger

1 large squid (or 2 small squid)

salt

1 tsp soy sauce

For the sauce

300 ml (1¼ cups) filtered water

2 tbsp sugar

2 tbsp sake

2 tbsp soy sauce

1 tbsp mirin

Preparation

Wash the sticky rice and leave to soak in a bowl of water for 1 hour.

Combine all the sauce ingredients and add the ginger slices.

Gut and clean the squid, removing the eyes and the mouth.

Cut off the head and the tentacles, then gently knead the tentacles with a small handful of salt to remove all the small hard chitinous rings on the tentacles. Wash and pat dry with kitchen towels (paper towels).

Cut the head and tentacles into small pieces; combine with the drained rice and the soy sauce.

Stuff the squid with the rice mixture so that it is about three-quarters full, then close with a toothpick. Do not overfill as the rice may not cook properly and may cause the squid to burst as it expands.

Put the sauce into a saucepan. Bring to a boil, then add the stuffed squid, cover and cook over a medium heat for 15–20 minutes, turning from time to time.

Remove the squid from the pan and cut it into bite-sized rings (about 1 cm / ⅜ in thick).

Simmer the sauce to reduce and pour over the sliced squid. Enjoy hot.

Difficulty ●●○

Serves 2

Preparation: 40 mins
Cooking: 10 mins

anko nabe

For the broth

1 l (4 cups) filtered water

1 sheet dried kombu seaweed (10 x 10 cm/ 4 x 4 in)

100 g (⅓ cup) miso paste

1 tbsp mirin

1 tsp sake

1 tsp soy sauce

2–3 slices ginger

¼ daikon radish, cut into thick slices

⅓ carrot, sliced diagonally

¼ Chinese cabbage, roughly chopped

2–3 fresh whole shiitake mushrooms, with a cross cut into the caps

½ bunch of roughly chopped chrysanthemum greens

2–3 spring onions (scallions), cut diagonally

300–400 g (10½–14 oz) monkfish (tail, skin, liver)

½ block of tofu, cut into large cubes

Optional

1 bowl of cooked white rice (hot or cold)

1 egg

⅓ bunch chives, chopped

Preparation

Pour the filtered water into a saucepan or an earthenware *donabe*, add the kombu and leave to soak for 30 minutes. Arrange the prepared vegetables on a large plate.

Cut the monkfish into bite-sized cubes, and plunge them into boiling water for 10 seconds. Arrange them on another plate.

Cook the rice (or use cold rice from the day before).

If possible, place the saucepan or *donabe* with the water and the soaked kombu over a single gas burner on the table, and turn to medium setting.

Leave to simmer for 2–3 minutes, remove the kombu, then add all the remaining broth ingredients. You can eat the kombu sliced and stir-fried with mirin and soy sauce to accompany a bowl of rice.

Add the prepared vegetables in the order listed, followed by the monkfish pieces. Skim to remove any foam if necessary, then add the tofu. The anko nabe is now ready to eat.

This is a nice sharing dish. You can start the meal by taking the ingredients directly from the saucepan or you can put the ingredients onto the diners' plates as you go. If the *anko nabe* becomes too dry, top it up with filtered water from time to time.

Optional

When all the vegetables and monkfish have been eaten, add the bowl of rice to the broth remaining in the saucepan. Break it up to distribute the grains throughout the pan, then cover and cook for 5–10 minutes. Beat an egg and slowly pour it in using a circular motion to combine it with the rice. Turn off the heat, sprinkle with the chopped chives and enjoy hot.

uni-ikura don

150–200 g (5¼–7 oz) salmon roe

2 tbsp soy sauce

1 tsp mirin

450 g (2¼ cups) sushi rice

560 ml (2¼ cups + 2 tbsp) filtered water

110 ml (scant ½ cup) rice or cider vinegar

1 tbsp sake

40 g (scant ¼ cup) sugar

12 g (2 generous tsp) salt

150–200 g (5¼–7 oz) sea urchins

shiso leaves (optional)

wasabi (optional)

Preparation

Marinate the salmon roe in the soy sauce and the mirin for 3 hours.

Cooking the sushi rice

Wash and rinse the rice gently without breaking the grains. Repeat two or three times, then drain in a colander.

Put the washed rice into a saucepan, add the filtered water, cover and leave to soak for at least 30 minutes before cooking.

Cover and cook over a high heat for 5 minutes to bring to the boil. Reduce the heat to low and simmer for 10 minutes. Turn off the heat and leave to rest, covered, for 10 minutes.

In a small bowl, mix the rice or cider vinegar, sake, sugar and salt. Spread the cooked rice over the surface of a large, flat tray.

Add the vinegar and mix gently, cooling the rice with a fan.

Presentation

Place the sushi rice in a bowl and arrange the sea urchins and salmon roe marinated in soy sauce on top.

Finely slice the shiso and use as a garnish with a little wasabi.

open
SAPPORO
営業中
サッポロ生ビール
黒ラベル

Ainu culinary culture: a rare gem worthy of preservation

The indigenous people of Hokkaido boast a rich culinary culture – but these traditions, much like their culture overall, is in peril, largely due to stigmatization by the government.

'Good conversations over delicious food are essential for preserving and promoting our culture. Instead of going to a museum, if you want to learn more about the Ainu, the best thing to do is sit down at a table, share a meal and talk.' Usa Teruyo is straight and matter-of-fact. She sincerely believes that you can discover and understand more about Ainu culture through its dinner plates than on any information board.

Usa Teruyo has owned Harukor, the only Ainu restaurant in cosmopolitan Tokyo, since 2011. Quietly tucked away in the Okubo district, a stone's throw from Shinjuku station, this hole-in-the-wall restaurant - it only has four tables - is a microcosm of her culture. Adorning the walls are a map of Hokkaido, the island she left with her family when she was ten years old and where, in Japan, most of her community live; a traditional indigo gown with a geometric pattern; and numerous posters of Golden Kamuy, a mega-popular manga whose heroes happen to be Ainu. All of this is set to the backdrop of traditional music. The menu contains all the dishes typical of these Northern people and their signature foods: fish, game, vegetables and wild herbs. Usa sources most of the ingredients directly from Hokkaido.

'There continues to be discrimination against our people. Many of them live very difficult lives. So we need to talk about our history, and, to a certain extent, this can be achieved by preserving our cuisine.'

JAPANESE COLONIZATION

So who are the Ainu? The Ainu are an indigenous people who initially inhabited the island of Hokkaido, Japan's northernmost island, which was then known as *Ainu Moshiri* (Land of the Ainu), and northern Honshu, Japan's main island. They also settled on the Kuril Islands and northern Sakhalin, both Russian territories.

That was until they started being pushed further and further north as a result of the Japanese empire's vague hopes of expansion. This community of fishermen, hunters and gatherers settled along the southern coast of Hokkaido, where the climate was warmer, and traded with the Japanese. The dawn of the Meiji Restoration in 1868 saw Japan's rulers start to colonize the island. Pioneers moved in and the Ainu who, until then, had been living in villages clustered around estuaries that brimmed with salmon and trout in the autumn, found themselves dispossessed of their land by virtue of an 1899 law on the 'protection of indigenous elders'. They had to leave their territories of abundant fish and game for the more mountainous regions in the centre of the island.

A CULINARY CATACLYSM

Forced to shift their focus to agriculture and livestock farming, the Ainu were no longer allowed to hunt deer on their land or fish for salmon in their rivers. Their animist bear ceremonies were similarly banned. Of course, all of this impacted their food culture: rice started to appear in their bowls, as did beans, potatoes and entirely new ways of seasoning. Until that point in time, animal oil, seaweed and salt had been their only flavouring agents, and *sayo* – Japanese millet – their main grain. The Ainu found themselves witnessing the gradual extinction of not only their traditions, but also their language, for they were only allowed to learn Japanese. Multiple instances of discrimination and stigmatization prompted a number of Ainu to conceal their origins, leading to the almost total disappearance of their culture and ancestral knowledge, which ceased to be passed down.

'Today, our culture is getting a lot more attention. But it's nowhere near enough. Some people even wonder if the Ainu really exist. What I want is for society to be aware of what the Japanese put us through,' says restaurateur Usa. 'There continues to be discrimination against our people. Many of them live very difficult lives. So we need to talk about

THE MAIN AINU DISHES INCLUDE:

- *Rataskep*: A mixture of vegetables and wild beans, stewed and mashed with pumpkin and animal fat.
- *Turep*: A wild lily, one of the most important ingredients in Ainu culture, eaten in a light and crisp tempura batter.
- *Oyakodon*: Salmon and salmon roe served with rice.
- *Mefin*: The internal organs of salted salmon.
- *Ciporimo*: A dish consisting of boiled potatoes and salt cod roe.
- *Pukusa* or *kitopiro*: Wild onions served boiled or marinated, usually with dumplings.
- *Ohaw*: A stock (broth) that acts as a base for dishes and is made from seasonal ingredients. There are different versions of it, served with meat or salmon.

our history. This can absolutely be achieved through education, but, to a certain extent, also by preserving our cuisine and arts.' not even his own. 'Tokyo does have an Ainu community centre, but it's difficult to freely socialize, talk and eat there; it's still a public building!'

WILD VEGETABLES AND MEATS

Usa Teruyo left Hokkaido as a ten-year-old, knowing nothing about her culture and being forced to hide her origins to avoid bullying and discrimination. She settled in Tokyo with her four siblings and her mother, who became involved with an Ainu cultural group. Her mother and grandmother opened a restaurant called Rera Chise ('wind house'). 'There was nowhere they could meet at the time.'

Once this closed, Usa and her mother opened the Harukor restaurant with one sole vision: to promote and introduce Ainu culture through food. However, as Usa's mother died soon after the restaurant opened, it is Usa's husband who, every day, takes the orders and serves the dishes of an indigenous people who are

Ainu cuisine primarily revolves around game, such as deer or bear - with the latter now only being served on very rare occasions - salmon and trout. All the meat and fish is smoked, boiled or stewed; unlike the Japanese, the Ainu eat very little raw meat or fish. These main stays are served with a variety of wild vegetables and roots, as well as berries and herbs, which are principally used for their flavouring and medicinal properties. They include *haskap* berries, *shikerebe-ni* bark and the wild garlic known as *kitopiro*.

When Usa thinks back to her childhood, one of the first things that come to her mind is *imo dango*, a dish based around sweet potato patties. 'I didn't even realize that my mother was cooking Ainu food for me. I had such little awareness of my own culture ...' Now a mother herself, Usa has gone to great effort to educate her daughter about Ainu craft and traditions. She has taught her songs and dances, introduced her to musical instruments and, of course, to Ainu food. 'I hold my ancestors very dear. I want to pass everything on to my children, especially as my mother and grandmother did so much for me.'

面白い

In 2008, the Japanese Parliament passed a resolution which acknowledged, for the first time, that the Ainu 'are an indigenous people with their own language, religion and culture', although this text amounted to little more than a token gesture.

In 2019, the controversial resolution from 1899 was replaced by a law on promoting Ainu culture, which promised to 'create a society that respects the dignity' of the minority. This law, the first of its kind, seeks to establish measures to support communities and boost the local economy and tourism.

While the situation has improved, there is still a noticeable disparity in income and education for Ainu people when compared to those of the rest of the population.

ゴールデンカムイ
ハルコロちゃん 野田サトル
2023.1

今が旬！
キトピロ天ぷら
釧路産
900えん
650 900 800
予約席
BACARDI
SAPPORO

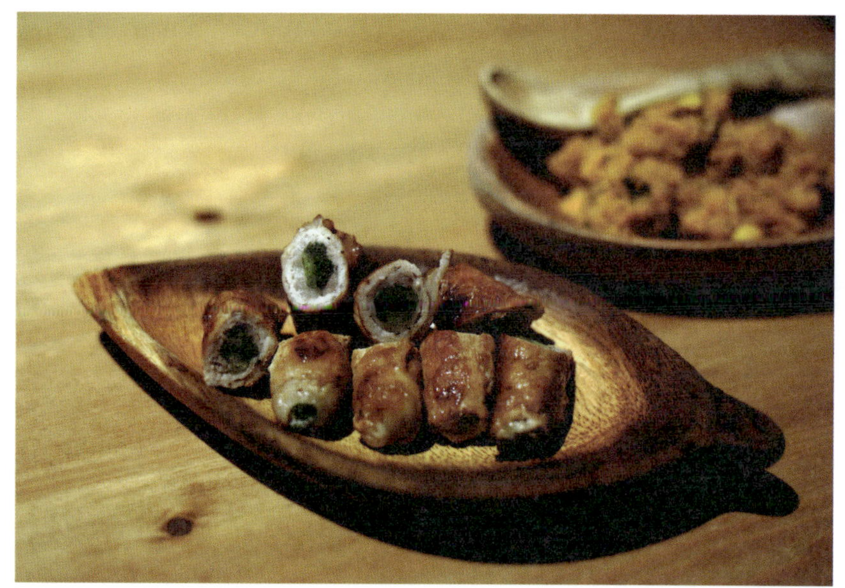

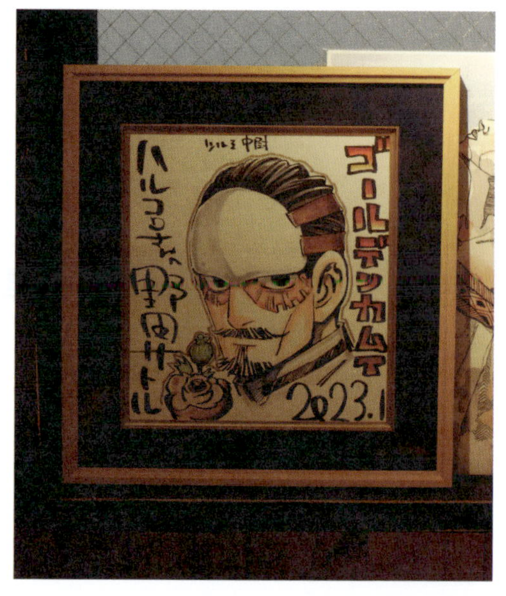

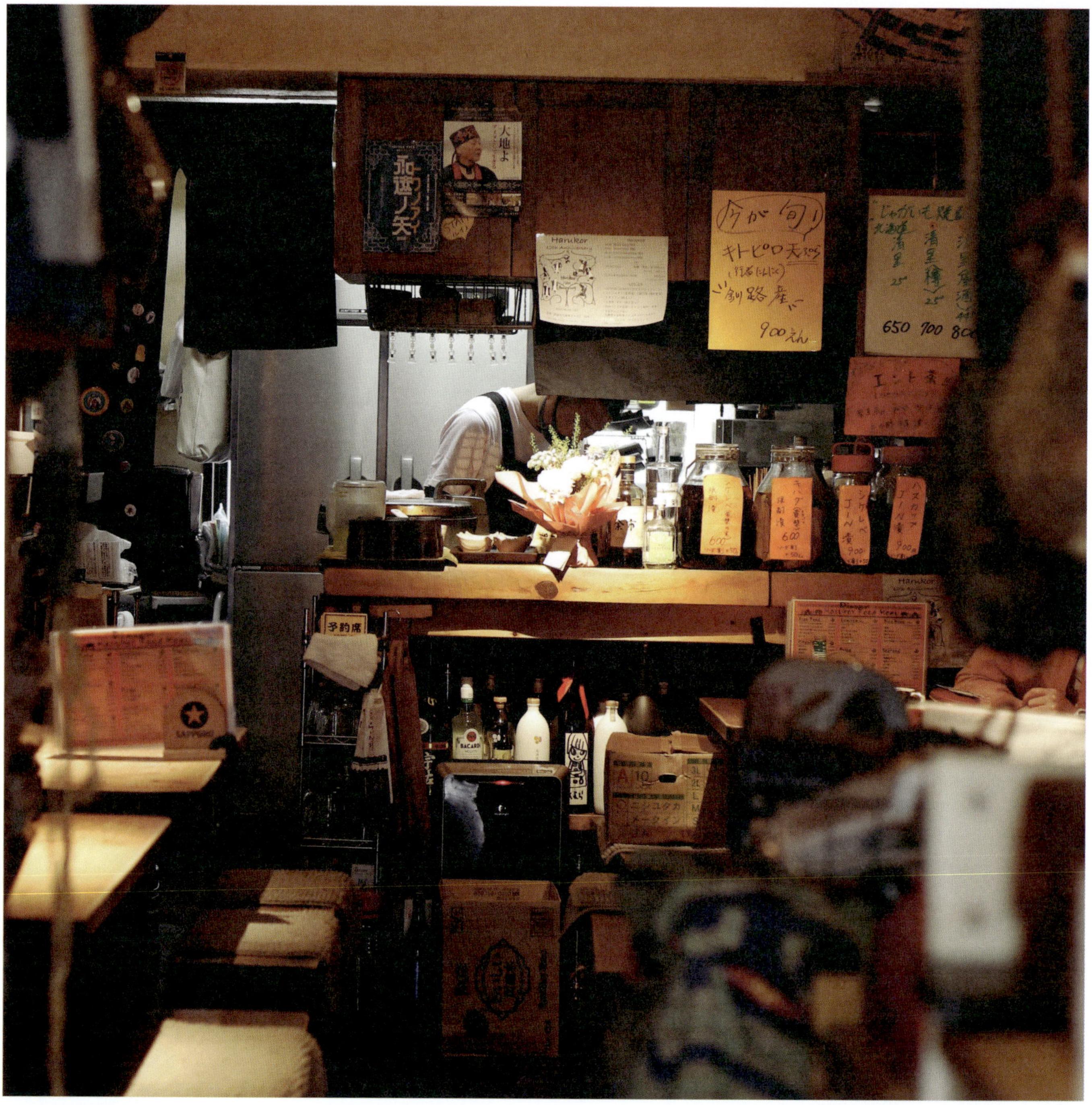

Difficulty ●●○

Serves 4

Preparation: 50 mins
Cooking: 20 mins

ishikari nabe

For the broth

1.5 l (6⅓ cups) filtered water

1 sheet dried kombu seaweed (10 x 10 cm/ 4 x 4 in)

80 g (generous ¼ cup) miso paste

2 tbsp mirin

2 tsp sake

30 g (2 tbsp) butter, or more to taste

½ onion, cut into thick semicircles

2–3 whole fresh shiitake mushrooms

4–5 choudou (or white cabbage) leaves, roughly chopped

2–3 spring onions (scallions), cut diagonally

½ bunch chrysanthemum greens, roughly chopped

200 g (7 oz) salmon head

salt

2 salmon steaks (about 200 g/7 oz) each

1 block of firm tofu, cut into large cubes

200 g (7 oz) *konnyaku* noodles, soaked in hot water and chopped

4 tbsp salmon roe

Preparation

Pour the filtered water into an earthenware pot or *donabe*, add the kombu and leave to infuse for 30 minutes.

Arrange all the prepared vegetables on a large plate.

Wash, descale and roughly shop the salmon head. Salt lightly.

Place the pot or *donabe* with the water and the soaked kombu over a single gas burner on the table and turn to a medium setting.

Leave to simmer for 2–3 minutes, then remove the kombu. Add the salmon head and all the remaining broth ingredients, except the butter. Increase the heat and skim any foam from the surface if necessary.

You can eat the kombu sliced and stir-fried with mirin and soy sauce to accompany a bowl of rice.

Add the salmon steaks and the vegetables to the pot in the order they are listed. Skim any foam from the surface of the broth if necessary. Then add the tofu, *konnyaku* noodles and butter. The *ishikari nabe* is now ready.

Serve in a bowl, garnished with the salmon roe.

Difficulty ●○○

Serves 4

Preparation: 10 mins
Cooking: 20 mins

chiporo imo

400 g (14 oz) potatoes

pinch of salt

120 g (4¼ oz) salty salmon roe

Preparation

Cook the potatoes in a pan of boiling salted water.

Roughly crush them while they are still hot.

Once the potatoes have cooled a little, sprinkle them with the salmon roe. Enjoy hot.

Difficulty ●●○

Serves 4

Preparation: 20 mins
Cooking: throughout the meal

genghis khan barbecued lamb and vegetables

600–700 g (1⅓–1½ lb) lamb meat, cut into bite-sized pieces

vegetable oil

For the sweet and fruity marinade

1½ tbsp sake

1 tbsp sugar

1½ tbsp mirin

½ tbsp honey

½ tbsp soy sauce

½ onion, grated

1 garlic clove, grated

½ apple, grated

1 tsp sesame oil

For the spicy miso marinade

2 tbsp sake

½ tbsp sugar

1 tbsp soy sauce

1½ tbsp miso

½ tbsp *gochujang* (chilli paste)

1 tsp ketchup

½ onion, grated

1 garlic clove, grated

1 tsp sesame oil

This is a Japanese table barbecue: marinated lamb and vegetables are cooked on a round hotplate which is domed in the centre and specially designed for optimal flavour. At home, the hotplate can be replaced by an electric plancha. It's the ideal meal to share with friends.

Preparation

Combine the ingredients for each marinade in a separate bowl. Use bowls that are large enough to hold both the meat and the marinade.

Marinating the meat

In separate bowls, combine all the ingredients for the sweet and fruity marinade and for the spicy miso marinade.

Divide the meat in half, and marinate each half in a different marinade for at least 1 hour. If there is not enough marinade, add more sake.

For the vegetables

1 onion, cut in fairly thick semicircles and separated into rings

2 leeks, sliced diagonally

100 g (3½ oz) spring onions (scallions), roughly cut into 4 cm (1½ in) pieces

100 g (scant 1 cup) beansprouts, washed and drained

⅛ choudou or green cabbage, cut roughly into cubes

2 (bell) peppers, cut into quarters lengthwise, seeds removed

⅛ pumpkin, cut into 5 mm (¼ in) slices

2 aubergines (eggplants), cut diagonally into 5 mm (¼ in) slices + vegetables of your choice

2 servings of *yakisoba* (or Chinese) noodles (optional)

Prepare the vegetables in the order in which they are listed.

Brush the plancha with a little vegetable oil. Place the meat in the centre and the vegetables around it and cook. Keep turning the meat and the vegetables, basting them with the juices and fat from the meat which will give added flavour to the vegetables. Eat the meat and vegetables as soon as they are cooked.

Optional

Sauté some *yakisoba* noodles with any remaining vegetables on the grill, and dress with the marinade to make a sauce.

Japanese seaweeds

Nori, kombu, wakame ... these are all absolutely indispensable seaweeds for anyone wanting to cook Japanese-style meals. Packed full of nutrients, they are also consumed for their medicinal properties. However, pollution and global warming are putting Japanese seaweeds at risk.

Whether floating delicately in a miso soup, wrapped around the rice of an *onigiri* or served as the finishing touch in a bento box, seaweed is an essential part of Japanese cuisine. While still consumed relatively meagrely in the West, it has been used as a garnish for Japanese dishes for centuries. Monks were the first to grow the famous *kaisou* (seaweed salad) in the 8th century – initially on bamboo stems in the shallow waters of bays and estuaries, using a technique known as *tenkusa* or 'suspended farming'. Seaweed was so important at the time that, in 701, a law was enacted allowing the people of Japan to use it to pay their taxes.

Several centuries later, seaweed moved beyond monastery kitchens and went mainstream. People all over Japan began consuming it, and farming intensified, particularly in Tokyo Bay. In 1670, aquafarmers planted bamboo stems in the sea – much like the monks had done a few centuries before – to attract clusters of seaweed spores. The stems were then moved to a river estuary, where nutrients in the water helped the seaweed grow. It was not until the technical improvements of the 20th century, however, that production really intensified. The bamboo stems were replaced with synthetic nets attached to bamboo rods, facilitating a larger farming area. This approach enabled nori seaweed production, for example, to increase 40-fold between 1940 and 1990. Japan produced more than 1.3 million tonnes (1.4 million tons) of seaweed in 2020, for a total value of more than 63 billion yen (approximately 367 million GBP/465 million USD).

JAPAN'S MAIN SEAWEED VARIETIES

Seaweed is a marine vegetable without any roots or leaves. It is classified by colour, ranging from brown and green to red and blue. Nori is a red seaweed, although its colour actually varies from purple to black. Wakame and kombu are brown varieties of seaweed.

Nori

This red seaweed is extremely high in protein, minerals and amino acids. In the 8th century, it was eaten fresh. This did not change until the Edo period (1603–1868), when nori started to be consumed primarily as dried leaves. This meant that it could be used for wrapping *onigri* (rice balls) and *maki* (a type of sushi). The seaweed can also be found in the form of flakes or powder, which are added to sauces, soups, salads, rice and broths as a flavouring agent. Nori is mainly grown in Tokyo Bay and in the bay of the Ariake Sea, in the north of Kyushu island.

1. Nori
2. Hijiki
3. Umibudo
4. Funori
5. Aonori
6. Wakame
7. Arame
8. Konbu

Kombu

This brown seaweed is particularly high in calcium. While it is usually eaten with fish, meat or in fondues, kombu is also an essential ingredient in dashi, the go-to stock in Japanese cuisine. This stock contains the precious umami flavour, which is obtained by mixing kombu seaweed with *katsuobushi* (dried skipjack tuna). Kombu grows in abundance off the coast of Hokkaido, Japan's northernmost main island.

Wakame

High in vitamins, calcium, fibre and antioxidants, this brown seaweed is the star in miso soup, one of the staple dishes of traditional Japanese cuisine, which can be eaten at any time of day. Wakame's taste is particularly mild, but distinctive and strong. This also makes it a perfect ingredient for salads. The seaweed is generally sold dried, and its preparation consists solely of soaking the sheets in hot water. The soaking causes it to change colour from a deep brown to a dark green. Wakame seaweed is farmed exclusively on the northern coasts of the archipelago, as it only grows in cold water.

SEAWEEDS ARE NUTRITIONAL BOMBS

Whether consumed dried or in a broth, seaweeds are veritable 'nutritional bombs', as described by Vincent Doumeizel, seaweed specialist and advisor on the oceans to the United Nations Global Compact. These sea vegetables are high in iron, vitamins A and C, protein, iodine and zinc. Indeed, some of them are the only vegetables at all to contain vitamin B12, which is otherwise primarily found in meat products.

'Several studies conducted in Japan by phycology[1] specialists have shown that all these marine resources can help prevent certain cancers of the breast, colon and prostate,' explains Vincent Doumeizel. 'And it is important to note that, unlike land-based plants, you don't need a lot of seaweed to get all the health benefits.' Another of seaweed's interesting bonuses is that - unlike plants - when seaweed is dried it retains its structure and nutrients perfectly.

[1] The study of algae

THE WEST IS BEHIND THE TIMES

'Why is it that only one region on the planet has learned to grow a food resource that doesn't require any soil, food or pesticides?' the algae specialist ponders.

Good question! Seaweed production in Asia has risen from 4 million tonnes (4.4 million tons) in 1990 to nearly 35 million tonnes (38.5 million tons) today. In the West, meanwhile, seaweed consumption remains modest at best, despite it making up around 10 per cent of the Japanese diet. There is another factor that may also explain this difference: 99 per cent of Asian seaweed is grown through marine phycoculture (algae farming), which has been in development since the early 20th century, whereas in the West, especially in Europe, most of the available seaweed is the result of wild harvesting. 'Westerners have remained foragers when it comes to the sea,' says Doumeizel. This has made it impossible to keep up with farming methods that are becoming increasingly sophisticated not only in Japan, but also in China, Indonesia and South Korea. Europe only makes up 1 per cent of global seaweed production.

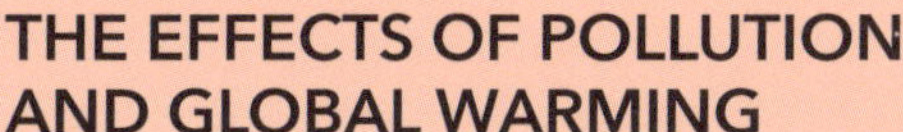

THE EFFECTS OF POLLUTION AND GLOBAL WARMING

The effect of global warming is starting to be felt along the 29,692 km (18,450 miles) of Japanese coastline. Rising sea temperatures, altered ocean currents and acidity build-up in the water are major factors affecting seaweed growth and quality.

One of the main effects of global warming is the rise in sea surface temperatures, which has a direct impact on seaweed. When the water temperature increases, it reduces the rate at which the seaweed grows, potentially compromising the harvest. And that is not all: warmer water can also encourage the growth of harmful algae that can damage both the farmed seaweed and the marine ecosystem.

DID YOU KNOW Nori is the most commonly used seaweed in Japanese cuisine and makes up around 60 per cent of total seaweed production in Japan. Wakame and kombu, meanwhile, make up approximately 25 per cent and 10 per cent respectively.

Global warming is similarly impacting seaweed farming through altered ocean currents. These changes affect the distribution of the nutrients needed for the seaweed to grow. As such, a group of researchers from Hokkaido University have warned that several varieties of kombu may completely disappear from Hokkaido's coastline over the next 70 years. If global warming continues at its current rate, sea water temperatures around the most northerly of Japan's main islands could, by 2090, have increased by 10°C (18°F) compared to their 1980 levels. ●

Umami,
the fifth taste that has conquered the world

Umami: three syllables for a flavour that has captivated taste buds with its moreish taste. Umami is a 'delicious taste', albeit with a reputation that is as savoury as it is controversial.

UMAMI AND DASHI STOCK

Dashi stock (broth) is one of the main bases of Japanese cuisine; it is used in the preparation of miso soup, stocks, sauces and many other dishes. Dashi is also one of the main condensed versions of umami, as it contains the trio of ingredients famed for tantalizing our taste buds: kombu seaweed, which is high in glutamate; dried skipjack tuna flakes *(katsuobushi)*, which are known to release inosinate; and dried shiitake mushrooms, which contain guanylate.

The Japanese word umami coined from a contraction of *umai* (meaning 'delicious') and *mi* ('taste') has been coveted by foodies of a certain palate for decades. It is one of the five basic tastes alongside sweet, salty, bitter and sour – a tight-knit circle which it joined only in the 1980s, but more about that later. Umami is thus a universal flavour, it just happens to be known by a Japanese name. Whatever your own mother tongue, the term is never translated, invariably remaining in Japanese.

This so-called 'delicious taste' sparks an almost irresistible urge to keep going back for more of the same, just to experience it one more time; it is a taste that lingers in the mouth and brings so much pleasure – is it Japanese? Yes. Kind of. Because, in the early 19th century, chemist Louis Jacques Thénard and food writer Jean-Anthelme Brillat-Savarin used the word 'osmazome' to describe a flavour almost identical to what we refer to as umami today. 'The greatest service chemistry has ever rendered to alimentary science is the discovery of osmazome, or rather the determination of what it was. Osmazome is the purely sapid portion of flesh soluble in cold water,' Brillat-Savarin wrote in *Physiologie du goût (The Physiology of Taste)*, published in 1825. 'Osmazome is the most meritorious ingredient of all good soups. This portion of the animal forms the red portion of flesh, and the solid parts of roasts. It gives game and venison its peculiar flavour.' Except that osmazome never really experienced the success of umami. And for good reason: while umami was discovered by a chemist, it is also heavily backed by the food industry and marketing. Let's rewind a bit.

'THE ESSENCE OF TASTE'

It's the early 1900s, the middle of the Meiji era (1868–1912). Japan had reopened to the world a few decades earlier and was now rapidly modernizing, industrializing and expanding its empire beyond its borders by adopting a colonialist policy. Kikunae Ikeda, a chemistry professor at Tokyo Imperial University, was interested in the umami flavour he could not link to any of the four basic tastes, and so examined the ingredients of the omni-present dashi stock. It was at this point that he discovered the glutamic acid extract known as glutamate. He patented the molecule he had just extracted - monosodium glutamate (MSG) - and managed to convince iodine manufacturer Suzuki to produce and market his discovery. *Ajinomoto*, 'the essence of taste' which acts as both a seasoning and a flavour enhancer, was born.

While its early days may have been rather underwhelming, this molecule soon found its way into the cuisines of Japan and its colonies, before spreading worldwide with the help of heavy marketing. In the 1970s, however, the tide turned, and glutamate, the synthetic flavour enhancer, saw its reputation plummet as consumers began shifting away from processed products. Nevertheless, the communications juggernaut that was the 'Made in Ajinomoto' campaign worked its magic and managed to reverse the trend: glutamate was redeemed, and the company even attempted to pass it off as a natural ingredient. The chemical MSG became umami. In 1980, Europe, the United States and Japan joined forces to make umami the fifth basic flavour - the only one in the

Unlike the four other tastes – bitter, sour, sweet and salty – which are adopted accordingly by the language using them, umami is never translated, remaining invariably in Japanese.

world to have its own information centre, the Umami Information Centre, a non-profit organization sharing vast scientific information on this subject. Needless to say, it is financed by leading players from Japan's MSG industry, which include ... *Ajinomoto*.

A FUSION OF AMINO ACIDS

This umami taste is linked to the presence of three amino acids: glutamic acid (the famous monosodium glutamate found in various plant or animal proteins), disodium guanylate (found in mushrooms) and disodium inosinate (found in pickled or dried fish). It is this fusion of these elements that makes umami. Each of its flavour enhancers, which can be sourced naturally, also has a synthetic version. These versions - E621, E627 and E631 - have a less dazzling reputation.

What exactly happens on our tastebuds that creates this delightful, irresistible urge to go in for a second helping? In 2009, researchers identified specific taste receptors for glutamate on the tongue. The process is therefore simple: our tastebuds, via the receptors, fixate on the glutamate and send an electric message to the brain. This message is associated with pleasure and triggers activity in the salivary glands. So there you have it: the secret is out.

THE PASSAGE OF TIME

Umami, this flavour of all flavours is - unsurprisingly - very popular among chefs, in both Japan and anywhere else in the world, because the ingredient that releases the umami flavour naturally is none other than time itself. Whether the umami is sourced from meat, fish or vegetables, it creeps in as food slowly cooks, ages, decomposes, is refined or fermented.

You don't necessarily have to try dashi stock to experience this 'delicious taste'. Simply nibble on a piece of Parmesan cheese or sprinkle some grated cheese onto pasta topped with tomato sauce; or enjoy a slice of roast meat; or just add a dash of soy sauce to your salad vinaigrette. An even more universal example, considering that so many newborn babies everywhere have already sampled it - breast milk is also very rich in umami.

The ingredient that releases this umami naturally is none other than time itself. Whether sourced from meat, fish or vegetables, umami creeps in as food cooks slowly, ages, decomposes, is refined or ferments.

OKINAWA

The culinary secrets of Okinawa's centenarians

Located in the far south of Japan and considered to be a tropical paradise, the Okinawa archipelago is one of the planet's 'blue zones'. What does that mean? Quite simply, that it is home to many more centenarians than anywhere else on earth. This longevity is due a variety of factors, one being nutrition.

There were 1,334 centenarians living in Okinawa in 2022. That is nine out of 10,000 residents. It is a ratio that has seen this most southerly region of Japan classified among a very small circle of 'blue zones', a term coined by *New York Times* journalist Dan Buettner to denote places with particularly high numbers of centenarians. There are only five in the world: Okinawa, obviously; the Nicoya Peninsula in Costa Rica; the island of Icaria in Greece; Loma Linda in southern California; and Sardinia in Italy.

While Okinawans are more than happy to lay claim to this longevity, they see the amusing side of it too. A stone tablet at the entrance to the village of Ogimi, in the north of Okinawa's main island bears the following inscription in Japanese characters: 'At 80 years of age, you are young. At 90, if your ancestors invite you to join them in heaven, ask them to wait for you to reach 100, then you can think about it.'

There were 1,334 centenarians living in Okinawa in 2022. That is nine out of 10,000 residents. Three factors are said to be key to this longevity: genetics, social habits and diet.

GENETICS, SOCIAL CONNECTION AND DIET

So what is the secret of long life according to Okinawa residents? What is it about this region that results in its people living longer and in better health than anywhere else in Japan, and indeed the world? To find out, we need to look at their lifestyle - something that has been closely examined by the scientific community for years, especially by the Okinawa Research Centre for Longevity Science. Three factors appear to be key to this astonishing longevity: genetics, social habits and diet. Despite all this, however, old age must never be sugar-coated. Granted, Okinawa has a particularly high number of centenarians, but it is important to note that, while most remain independent until their mid-90s, one-third of them are very ill or even disabled.

OKINAWA AND THE US OCCUPATION

On 1 April 1945, tens of thousands of GIs descended upon the beaches of Okinawa for the impending attack on Japan's main archipelago. After 82 days of fierce combat, the United States took control of the territory. While US occupation ended in 1952, it was not until 1972 that the islands of Okinawa were returned to Japan. However, the US military still maintains its bases there, serving as training camps as well as strategic bridgeheads. The numbers speak for themselves: While the entire Okinawa Prefecture only makes up 0.6 per cent of Japan's surface area, more than 70 per cent of all US military facilities in Japan are located there in terms of the area covered.

The food eaten by the Okinawans is not always the same as that found on dinner plates elsewhere in Japan, although this culinary gap has been closing since the end of World War II. Before 1945, the traditional Okinawan diet was influenced by a mixture of Japanese, Chinese and Southeast Asian cuisine: a fusion known as *champuru*, which can indeed be translated as 'mix'. Very little white rice, if any, was eaten in Okinawa. The star ingredient instead was the sweet potato, several varieties of which were grown in the tropical archipelago following their introduction, via trade with the Netherlands, in the early 17th century.

A DIET THAT IS SEMI-VEGETARIAN

As well as the sweet potato, other staple foods included root vegetables, leafy green vegetables, soy-based products and miso soup - all usually steamed or stewed. These foods were coupled with only small servings of lean meat and fish, ensuring the majority of the diet was plant-based - always seasoned with herbs and spices or skipjack tuna stock (broth) rather than salt. As a result the traditional Okinawan diet is high in minerals, essential vitamins and antioxidants, much like its other healthy counterparts such as the traditional Mediterranean diet. These diets significantly help to reduce the risk of cardiovascular disease, chronic illness and certain cancers.

Another particularity of the traditional Okinawan diet is the practice of what is known in these parts as *hara hachi bu*, a simple doctrine consisting of 'eating until one is 80 per cent full.' Meals typically consist of a variety of small dishes and people stop eating before they feel completely full. *Nuchi gusui*, the notion of seeing food as 'medicine', is another key pillar of the island's culinary culture. The various typical dishes here mix 'classic' fruit and vegetables with herbs and spices that have medicinal properties. These include *getto*, a flowering plant which produces red berries and is high in antioxidants, and

umibudo, a seaweed grown exclusively in the archipelago and which resembles a small bunch of grapes. It is a veritable power pack of nutrients, and is also high in iron, magnesium and minerals.

THE IMPACT OF THE AMERICAN OCCUPATION

While this traditional diet is still followed by most of the elderly residents today, the ingredients used in Okinawan dishes have undergone a few changes since the end of World War II and the subsequent US military occupation. Sweet potato has slowly given way to rice, and supermarket shelves are now stocked with imported products. The younger generations are moving away from the traditional diet, instead consuming more processed foods high in fast-acting sugars, saturated fats and sodium. Not surprisingly, these changes have had an impact on healthy human ageing, as the Okinawa Research Centre for Longevity Science is already starting to notice.

Simply subscribing assiduously to a semi-vegetarian or Mediterranean diet is not everything, however. As mentioned earlier, a combination of factors is responsible for so many people in this part of the world reaching 100 years of age. Genetics also plays a role. It has been proven that most Okinawans carry a variant of the Fox03 gene, a gene which is important for human longevity and that is involved in metabolic regulation and cell growth, consequently reducing the risk of cancer and many other age-related illnesses.

Social connections, which are very tight in this archipelago, also appear to play a major part in healthy ageing. While interpersonal networks in Japan primarily revolve around the close family, it seems to be friends and neighbours who carry more weight in this chain of tropical islands. In Okinawa, it is all about *moai*, a tradition encouraging the development of close social relationships within a small group of people who support each other emotionally, physically and financially whenever the need arises, thus preventing members from feeling isolated.

The longevity of the Okinawans is the product of a precious mix of factors that could - and probably should - serve as inspiration for Western societies. However, as Professor Donald Craig Willcox from Okinawa International University is keen to stress, 'we still need many more years of research to understand the exact role played by each of these factors and to thus uncover the secret of the Okinawa archipelago's elixir of youth.' ▬

Difficulty ●●○

Serves 2

Preparation: 40 mins
Cooking: 55 mins

juuchii

300 g (1½ cups) sushi rice

4 dried shiitake mushrooms

20 g (generous 1 tbsp) cooked *hijiki* seaweed (or 1 black fungus, rehydrated in water and finely chopped)

1 carrot

50 g (2 oz) *kamaboko* or *surimi* (imitation seafood)

For the cooking broth

500 ml (2⅛ cups) water

200 g (7 oz) pork belly, in one piece

2 tbsp soy sauce

2 tbsp mirin

1 tbsp sake

2 tsp dashi powder

Okinawa miso soup, to serve

Preparation

Wash and rinse the rice gently without breaking the grains, leave to soak in water for at least 30 minutes, then drain.

Cut the stems off the dried shiitake. Soak the caps in 200 ml (generous 1 cup) hot water for 30 minutes, then cut them into 1 cm (⅜ in) cubes.

Drain the *hijiki* (or rehydrated and finely chopped black fungus) in a colander.

Peel the carrot and cut it into 1 cm (⅜ in) cubes. Cut the *kamaboko* or *surimi* into 1 cm (⅜ in) cubes.

To make the broth, bring 500 ml (2⅜ cups) water to the boil in a saucepan. Add the pork belly and cook for 30 minutes over a medium heat. Skim any foam off the top if necessary. When it is cooked through, remove the meat from the pan and reserve the cooking water.

Once the pork has cooled, cut it into 1 cm (⅜ in) cubes.

Put the drained rice into a rice cooker or saucepan. Measure the stock from cooking the meat and add the cooking broth ingredients so that the total volume is 400 ml (1⅔ cups). Pour the broth over the rice.

Add all the other chopped ingredients to the rice, mix and cook. If you are cooking the rice in a saucepan, cook over a high heat for 5 minutes, then reduce the heat to low and simmer for 10 minutes. After cooking, turn off the heat and leave to rest for another 10 minutes with the lid on.

Once the rice is cooked, mix everything together and serve in a bowl. Enjoy hot with Okinawa miso soup.

Difficulty ●○○

Serves 5

Preparation: 2 hours
Cooking: 3 hours 50 mins

okinawa soba

For the Okinawa noodles

1 tbsp bicarbonate of soda (baking soda)

2 tsp salt

1 egg

200–230 ml (generous ¾ to scant 1 cup) filtered water

500 g (3⅔ cups) plain (all-purpose) flour

2–3 handfuls of potato starch, plus for dusting

1 tbsp vegetable oil

a pinch of salt

For the soba broth

1.5–2 kg (1½–4½ lbs) pork bones (ribs, back, etc.)

200 g (7 oz) pork belly, in one piece

200 ml (generous ¾ cup) katsuobushi dashi stock

2 tbsp salt

2 tbsp soy sauce

3 tbsp awamori

3 tbsp demerara sugar

3 tbsp soy sauce

10 kamaboko or surimi (imitation seafood) slices

2 spring onions (scallions) or ½ bunch of chives

pickled pink ginger (optional)

pickled chilli (chili pepper) in awamori sauce (optional)

Making the Okinawa noodles

In a small bowl, mix the bicarbonate of soda (baking soda), salt, egg and water. Sift the flour into a large bowl, then add the contents of the small bowl, using a circular movement.

Mix the ingredients together using chopsticks, then knead for 10 minutes with your hands.

Once the dough is a smooth, uniform mixture, form into a ball and put it in a resealable plastic food (zip lock) bag. Seal the bag and leave to rest for 1–1½ hours.

Dust the work surface and your hands with some of the potato starch to prevent the dough from sticking. Divide the dough into quarters. Use a rolling pin to flatten the dough until it is 1–2 mm (about ¹⁄₁₆ in) thick. Cut into 3–4 mm (⅛–¼ in) wide ribbons to make the noodles. Add more potato starch to prevent the noodles sticking together.

Making the soba broth

Clean the pork bones in boiling water, then put them into a saucepan together with the pork belly. Add enough water to cover everything completely. Cook over a medium heat. Once the water has come to a boil, skim the surface and reduce the heat. Simmer over a low heat for 2–3 hours, skimming regularly, until the broth has reduced by half.

Remove the pork belly and reserve, skim any excess fat from the surface of the broth if necessary, and strain it. Add the dashi stock, salt and soy sauce. The soup is now ready.

Cook the pork belly together with the awamori, brown sugar and soy sauce for 30–50 minutes, until you obtain a nice shiny colour. Cut into slices.

Cut the kamaboko into slices and chop the spring onions (scallions) or chives.

Bring a large saucepan of water with a pinch of salt to a boil, add the noodles and cook for about 2 minutes. Shake them before putting them into the water to remove some of the potato starch. The noodles are cooked when they rise to the surface. Drain.

Combine the soup and noodles in a bowl, and garnish with slices of pork, kamaboko and spring onions (scallions) or chives. If you like, add some pickled pink ginger and a little pickled chilli (chili pepper). Enjoy hot!

Difficulty ●○○

Serves 2

Preparation: 10 mins
Cooking: 10 mins

ninjin shirishiri

2 carrots

1 tin (can) tuna (in springwater)

1 tbsp vegetable oil

1 pinch each of salt and black pepper

1 tsp soy sauce

1 tbsp *kombu* dashi powder

2 eggs, beaten

rice, to serve

Preparation

Grate the carrots. Drain the tuna.

In a frying pan, heat the oil and sauté the grated carrots, then add the tuna and cook lightly.

Add the salt, pepper, soy sauce and dashi powder; continue cooking.

Pour in the beaten eggs, let them cook a little, then turn off the heat. Serve with or on top of rice. It's delicious!

山荘
なぎさ
SANSOU NAGISA
先導師
旅館
小笠原
電話 0463-95-2753

Journey to Oyama, land of the gods and of tofu

Packed full of plant protein and a perfect alternative to meat products, tofu is one of the iconic ingredients of Japanese cuisine. While consumption is on the rise, the number of small artisanal factories is dwindling by the year.

Artisanal tofu producers Takuya Aihara and Mika Shimizu are well worth meeting. This requires leaving the labyrinthine megacity that is Tokyo and taking a train journey of just over an hour to Isehara station in Kanagawa Prefecture, before getting on a bus that slowly meanders its way through the city centre and then continues on its route through fields. As the miles roll by, houses become scarcer, giving way to wide open spaces where lush vegetation takes back the reins. Half an hour later, the coach doors open at Oyama, a tiny village clinging to the slopes of the sacred mountain that shares its name. Here, time seems to have stood still, moving gently to the rhythm of the water that rushes down the hillside and splits the village in two. In the lanes are a handful of shops, which remain operational largely as a result of the many organized pilgrimages to the shrine at the top of the mountain.

Thanks to the presence of the shrine, Oyama is known for its sacred mountain, but also for the superiority of its tofu, which primarily owes its taste and sweetness to the quality of the local water. Every March, the town holds a *matsuri* ('festival') dedicated to this soy product. Takuya Aihara and Mika Shimizu are the magic pairs of hands using artisanal methods to prepare several different varieties of tofu every day. Since June 2006, they have invented plant-flavoured recipes to complete the range of 'plain' tofu – the most traditional version – made in the 20-square-metre (215-square-foot) boutique workshop they run in the area.

Takuya Aihara and Mika Shimizu are village locals who began their operations in a *ryokan*[1] belonging to Takuya's family: he worked in the kitchen and she as a chambermaid. They served the famous *kaiseki* cuisine, the most authentic form of Japanese gastronomy, involving a vast array of different dishes. 'We noticed that travellers particularly enjoyed the tofu dishes. So we decided to have a go at enabling our customers to

[1] A traditional Japanese inn.

take it with them, as a souvenir,' Mika explains. Together with Takuya, she learned tofu-making skills and secrets from a local tofu maker in the village, who was preparing to shut up shop. A few months later, they opened their own factory just opposite the *ryokan*, and for the last 17 years, their days have been spent moving to the almost metronomic beat of tofu, and, at 45 and 49 years of age respectively, the duo is still eager to discover new recipes.

PRECISION RULES, OK?

It takes about eight hours to create a block of tofu, and that's not counting the preparatory work. Every evening, before shutting their shop, Takuya and Mika carefully sort through the soya beans (soybeans) before soaking them in water for a duration of anything between one and 18 nights, depending on the type of tofu they want to produce. 'We only use soy from Hokkaido, because we believe it's the best in the country. It has a taste that is very dense, but at the same time also subtle and delicate,' Mika explains. Early in the morning, Takuya heads to the back room and starts preparing the tofu. 'Its quality essentially depends on the quality of the ingredients that are used, because there are only very few of them. All you need to make tofu is soya beans (soybeans), water and a coagulant known as *nigari*, which is obtained from seawater and is therefore very high in minerals.' Once the beans have been removed from the water, they are crushed, then mixed with water to create a soy soup of sorts which is known as *go*. First you boil it, then you separate the pulp, known as *okara*, from the soy milk and add a coagulant to the latter to solidify it.

FIRM OR SILKEN TOFU

What happens next depends on the type of tofu that is desired, Takuya explains. 'If you want silken tofu, or *kinugoshi*, you need a more concentrated soy milk, so you add only a small amount of water, then you pour this milk into an unperforated mould, mix it well with the *nigari* and leave it to slowly solidify over several hours. The resulting product, the *kinu*, is neither pressed nor strained, but just packed.'

Making firm tofu, called *momen*, however, is quite different. 'Once the soy milk has solidified, you crumble it, then spread it over a cotton cloth and place the whole lot into a perforated mould. The mixture is then pressed firmly to extract the desired amount of water. This is what determines the firmness of the tofu,' Takuya continues. The mixture is then moulded and cut for packaging. 'The cutting is always done in a tray of water,' Mika explains. 'This prevents the tofu from spoiling. The water makes the knife blade less coarse and sharp, making for a softer cut.'

The pair shares all the tasks of the preparation, packaging, sale and delivery of their tofu to both private individuals and chefs in the surrounding area. Their recipes include silken tofu, a very soft tofu whose consistency is akin to that of yoghurt or cream, and whose taste can be enhanced simply by adding a drop of soy sauce or a pinch of salt. 'The saltiness brings out the softness of this type of tofu,' Mika says quietly.

The pair's firm tofu, meanwhile, comes in a classic version, as well as a number of plant flavours: *yomogi*, with its hints of mugwort leaves; *hojicha*, which conjures up the taste of green tea roasted on cedar wood; *murasaki imo*, which recalls sweet potato; and *kurogoma*, a dark grey tofu that tastes like black sesame. 'But tofu is a food whose taste, texture and firmness vary dramatically from season to season. No two artisanal tofus are the same. Air and water temperature, bean freshness and hydrometry all impact the finished product,' Takuya is quick to point out.

ARTISANAL PRODUCTION UNDER THREAT

Consumption of this high-protein food continues to rise in Japan. According to a study by the Japanese Ministry of Internal Affairs and Communications, tofu is the leading soy-based product purchased by households, ahead of *natto*. Household consumption has increased by 4.6 packets of tofu a year over the last 20 years. However, this trend also means that there are fewer and fewer artisanal tofu producers to be found. Faced with the consistently lower prices of large-scale producers and specialized co-operatives, who sell their products through major supermarkets and grocery shops, independent producers are struggling to keep up. The numbers speak for themselves. According to Zenkoku Tofu Rengokai, the Japanese national association of tofu-makers, there were only 5,713 artisanal producers in the year 2019, as opposed to 51,600 in 1961.

The quality of tofu essentially depends on that of the ingredients, because there are very few of them. All you need to make tofu is soybeans, water and a coagulant known as nigari, which is obtained from seawater and thus very high in minerals.

面白い

TOFU IS NOT ORIGINALLY A JAPANESE FOOD

Tofu first made its appearance in the archipelago in the 8th century, when the Japanese intellectuals and monks who had been sent to China returned to Japan. Tofu consumption noticeably started to increase, particularly at monasteries, during the Kamakura period (1185–1333), when Zen Buddhism took root in the country. In the early days of the Edo period (1603–1867), tofu remained a food consumed mostly on special occasions, such as *Obon* or New Year, and especially among the upper classes. It became more accessible to the masses in the mid-18th century, in particular thanks to the publication of *Tofu hyakuchin (100 Tofu-Based Dishes)*, which, over several hundreds of pages, details recipes for cooking and enjoying tofu, whether raw, cooked, boiled, toasted or fried.

湧水工房
YUSUI KOUBOU
大山豆腐
OYAMA TOFU
おから無料で
差し上げます。
You may have a free tofu refuse.

PayPay
大山とうふ
せいぞうはんばい
ゆうすいこうぼう
TAKE OUT
ゆうすい こうぼう
湧水工房
Twitter
@yusui_oyama

champuru goya

½ block tofu (150–200 g/ 5¼–7 oz)

½ or 1 small bitter melon (*gōyā* or *nigauri*)

¼ tsp plus 1 pinch of salt

½ tsp sugar

100 g (3½ oz) thinly sliced pork belly

ground black pepper

1 tbsp vegetable oil

1 tbsp sesame oil

1 egg

2 tsp soy sauce

rice, to serve

The Okinawan tofu traditionally used in this recipe is denser and firmer than the tofu we normally find in the West. To prevent it from breaking up while cooking, you need to make it firmer by pressing it and reducing its water content. To do this, choose a firm tofu, wrap it in a square of cheesecloth or paper (kitchen) towel. Place the wrapped tofu in a colander and weight it down with a plate on top. Leave for 1 hour for the water to drain out.

Once pressed, use your fingers to tear the tofu into bite-sized pieces.

Preparing the bitter melon

Cut the ends off the bitter melon, halve it lengthways, remove the seeds and the soft white flesh using a spoon. Cut the bitter melon into 5 mm (¼ in) semicircles.

Put the bitter melon slices into a bowl with the salt and sugar and mix with chopsticks. Set aside for 5 minutes to drain and remove the bitterness of the vegetable. (If you want to keep its bitter taste do not add the sugar.)

Cut the pork belly slices into strips 3–4 cm (1¼–1½ in) wide, then season with the salt and pepper.

Heat the vegetable oil in a frying pan, add the tofu and cook over a medium heat until lightly browned. Set aside on a plate.

Add the sesame oil to the same pan and sauté the bitter melon over a medium heat. Turn off the heat before it is completely cooked – it will continue to cook with the other ingredients. Set aside on a plate.

In the same pan, cook the pork slices on both sides. When the pork turns brown, add the cooked tofu and the sautéed bitter melon.

Sauté with a pinch of salt and pepper. Then beat the egg and pour over the ingredients in the pan so that the entire surface is covered. Wait a few seconds, so the egg doesn't break into small pieces, but instead forms large pieces that hold the other ingredients together.

Finally, add the soy sauce, mix lightly and turn off the heat. Enjoy hot with or on top of rice.

Difficulty ●○○ Serves 2 Preparation: 15 mins
Cooking: 15 min

tofu miso soup

½ tbsp vegetable oil

¼ onion, not too finely sliced

½ slice (about 50 g/1¾ oz) pork loin cut into strips

¼ carrot, cut into large slices

400 ml (1⅔ cups) *katsuobushi* dashi stock

2 choudou or white cabbage leaves, roughly chopped

50 g (scant ½ cup) *shimeji* or mushrooms, cut into bite-sized pieces

50 g (½ cup) beansprouts, washed and drained

1 block (about 200 g/ 7 oz) Okinawa or solid (extra-firm) tofu, cubed

2–3 tbsp miso paste

2 eggs

½ bunch of chives, chopped

Preparation

Heat the oil in a frying pan, add and lightly sauté the onion, pork and carrot.

Add the dashi stock and bring to a boil. Add the choudou, mushrooms, beansprouts and tofu.

Add the miso paste and stir gently until it has melted.

One at a time, carefully break the eggs on top of the ingredients in the pan. Cover the pan and leave the eggs to cook.

Sprinkle with the chopped chives and enjoy hot with rice.

Difficulty ●●○ Makes 1 kg (2⅛ lbs) tofu Preparation: 10 days

yo tofu

330 g (1¾ cups) red koji rice (red yeast rice) or miso koji

50 ml (generous 3 tbsp) *awamori* + more if needed to rinse the tofu (or shochu at 40°C/104°F or more)

40 g (⅓ cup) + 1 tsp salt

1 tsp sugar

1 kg (18 oz) Okinawa tofu (or extra-firm tofu if not available)

Preparation

Soak the koji rice in the awamori for 10 days. Once the koji is softened, grind it using a pestle. (If you cannot find red koji rice you can make this recipe without it.)

Add the salt and sugar to make the marinade.

The Okinawa tofu traditionally used in this recipe is denser and firmer than the tofu we normally find in the West. To prevent it from breaking up while cooking, you need to make it firmer by pressing it and reducing its water content. To do this, choose a firm tofu, wrap it in a square of cheesecloth or paper (kitchen) towel. Place the wrapped tofu in a colander and weight it down with a plate on top. Leave for 1 hour for the water to drain out.

Pat it dry, cut it into 2 cm (¾ in) cubes and leave in a colander in the shade for a day to dry out, turning it from time to time. If it is very hot, keep it in the fridge.

Sprinkle the dried tofu cubes with a little salt.

Drain the tofu in a colander in the shade for a day again, turning it every 2 hours, or keep it in the fridge if it is hot.

Once the tofu is dry, rinse it with the awamori.

Rinse an air-tight container with boiling water, then dry it. Add the marinade and the tofu cubes, making sure the tofu is well covered.

Close the container tightly. The preparation is now finished. The yo tofu can be eaten after 2 months, but will be better after 6 months. It is traditionally enjoyed in small quantities using a cocktail stick.

オリオンビール
Orion
沖縄
魅惑の島々へ
宮古
久米仙
オリオン麦職人

Okinawa, a tropical paradise with a US flavour

Occupied by the American armed forces from the end of World War II until 1972, the Okinawa archipelago is still home to a number of US military bases – a presence that has influenced its food culture among other things.

'Born in America, raised in Okinawa': The Blue Seal ice-cream brand, with its slogan and orange-and-blue wave-themed logo, is a perfect example of the American influence on the islands of Japan's far south. Its history goes like this: in 1948, the American company Foremost Blue Seal established one of its factories at the Tengan military base in Uruma so that it could supply dairy products to the troops and add some American flavour to this tropical Japanese island. Initially reserved exclusively for Americans, these ice creams became available to local Okinawans in 1963, even though dairy products had not traditionally been a part of their diet. Today Okinawa boasts ten of the brand's shops. Its logo is plastered everywhere from restaurants to convenience stores, and Blue Seal is now under local management.

In what has been another evolution, many of the 30 flavours on offer at Blue Seal ice cream parlours are made using regional ingredients, meaning that you will find here options such as lime, known as *shikuwasa*, sweet potato and even a bitter melon called *goya*. 'Okinawa has been heavily impacted by colonization, but the Okinawans have utilized

FROM INDEPENDENCE TO ANNEXATION BY JAPAN

Closer to Taiwan than to Tokyo, this chain of islands was initially an independent kingdom - the Ryukyu kingdom - which primarily traded with China and Japan. However, in 1609 the Shimazu clan from the island of Kyushu invaded Okinawa, and the islands were incorporated into Japan's feudal system. In 1872, Okinawa became the territory of Ryukyu, before finally being annexed by the Japanese government in 1879. When it comes to food culture, this has resulted in a prevalence of sweet potato farming, since the climate and local topography meant that rice could not be grown here.

their unique traits to innovate and turn their culture into the hybrid culture it is today,' explains Takeshi Watanabe, a professor of East Asian studies who specializes in analysing Japanese culture through its culinary traditions.

FROM INDEPENDENCE TO AMERICAN OCCUPATION

Generally, when people talk about Okinawa, it is in relation to its gloriously white sandy beaches and clear waters, or the incredible longevity of its residents – the island is home to a particularly high number of centenarians. However, this tropical paradise for tourists, be they Japanese or foreign, has also witnessed a number of major historic events. During World War II, between April and June 1945, it was the scene of the Battle of Okinawa, when the Americans, in a bid to intensify their strikes, used the little islands as a base for their final attack on Japan. Ninety per cent of the island's main buildings were destroyed at the time, and nearly 150,000 of its civilians killed. After the war, the mini archipelago came under the administration of the United States, which occupied it via its military bases. It was not until 1972 that Japan regained control of Okinawa, but the American presence remains strong. The figures speak for themselves: while the islands of Okinawa only make up 0.6 per cent of Japan's surface area, they are still home to 56,000 American citizens and 70 per cent of Japan's total number of US bases.

ROOT BEER, HAMBURGERS AND SPAM

The American occupation has obviously left its mark on the island's culture, and most notably on its food culture. While Blue Seal is a perfect synthesis of the two civilizations, there are other examples too. Okinawa was introduced to fast food in the early 1960s through the A&W chain of fast-food restaurants. A&W chose the island as the location of its first franchise outside the United States. And so it was that root beer (a soft drink flavoured with a mix of vanilla, liquorice and nutmeg), hamburgers and curly fries descended upon Okinawa. Locals placed orders at drive-throughs while listening to the American Forces Network radio broadcast from the military base. Even today, the islands are dotted with 26 establishments that look as if they have come straight out of the 1960s.

And that's not all. The palates of the Okinawans were introduced to new tastes that began to take over supermarket shelves to ease the deployed soldiers' homesickness. These included SPAM (tinned pork fat and meat that can be eaten cold, heated or cooked) and a tinned ham known as 'luncheon meat'. The latter became popular during the war, and unlike beef, pork has gradually found its way into typical Okinawan dishes such as *goya champuru* (a stir-fry of bitter lemon, tofu, egg and now pork), but also *onigiri*, tempura and miso soup. Indeed, it continues to be successful, with Okinawans today, accounting for more than 90 per cent of Japan's total luncheon meat consumption although the island only makes up 1.1 per cent of the country's population.

Takoraisu, a dish combining Tex-Mex beef with Japanese rice, is another example. 'Many of the – often Hispanic – American soldiers based in Okinawa during World War II wanted a dish that reminded them of the Tex-Mex flavours they were accustomed

'Okinawa has been heavily impacted by colonization, but the Okinawans have utilized their unique traits to innovate and turn their culture into the hybrid culture it is today.'
Takeshi Watanabe

to in their South-Western homelands,' Professor Watanabe explains. 'They used whatever was at hand to prepare simple tacos made from seasoned minced (ground) beef and cheap vegetables. These military-base tacos became omnipresent across Okinawa.' Local chefs then took over the reins and combined the taco garnish with short-grain rice. '*Takoraisu* thus represents the chefs' acceptance of the Japanese and American influence, while also expressing a cultural element specific to the island of Okinawa. Incidentally, the dish is now considered to be distinctly Okinawan,' Takeshi Watanabe says.

AN OKINAWAN ENCLAVE IN TOKYO

Japan's main island, Honshu, is itself also home to enclaves of Okinawan culture. One example of such an enclave can be found in the Kabukicho entertainment district of downtown Tokyo. Tucked away on the third floor of a building is a restaurant where, come nightfall, the sounds of Okinawan music and singing ring out. Its culinary offering naturally includes *goya champuru*, but also *soki soba* served with pork and, of course, the famous 'luncheon meat'. In terms of drinks that are available here, you will find *awamori*, a rice-based alcohol that is produced exclusively in Okinawa, everywhere and free-flowing. You'll be warmly welcomed at Okinawa Paradise, for example, a colourful and lively little place amply fitted out with paper lanterns bearing the logo of Orion Breweries, the local beer brand. Its owner is Shingo Tamaki, a native of the tropical archipelago of Okinawa – located more than 1,500 km (930 miles) away.

Clutching his *sanshin*, a stringed instrument used to accompany the folk songs of the Ryukyu Islands, and readjusting his traditional clothes, Shingo Tamaki is a reminder of the urgent need to create and preserve establishments like his in the megacity. 'It's like a point of contact for the Okinawans who have had to leave their island to find work, or for Okinawans who are simply passing through Tokyo. It enables us to get together and celebrate and preserve a part of our culture,' he explains. That is also why he organizes traditional music or singing concerts several times a week. 'Singing, playing the *sanshin* and eating Okinawan dishes all helps to keep our culture alive. Okinawa is resilient, and it's important to demonstrate this.'

NOMIMONO

Sado, the Way of Tea

Tea ceremonies are a traditional Japanese art form. They have influenced many other aspects of Japanese culture too, most importantly architecture, landscape painting and pottery.

Attending a tea ceremony means participating in one of Japan's most iconic traditions. It means discovering a world where time appears to have stood still, where every gesture counts and where there is no room for chance. It is a systematic, centuries-old dance that continues to be carefully passed down through the generations to this day. Preparation, serving, tasting ... Describing its various steps and symbolic stages in detail would make for tedious reading and ruin the magic and sanctity of those moments. It is still worth noting, however, that these ceremonies are steeped in a history which is inextricably linked with Buddhism, the evolution of women's roles over the centuries, architectural creations and even manufacturing - all elements that allow us to learn a little more about Japanese society.

It started with the tea itself, which came straight from neighbouring China via Buddhism. In the 8th century, tea was primarily consumed for its medicinal properties. At the time, it was drunk as an infusion, just as it was in mainland China. It was not until the 12th century and the Kamakura period (1185–1333) that the precious green tea powder - the famous matcha - was imported into Japan, once again from China. This was all thanks to Eisai, the founder of the Rinzai school of Japanese Zen Buddhism. The green tea powder was initially closely guarded within the walls of Buddhist temples where it helped the monks to meditate.

TEA-GROWING IN JAPAN

Japan's tea-producing regions are primarily concentrated in the south of the country. The main area is Shizuoka, near Mount Fuji, where 40 per cent of Japanese green tea is grown and harvested. Another tea-growing stronghold is the island of Kyushu, where the volcanic soils and subtropical climate add a multitude of flavours to the teas. Finally, there is Uji, Japan's ultimate tea town. This is where the famous *sencha* and matcha are grown, but also *gyokuro*, which can be translated as 'jewel dew'. *Gyokuro* is a dark tea harvested in the spring, and is considered to be Japan's most prestigious variety of tea.

DRINK OF WARRIORS AND ARISTOCRATS

Matcha became more accessible during the Miromachi period (1336–1573) which followed soon after. It was deemed an essential drink at warriors' and rulers' *chakai* banquets, where the matcha and sake would flow freely and, under the pretext of socializing, the elites would flaunt their finest clothes. These festivities were brought to a halt a century later, when tea master Murata Shukō (1423–1502) banned sake consumption at banquets and instead advocated for *wabi-cha* ceremonies, in which minimalism was king and any ostentation was prohibited. This is when the foundations for today's tea ceremonies were laid. In the 16th century, another tea master, Sen no Rikyū (1522–1591), established the guidelines for the ceremonies (seven in total). From then on, they became events where spirituality ruled, and where the cardinal values of purity *(sei)*, serenity *(jaku)*, harmony *(wa)* and respect *(kei)* were always honoured. He wrote:

'Make a satisfying
bowl of tea; lay the charcoal
so that the water boils
efficiently;
Provide a sense of coolness
in the summer
and warmth in winter;
Arrange the flowers
as though they were
in the field;
Be ready ahead of time;
Be prepared in case
it should rain;
Act with utmost
consideration
toward your guests.'

THE BIRTH OF THE TEA HOUSES

Tea ceremonies and, more broadly, the 'way of tea' known as *sadō*, also gave rise to other essentials of Japanese culture beyond these rules – the most important being the tea houses. An architectural style emerged known as *chashitsu*, a combination of *cha* ('tea') and *shitsu* ('room'). The houses consisted of two spaces: one where the tea was sampled and one where the host prepared the ceremony. Spanning a total area of two tatami mats (the tatamis have dimensions of about 91 x 182 cm/ 35¾ x 71½ in), these *chashitsu* had front doors measuring about 51 x 69 cm (20 x 27 in), located 30 cm (11¾ in) off the ground, which forced the lords to remove their swords and enter with bowed heads before meeting the tea master. Hierarchy and social differences faded into oblivion in these spartan, rustic-looking rooms.

As tea houses continued to develop, so too did a very specific form of garden design known as *roji*. Unlike dry gardens or gardens for strolling created for the sole purpose of being seen and contemplated, a *roji* that is, the 'garden leading to the tea house', was a thoroughfare of sorts. People passed through it to reach the space where the ceremony was being held. It was intended to be a place of transition where guests prepared their minds for the ceremony that was about to commence. The *roji* featured three distinct elements: the *tsukubai* basin for purifying the hands and mouth before attending the ceremony, the *ishi doro* stone lanterns, and the famous *tobi ishi* Japanese stepping stones that enabled visitors to walk around the garden without damaging the soil. Contemporary Japanese gardens continue to be inspired by this specific aesthetic to this day.

THE RISE OF POTTERY

Another form of art to be influenced by tea ceremonies was ceramics. Tea was initially drunk in Chinese bowls decorated with a celadon glaze or made from white porcelain, though usage changed as the ceremonies were increasingly pared down. In the 16th century, tea masters began to favour ceramics that were more rustic and less uniform, including terracotta raku bowls (raku is a Korean glazing technique that emerged in the Kyoto region in particular) and stoneware bowls straight out of the kilns from the Bizen region on Kyushu. The latter were not glazed, giving the pottery a matte finish.

TEA IN NUMBERS

In 2021, an area of 39,000 ha (96,000 acres) was farmland, as opposed to 61,000 ha (150,734 acres) in 1980, the year in which tea-growing saw its greatest expansion. In 2021, Japan exported a record 5,274 tonnes (5,813 tons) of tea (20 years earlier this was 599 tonnes (660 tons).

A CASE OF GENDER?

The 'way of tea' was originally exclusively open to men. Tea houses were the domain of lords and samurai, where women had no place. It was not until the Meiji era (1868–1912) that the country opened to the world and women started to set foot in tea houses. This universe then turned distinctly more feminine, and women were allowed to become tea mistresses, albeit solely for the simplest of preparation styles. Only after World War II did tea education become more accessible to women, enabling them to become fully fledged ceremony mistresses for *chanoyu*, which literally translates as 'hot water for tea'. Incidentally, these days more women than men continue with this traditional Japanese art.

Incidentally, these days more women than men continue with this traditional Japanese art.

matcha tea and variations

dalgona matcha ①

1 egg white
2 tsp sugar
1 tsp matcha tea powder
2 tsp lukewarm water
2 tbsp whole milk

Preparation

In a bowl, whisk the egg white with the sugar.

In a second bowl, dissolve the matcha powder in the lukewarm water to obtain a runny, smooth paste.

Add the paste to the beaten egg white and whisk until smooth to make a foam.

Divide the milk between two cups and top it with a layer of the matcha foam.

frothy iced matcha ②

300 ml (1¼ cups) whole milk
crushed ice
1 tsp matcha tea powder
2 dashes of vanilla syrup
whipped cream (optional)

Preparation

Pour the milk into a bowl, then fill it almost to the brim with crushed ice.

Add the matcha and vanilla syrup to the iced milk. Mix everything for 1–2 minutes.

Strain the frothy matcha into two cups and top with whipped cream (optional).

500 ml (2 cups) whole milk

1 tsp matcha tea powder

2 tsp honey

matcha latte ③

Preparation

Heat the milk over a low heat, then pour it into a blender with the matcha and the honey.

Blend until you have a thick foam.

Divide the milk mixture between two cups using a spoon.

Top the drinks with the milk foam.

Difficulty ●○○

Makes 1 l (4¼ cups)

Preparation: 2 days
Cooking: 5 mins

hokkaido milk tea

1 l (4¼ cups) whole milk
4 black tea bags
4–6 tsp brown sugar

Preparation

Pour 250 ml (1 cup) milk into a saucepan. Add the tea bags and the sugar.

Heat until the liquid simmers. Stir to dissolve the sugar.

Remove the pan from the heat and add the remaining milk.

Place in the refrigerator for 2 hours.

Remove the tea bags and enjoy.

This tea can be kept in a bottle in the refrigerator for 3 days.

sakura latte

250 ml (1 cup) milk

2 tbsp sakura latte powder

1 tbsp honey

60 ml (4 tbsp) crème fraîche

Preparation

Heat the milk in a saucepan. Add the sakura latte powder. Mix well until the liquid is simmering.

Remove from the heat, add the honey and stir well.

Pour the crème fraîche into a separate bowl and beat it until frothy.

Pour the sakura-infused milk into a cup, then delicately place the cream mousse on top, using a tablespoon.

Sake, nectar of the gods

Sake is the first alcoholic beverage that springs to mind when you think of Japan. And although it is being consumed less and less often there, the world of sake has undergone a revolution of sorts in recent years, with an increasing number of women becoming involved in its production.

Sake fills the glasses of Shuhei Hirayama and his friends as they discuss his daughter's future marriage in Yasujirō Ozu's *The Taste of Sake* (1978). The bride, the heroine in Quentin Tarantino's *Kill Bill* (2003), similarly orders a glass of sake from swordsmith Hattori Hanzo in an Okinawa sushi bar. And sake also features in Makoto Shinkai's animated film *Your Name* (2016), where young Mitsuha prepares the famous *kuchikami no sake* using her ancestors' method. Sake is omnipresent in Japanese cinema, from pop culture anime to arthouse films old and new. Beyond the cinema screens, it adorns the tables of the popular afterwork drinking establishments known as *izakayas*, while also featuring on the menus of Tokyo's finest restaurants.

This fermented beverage is undeniably synonymous with Japan, where it is known as *nihonshu*, which translates literally as 'Japanese alcohol'. In Japan, the term 'sake' is used to denote any alcoholic beverage, whether it be *nihonshu*, beer or whisky. In times past, sake served as an offering to the Shinto gods and as a means of communicating with them. Today, this 'nectar of the gods' is what people drink on special occasions. Participants in religious festivities, such as the bearers of miniature shrines, purify their bodies by drinking offerings of sake. At Shinto weddings, the couple exchange three cups of sake while saying their vows, and during New Year celebrations people use sake to toast what is known as *o-toso* – an act intended to keep evil spirits trapped in the year just gone and ensure long life for those who indulge in a sip.

PRODUCTION SECRETS

What exactly is sake? Well, it is a fermented alcoholic beverage made from water, rice and *koji*. Its base constitutes grains of polished rice, which are then washed, soaked, drained, steamed and cooled. Part of the rice is infused with *koji* fungus spores that, over the course of three days, turn the starch into sugar. This produces the *koji-mai* used to ferment the sake. During this step the *koji-mai*, cooked rice and spring water are mixed together to create *shobo*, to which yeast can be added, if desired, to accelerate the fermentation process.

The entire mixture is then placed in a vat, to which rice, water and *koji* are added alternately. The process ends with pressurization and filtration (and sometimes also pasteurization and a period of ageing), and then the sake is ready to be enjoyed.

魔王
なかむら
佐藤
兼八
中々
三岳
mono
4-2

Sake can be consumed cold, like white wine, between 5 and 10°C (41 and 50°F), at room temperature or even hot (between 30 and 55°C /86 and 131°F), particularly when accompanying winter dishes.

THE RETURN OF THE *TOJI* WOMEN

The sake world is essentially a masculine one. Of the 1,200 *toji* (master sake brewers), only about 20 are women, although this number is on the rise, considering it was zero in 1980! However, things were not always like this. A look back at the recipes that first mention *nihonshu* reveals that women played a pivotal role in sake production. Texts from the 6th century refer to the fact that women were the ones producing sake at Shinto shrines (just like the heroine in the 2016 film *Your Name*), chewing and spitting out the grains of rice to trigger the fermentation process with their saliva. Two centuries later, women appeared in records as brewers on a par with men.

So what caused women to be excluded from breweries? Some historians trace their gradual eviction back to the Edo period (1603–1867), which cemented the belief that women were impure because of their menstruation and the acidity of their sweat. It was deemed that these factors spoiled the production process and thus ultimately the taste of the sake. Women were completely excluded from breweries as a result of the new social structure promoted during the Meiji Restoration period (1868–1923); while economic structures were transformed, women were relegated to the home, which became a solely domestic space, having previously been a place where family life and business coexisted.

Since the end of the 20th century, however, women have been returning to the breweries. One of them is Miho Imada. After a career on the cultural scene, namely as a producer of *nō* theatre, she took over the reins of Imada Shuzo, the 150-year-old family brewery in Akitsu in Hiroshima Prefecture. This amazing journey saw Miho Imada feature on the BBC's prestigious list of '100 inspiring and influential women from around the world' in 2020. The *toji* women are getting things done. In 2018, 12 of them created the *Kura Jo* group to promote their sake production and, in so doing, raise awareness about the sexist stereotypes that still exist in the sake industry.

A DROP IN CONSUMPTION

As iconic as sake is, its consumption in Japan is decreasing. Gone are the glory days of the past when it flowed thick and fast. While the country boasted some 4,000 sake breweries in the 1970s, this number had dropped to no more than 1,200 in 2021. Despite the introduction of World Sake Day on 1 October, and the Japanese government's launch of the Sake viva! campaign to encourage the people of Japan to drink more of its national alcohol in 2022, sake consumption (as that of other alcoholic beverages) is falling in the country, having declined from 100 litres (26½ gallons) per person in 1995 to 75 litres (20 gallons) in 2020.

While exports may only make up 6 per cent of the overall production volume, sake is now also enjoyed outside the archipelago, with the top three importing countries being China, the United States and Hong Kong. In Europe, the largest number of sake consumers can be found in France, where the consumption of this drink is a rapidly growing trend; in 2021 imports there rose by 127.9 per cent.

HOW TO UNDERSTAND THE NAMES

Sake names depend on two factors: the degree to which the rice has been polished and whether or not alcohol has been added.

- *Honjozo shu* contains rice that is at least 70 per cent polished.
- *Ginjo shu* contains rice that is at least 60 per cent polished.
- *Daiginjo shu* contains rice that is at least 50 per cent polished.

If you find the term *junmai* on the label, you are dealing with a sake that has not had any alcohol added. *Junmai daiginjo shu* is considered to be the tastiest sake, because the more polished the rice, the better the sake is supposed to be.

Difficulty ●○○ Serves 1 Preparation: 5 mins

ginger sake

ice cubes
40 ml (scant 3 tbsp) sake
ginger beer, as desired
5 pink peppercorns

Preparation

Fill a spritz glass with ice cubes. Add the sake and top with the ginger beer.

Garnish with the pink peppercorns.

Difficulty ●○○ Serves 1 Preparation: 5 mins

pink umeboshi

50 ml (generous 3 tbsp) white tequila
25 ml (scant 2 tbsp) lime juice
15 ml (1 tbsp) sugar syrup (simple syrup)
5 ml (1 tsp) *umeboshi* (plum) jam
crushed ice

Preparation

Place all the ingredients in a cocktail shaker.

Add the crushed ice.

Shake vigorously and strain into a martini glass to serve.

左門
左門
左門
左門
車麩
ねぎ
薩摩揚げ
はんぺん
大根
名古屋コーチン
半熟卵
三角軟骨
せせ
ねぎ間
鶏むね
もも
ぼんじり
砂肝
手羽先

No.1
強炭酸
WILKINSON
LEMON
刺激、強め。
MITSUYA CIDER
SINCE 1884
ずっと受け継がれていく
日本品質
「水」「香り」「製法」
MITSUYA CIDER
SINCE 1884
ずっと受け継がれていく
日本品質
「水」「香り」「製法」
1本で1日分のビタミン!
MATCH
MATCH
ゴクゴク飲める微炭酸
つめた〜い
600ml
Asahi
天然水
NATURAL MINERAL WATER
生茶
摘みたて生茶葉のようなあまみ、香り
555ml
KIRIN
午後の紅茶
おいしい無糖
Darjeeling Tea
食事のお供やリフレッシュに
常温になっても、うまい
FIRE
ONEDAY
Black
[無糖]
600ml
無糖
ボスのフルーツオレ!
CRAFT BOSS
Since 1992
果実つまったフルーツオレ
果物とミルクで
元気チャージ!
後味すっきり!
カルピス
Water
甘ずっぱいがあふれてる
贅沢でクリーミー
北海道産生クリーム
カルピス
THE RICH
上質な濃さ
つめた〜い
ICE
贅沢な微糖
ボス史上最高深煎り
NEW 深煎り豆増量
PREMIUM BOSS
ボス史上最高深煎り
NEW 深煎り豆増量
PREMIUM BOSS
Asahi
特製
WONDA
カフェオレ
コーヒー飲料
ミルクがおいしいカフェオレ
キレ・コク際立つ
Asahi
GOLD PREMIUM
WONDA
金の微糖
高級豆で、いい休憩を
Asahi
WONDA
Morning Shot
BLACK
朝専用ブラック
おはようございます!
WONDA
Morning Shot
朝専用
徹底的に
極
微糖
WONDA
丸福珈琲店
つめた〜い

Japan – vending machine heaven

What's something you will just as easily find on the streets of Tokyo as you will on a winding road among the rice paddies or at the top of Mount Fuji? A vending machine, obviously!

Known as *jidohanbaiki*, which is often shortened to *jihanki*, the majority of Japan's vending machines – 57 per cent, to be precise – sell drinks. A single machine can contain cold drinks, such as fruit juices, water or soft drinks (sodas) as well as hot drinks like coffee and tea; the ratio varies depending on the season. Some machines even sell tins (cans) of beer or sake. And plenty of other food products are also available here, such as fruit, soup, freeze-dried ramen and dashi (the stock commonly used in miso soup).

BURGERS, OYSTERS AND CAKES IN A TIN

But that's not all! Some of the vending machines sell far more mind-boggling foods, including hamburgers that come out of the machine hot. Or the Hiroshima speciality of fried, crumbed oysters. Occasionally, you can find machines selling cakes in a tin (can). The cakes are made of crème fraîche from Hokkaido as well as mascarpone – an innovation conjured up by the Gaku restaurant chain. Vending machines are also a way for some businesses to sell their wares without having to rely on traditional shops. In January 2023, for example, the whale-meat seller Hideki Tokoro set up

In 2020, just over 4 million vending machines were identified in the archipelago by the Japanese Association of Vending System Manufacturers, this means one for every 30 inhabitants – with a staggering turnover: 34 billion GBP (43 billion USD) per year.

several machines across Tokyo and Yokohama, with the aim of installing around 100 machines by 2027. Whaling, and consequently eating whale meat, was banned in 1986 (officially, if not in reality – some people continued to find legal loopholes to get around it) following a historic campaign by the non-governmental organization Greenpeace and the Japanese government's involvement on the International Whaling Commission. However, whaling in the Japanese archipelago was permitted once again following the country's resignation from the commission in 2019. While supermarkets are still uncomfortable with the idea of selling the meat of this protected species, vending machines are an effective plan B for the company.

CUTTING-EDGE MACHINES

Japan's first vending machine was made by Tawaraya Takashichi in 1888 so that it could sell cigarettes automatically. Sixteen years later, a wooden vending machine was invented that sold stamps and postcards. However, it was really from the late 1960s onwards that vending machines began to take over the landscape. Industrial production launched in 1967, as the railways association started to introduce *jihanki* for train tickets. It was also around this time that Japan began the large-scale minting of the 100-yen coin, an indispensable piece of change for anyone wanting to use these machines. The 1970s brought a watershed moment when Sanden Retail Systems and Pokka Sapporo

A TOUR OF JAPAN

A BIT OF EVERYTHING FOR EVERYONE

Japan's vending machines don't just sell food and drink, you can also buy a range of other items from them, including umbrellas, newspapers, magazines, toys, disposable nappies (diapers), cigarettes, masks, DVDs and pet accessories, as well as condoms and sex toys ...

joined forces and created the first vending machine capable of selling both hot and cold drinks. Within just a few months, models of this type of machine had been installed right across the Japanese archipelago.

Innovations continue to this day. Some machines, namely those in Tokyo's Shinagawa station, have facial-recognition systems equipped to detect a customer's gender and age, enabling them to offer the most appropriate drink based on the weather and time of purchase. These *jihanki* have also had to adapt to the energy crisis. Over the past 20 years, the companies have managed to cut their electricity consumption by 70 per cent through using the heat generated by the refrigeration system to heat the hot drinks and reducing the drinks' refrigeration level during times of peak electricity consumption.

A LARGE COMMUNITY OF FANS

Now inextricably linked with the Japanese identity, these machines have sparked great interest in internet chat forums and on social media, with fans providing information on both broken and newly installed machines, or making lists of those selling more outlandish items of food and drink. Makoto Nomura is one such fan. The self-professed *jihanki* enthusiast discovered and fell in love with the machines on his way home from high school and has been following them for more than 30 years. 'There were hamburger machines along my route. As I began paying closer attention to the other machines I came across, I found some selling udon, some selling toast and even some selling miso soup. This kick-started my interest in *jihanki*,' he recalls. In 1995, Makoto launched a blog dedicated to the machines. It is a passion he continues to feed to this day via his site, but also on Instagram and X (formerly Twitter), using the handle @24jihanki. When asked about his most memorable discovery, he is quick to respond: 'I remember a vending machine selling curry and rice. I was blown away when I saw it for the first time about 20 years ago. You put your money in, you choose your product and the machine then serves it on a plate with curry and rice. It's as if there's a human being inside the machine,' he marvels. 'But those particular machines are rare and malfunction easily, which is why there is currently only one in existence.' To find it, you'll need to head to the city of Sagamihara, in Kanagawa Prefecture.

Vending machines have also captured the attention of artists, including photographer Eiji Ohashi, who dedicated two entire photo series to them – *Being There* and *Roadside Lights*. 'A few years ago, I was driving through a snowstorm. Caught in a white vortex, I lost all sense of space, but the familiar lights of the vending machines guided me. Vending machines have been special to me ever since. They're a window through which I see the world,' the Hokkaido-born photographer explains, before pointing out another feature of these machines: 'When the great Tohoku earthquake and tsunami struck in 2011, vending machines were the first things to be re-installed once the buildings and debris had been cleared away in Iwate and Miyagi Prefectures.' This was indeed the case and for one simple, non-profit-related reason: some machines are able to operate without power, enabling residents to stay hydrated and fed while awaiting more substantial aid. There are also some *jihanki* that, thanks to a remote management system, are able to supply drinks to earthquake victims free of charge.

Drinks – an overview

All kinds of drinks can be found inside Japanese vending machines. Here is a small selection of those you can buy from (almost) any machine in the country.

① **White coffee** – If there's one essential item sold by every vending machine, it's BOSS coffee. Pictured here is the white coffee version in a mini tin (can) (185 ml/ 6¼ fl oz). A chilled coffee that's not too strong is the perfect way to start the day. In winter, a hot version is available. How do you tell them apart? If the label on the can is blue and says つめたい it's a cold drink. Conversely, if the label is red and says あたたかい your coffee will be hot.

② **Fizzy lemon drink (soda)** – Launched by Suntory, C.C. Lemon is the third most popular drink in Japan. This sour sparkling drink delivers a vitamin C boost, with the brand claiming the 330 ml (11fl oz) tin (can) contains the equivalent of 28 lemons. When the product was released in 1994, Suntory signed a partnership agreement with *The Simpsons* and, for a time, C.C. Lemon became the go-to drink of Springfield's most famous animated family.

③ **Yuzu drink** – Yuzu is Japan's national citrus fruit. This drink fuses the sourness of yuzu with honey to add a touch of sweetness. And it is instantly recognizable thanks to its yellow packaging which features a smiley-faced yuzu. There is one requirement, however: for the best flavour, it needs to be consumed very cold.

④ **Ramune lemonade (soda)** – With its distinctive glass bottle that narrows at the neck and its lemon bubble-gum flavour, Ramune lemonade is synonymous with summer. Opening the bottle is a spectacle in itself, but we won't say any more, because that conundrum is all part of the taste experience!

⑤ ***Sencha* tea** – *Sencha*, which means 'infused tea', is a Japanese green tea. It can be drunk hot or cold, but is only ever cold when sold in bottles from vending machines. With its strong plant-like flavour that is reminiscent of fresh grass or seaweed; it is the perfect companion for hot summer days. As this drink contains no sugar, some may find its taste rather bitter.

⑥ **Milk drink** – Calpis カルピス is a drink made from water, powdered milk and lactic acid. It is most commonly sold as a concentrate that needs to be diluted with water or milk. It can also be used to add flavour to the Japanese shaved-ice dessert known as *kakigori*. Ready-diluted varieties of the Calpis milk drink are also available in the form of Calpis Water (カルピスウォーター) and the sparkling Calpis Soda (カルピスソーダ).

⑦ **Melon-flavoured sparkling drink (soda)** – Fans of sugary beverages with a distinctly chemical flavour will love this carbonated melon drink. For everyone else, it's probably better to stick to more natural-tasting fruit juices. This soft drink, which is particularly popular with children, also features on the menus of many family restaurants across Japan.

⑧ **Grape juice** – The little sugar-sweet bomb that is Tubu Budou grape juice has a huge surprise hiding inside its bottle: chunks of fruit similar to those found in aloe-vera drinks.

⑨ ***Mugicha*** – *Mugicha* is a barley tea, though it is probably more apt to call it an infusion, as this drink does not contain a single trace of actual tea. With its roasted flavour, *mugicha* is an indispensable drink during Japan's hot, humid summers. Please note, however, that it is not recommended for people with a gluten intolerance.

BOSS
Café au Lait
1

Vitamin
C.C
Lemon
Super Vitamin C
ビタミンC
レモン70個分
SUNTORY
2

土佐れいほく
わんぱく
ゆず
じゅーす
3

HATA
4

SANGARIA
あなたの
お茶
5

CALPIS
カルピス
ウォーター
6

MELON SODA
メロン
ソーダ
Gettin' Cool!!
7

粒ぶどう
TUBU
BUDOU
8

SANGARIA
あなたの
香ばし
麦茶
Barley Tea
9

The Japanese whisky boom

Having recently celebrated its centenary, Japanese whisky has become a global benchmark. Yet despite regularly being awarded the first prize in international competitions, it now seems to have become a victim of its own success.

'Japanese whisky is more liberal than British or American whisk(e)y in terms of casks and methods.'

Yuji Kawasaki

1923-2023. *'For relaxing times, make it Suntory time.'* It's 2003. In front of Sofia Coppola's camera, Bill Murray is playing Bob, an American actor invited to Tokyo to film a commercial for the Suntory brand and its Hibiki 17 Year Old. This classic scene from *Lost in Translation* shines a light on a drink still relatively unknown in the West: Japanese whisky. However, Bill Murray wasn't the first to extol the virtues of Japanese malts. Other actors have also tried to do so in genuine commercials, namely Orson Welles for Nikka in 1979 and Sean Connery for Suntory in 1992.

In the early 2000s, when Bill Murray and his glass of Hibiki were projected onto cinema screens around the world, Japanese whisky was at an all-time low. Japan's annual consumption was only around 150,000 litres (40,000 gallons) - a far cry from the record 408,000 litres (108,000 gallons) of 1983. Suntory's famed Hibiki 17 Year Old sold for just over 9,000 yen, or around 50 GBP (65 USD). Today, that same bottle sells for about 425 GBP (540 USD). This is because this beverage, with its high price label, is virtually impossible to find in bars. In 2020, the Japanese whisky giant stopped supplies of some of its bottles, including Hibiki and Hakushu, after it deemed it impossible to keep producing them off the back of their tremendous success on both the national and international markets. The reason? A premium whisky needs to age in a cask for between five and ten years. The distilleries did not have enough stock, and the malt's international popularity could not have been predicted in the darker days of the early 2000s. 'Global demand for Japanese whisky has exploded over the last decade - bottles like Yamazaki 18 Year Old, which previously sat on shelves collecting dust with its price tag of 78 GBP (100 USD), now cost five times as much and are virtually impossible to find,' explains Mamoru Tsuchiya, a whisky expert and director of the Japan Whisky Research Centre. The year 2020 saw the export value of Japanese whisky eclipse international sake sales for the first time ever, and this trend has continued ever since.

FROM HIGHBALLS TO CHIC COCKTAILS

The final years of the 2000s coincided with whisky's return to grace. 'In Japan, it was originally considered a special after-dinner drink. Until the 1980s, primarily due to customs laws, it had a strong reputation as a "luxury Western liqueur",' explains Yuji Kawasaki, an acclaimed whisky critic and creator of the *One more glass of whisky* blog. At that same time – and still to this day – whisky became the go-to evening drink for workers, who would down one highball after another. These whisky and soft-drink-based cocktails were 'slightly cheaper than beer. They were also seen as being healthier than beer, given they did not contain sugar or purine,' Kawasaki adds.

As well as this everyday consumption, Japanese whisky is also in the process of earning its stripes as a luxury beverage. Japanese single malts and blends are now beginning to receive medals in international competitions, stealing the spotlight from their Scottish and Irish counterparts. In 2008, for example, two Japanese whiskies received the awards for best single malt (Yoichi) and best blended whisky (Hibiki 30 Year Old). And yet Japanese whisky is still only about 100 years old.

'BLACK SHIPS' AND GALLONS OF WHISKY

One has to go back to 1853 to find the first trace of whisky in the Japanese archipelago. At the time Commodore Perry, an American naval officer, was conducting a military expedition to Japan in a bid to force the country to throw open its

diplomatic doors and borders to the West. In the holds of Perry's ships were crates of this tempting amber-coloured drink. He offered 58 gallons (70 US gallons) to the imperial court and it turned out to be a success. It was not until the 1920s, however, that Japan began producing whisky itself, after a detour via Scotland.

'If we're going to try to define Japanese whisky, we could say it's a whisky created by people who grew up eating Japanese food all the time, following the four seasons of Japan's climate and who are relatively sensitive to natural flavours.' Yuji Kawasaki

By the year 1918, the Japanese company Settsu Shuzo had started to distil an ersatz whisky. Masataka Taketsuru, a young chemist, was sent to Scotland to explore and study the whisky distillation process there. Having spent two years training at various distilleries, he returned to Japan and was hired by Kotobukiya, a Japanese whisky producer. It was here that he met Shinjiro Torii, and the pair would later team up to establish Yamazaki, the country's first whisky distillery. They produced Shirofuda, the brand's first Japanese whisky. Several differences of opinion resulted in the two men parting ways: Shinjiro Torii remained in Kansai and changed the company's name to Suntory, while Masataka Taketsuru headed to the north of the country and founded Yoichi, the first distillery to be run by the Nikka company. And so it was that Japan's two major whisky brands were born.

FLEXIBLE PRODUCTION REGULATIONS

What makes a whisky distilled in Japan unique? 'That's a very good question', says critic Yuji Kawasaki. 'Japanese whisky is more liberal than British whisky or American whiskey in terms of casks and methods,' he explains, adding that, 'if we're going to try to define Japanese whisky, we could say it's a whisky created by people who grew up eating Japanese food all the time, following the four seasons of Japan's climate and who are relatively sensitive to natural flavours. I think the focus needs to be not on the whisky itself, but on the person who produced it. After all, it's the "nose" that determines the whisky's character, whether it is a single malt or a blend.'

So one has to be careful, because, unlike most whisky-producing countries, Japan has very few regulations on what constitutes a whisky and what makes it Japanese. While the Japanese government did introduce official definitions for whisky made in Japan in 1989, it was in the interests of the industry, which at the time was monopolized by a few large distilleries, to keep legislation flexible. Mamoru Tsuchiya, who we spoke to earlier, thus embarked on a crusade to further standardize the production regulations governing this yellow nectar in order to prevent its value and reputation from declining both in Japan and around the world. 'We can use imported barley or malt, but the brewing, saccharification, wort production, addition of the yeast, fermentation to obtain the wash, wash-distillation and ageing in the cask all need to take place here, in Japan, in order for the whisky to be labelled as Japanese. That is the standard for whisky worldwide. If a single step of this process does not take place in Japan itself, it is definitely not Japanese whisky.'

These recommendations were followed by the Japan Spirit and Liqueurs Makers Association, and the latter ratified them in April 2021. Companies operating in the sector had a deadline of 21 March 2024 to ensure their labels complied with the rules. Some soon started to modify their labelling and it is now not uncommon to see terms such as 'world blends', which implies a combination of imported and Japanese ingredients. Despite these constraints, critic Yuji Kawasaki has a positive outlook: 'A number of new distilleries have popped up in Japan over the last ten years. If we look back at history, we can see that it was the newcomers who made Japanese whisky what it is today and I expect more and more unique, delicious Japanese whiskies will be produced in the future.'

WHISKY TERMINOLOGY

The three base ingredients of whisky are water, grains and yeast.

Pure and single malts only use barley. Bourbon, blends, *rishi* whiskies and Canadian whiskies are made by mixing several different grains.

- ***Blend***: A whisky produced by various distilleries.
- ***Double wood***: A term used to describe whiskies aged in two types of casks.
- ***Mashbill***: A mix, as a percentage, of grains making up a whisky.
- ***Pure malt***: Whisky made exclusively from malted barley.
- ***Single cask***: Whisky from a single cask.
- ***Single malt***: Whisky produced by a single distillery.

さつま
本格焼酎
白波
黒白波
ほの甘く、香り立つ。
黒白波
ほの甘く、香り立つ。
黒白波
黒白波

Shochu, the great unknown

The distilled alcohol symbolic of southern Japan struggles to build its profile outside the country. Unlike sake, which is produced solely from rice, *shochu* can be made from a multitude of ingredients, including sweet potatoes.

Whenever you sit down to dine at a restaurant or *izakaya* (bar) on the island of Kyushu, there is a good chance that, even if you have ordered a glass of sake, you will be served a beverage identical to it but which is actually *shochu*. Locally, this alcoholic drink is the star of the show, its consumption far outpacing that of sake. So what are the differences between the two if any? Well, firstly, sake is a fermented alcohol, whereas *shochu* is distilled. Then it's all about the base ingredients. Just like sake, water and *koji* (a ferment) are key, except that sake is produced exclusively using rice, while *shochu* can be made with more than 50 different ingredients, the most common being barley, rice and brown sugar, but often also including sweet potatoes.

The island did its best to make sake, but its subtropical climate means that the winters are too mild to produce high-quality alcohol. *Shochu* came to Kyushu from China, via the Ryukyu Islands that today form part of the Okinawa archipelago. A fisherman named Riemon Maeda brought the first Okinawa-grown *satsuma imo* (sweet potato) to the island aboard his little boat. Market gardeners began farming the new vegetable and this soon proved to be a profitable venture thanks to the region's climate and soil quality. *Imo shochu*, or sweet potato-based *shochu*, has filled bottles in Japan since the 16th century. This was also the time, the year 1559 to be precise, that the first mention of the drink was made – a carpenter from Kagoshima who had filed a complaint against his employer included in his report a sentence that was surprising to say the least. 'The boss was so stingy, he wouldn't even offer us a glass of *shochu*,' it read.

SHOCHU IN NUMBERS

Of the 852 *shochu* distilleries in Japan, 350 are located on Kyushu. Kagoshima Prefecture alone is responsible for 40 per cent of national *imo shochu* (sweet potato *shochu*) production. In fact, 99 per cent of the Japanese *shochu* produced in 2020 came from the island of Kyushu and the Okinawa archipelago.

SHOCHU, ALCOHOL FROM THE SOUTH

Kagoshima Prefecture, in the far south of Kyushu, is the primary producer of the famed sweet potato *shochu* known as *satsuma shochu*, which was incidentally the first Japanese alcohol to benefit from a geographical indication, a valuable identifier (just like the one used for French champagne) of a product's geographic origins, but particularly also its quality and reputation. So off we head to the tip of the island, specifically the coastal town of Makurazaki, one of the birthplaces of this famous brew. Getting there from Kagoshima means taking a local train that slowly snakes its way through the countryside on a single-track railway. After 37 stops and 2 hours 50 minutes of travelling time, with tree branches seemingly smacking at the windows in some of the more remote parts, we reach the East China Sea, where the lapping waves mark the end of the journey. As soon as we arrive in Makurazaki, the tantalizing smell of smoked fish hits our nostrils, for the town is also known all over the island for its skipjack tuna.

A few minutes' walk away, the imposing Satsuma Shuzo Meijigura distillery comes into view with its expansive white cement walls and its ornate roofing with traditional silvery-grey Japanese tiles that glint in the sunlight. Katsuhiro Hisahara, his clothes protected by a large blue apron, is on duty at the entrance. He gives a succinct summary of the distillery's history. Satsuma Shuzo Meijigura has been manufacturing shochu since 1936. Its speciality is the sweet potato variety of the drink - but not just any old one. 'For Satsuma Shiranami, our flagship product that has been made here since 1955, we only use sweet potatoes known as *kogane sengan*, whose flesh is paler - more yellow than orange - and known to be softer and more tender,' Katsuhiro explains. The distillery works exclusively with local growers whose sweet potatoes are farmed sustainably, that is with minimal treatment and processing. 'In peak season, which starts in the autumn, we receive up to 7.5 tonnes (8.2 tons) a day. They are sorted manually by our employees, before being chopped and steamed,' Katsuhiro adds.

VOLCANIC INFLUENCES

A number of preparation stages then ensue. The *shochu* is fermented by the *koji*, which can be 'white', which is mild and neutral; 'black', which adds an almost earthy taste; or 'yellow', which has a floral flavour. The *toji* or 'shochu master' chooses the *koji* based on the flavours he wants the finished product to have. The *koji* and water are then mixed with the sweet potato. 'That's why water quality is very important when making *shochu*,' Katsuhiro Hisahara explains. 'In Kagoshima Prefecture, we have exceptionally pure mountain water that is filtered by volcanic ash.' This marks the start of the fermentation process, which will take about two weeks, after which the alcohol content by volume is between 15 and 19 per cent. It is placed in wooden stills for one single round of distillation. The entire contents are then aged in clay pots for at least three years.

Behind the large bay windows, artisans continue to put the large wooden pallets into storage. Katsuhiro Hisahara is keen to share a little anecdote. During the Edo Period (1603–1867), shochu was one of the gifts most beloved by the shoguns. 'Alcohol was used both as a drink and as a makeshift disinfectant for sword injuries.' So it would seem that the renaissance of sweet potato *shochu* in Japan was aided by an innovation made by the Satsuma Shuzo Meijigura distillery. 'In the late 1970s, *oyuwari*-style *shochu*, a mix of alcohol and hot water, was all the rage, but in the 1980s, we came up with the *roku-yon*, which is six (*roku* in Japanese) parts *shochu* to four *(yon)* hot water. This mixture soon became a hit, resulting in the sweet potato-based *shochu* gaining popularity well beyond the borders of our southerly province!'

か

To find out more

Here is a selection of books and films that may accompany you on your journey of discovery of Japanese culinary culture. Below you will find references that I refer to in my articles or written by the people who were interviewed. I have listed others because they caught my attention as a reader or viewer. Obviously, this list is very subjective, and therefore not exhaustive by any means.

NOVELS AND ESSAYS

- *Coffee life in Japan*, Merry White, University of California Press, 2012
- *Fade*, Ryoko Sekiguchi, Éditions Argol, 2016
- *Konbini. La fille de la supérette*, Sayaka Murata, éditions Gallimard, 2019
- *L'astringent*, Ryoko Sekiguchi, Éditions Argol, 2012
- *La cantine de minuit*, Yarō Abe, Le Lézard Noir, 2017
- *La révolution des algues*, Vincent Doumeizel, Éditions des équateurs, 2022
- *La saveur des ramen*, Eric Khoo, 2018
- *Le saké, une exception japonaise*, Nicolas Baumert et Jean-Robert Pitte, Éditions Rabelais, 2011
- *Les carnets de table d'un amateur de cuisine japonaise*, Arashiyama Kozaburo, Éditions Picquier, 2022
- *Les herbes sauvages, récit d'un cuisinier*, Hisao Nakahigashi, Éditions Picquier 2022
- *Nagori, la nostalgie de la saison qui s'en va*, Éditions P.O.L, 2018
- *Notes d'Okinawa*, Oe Kenzaburo, Éditions Picquier, 2019
- *Tombent, tombent les gouttes d'argent - Chants du peuple Aïnou*, Éditions Gallimard, 1996
- *Un amour de bento*, Shiori et Nao Kodaka, Pika, 2012
- *Un sandwich à Ginza*, Yoko Hiramatsu, Éditions Picquier, 2021

PICTURE BOOKS

- *Hôtel Okinawa*, Greg Girard et Marc Feustel, The Velvet Cell, 2017
- *Kissa by kissa*, Craig Mod, Special Projects, 2020
- *Le guide du saké en France*, Adrienne Saulnier Blache et Ryoko Sekiguchi, Éditions Keribus, 2018
- *Paris Tokyo, la pâtisserie franco-japonaise*, Pâtisserie Tomo, Hachette Pratique, 2021
- *Tokyo Stories, à la découverte de la cuisine japonaise*, Hachette Pratique, 2020
- *Whisky japonais, la voie de l'excellence*, Brian Ashcraft, Synchronique Ed., 2021

MANGA AND CARTOONS

- *Golden Kamui*, Noda Satoru, Ki-oon, 2016
- *La Cantine de minuit*, Yarō Abe, Le lézard noir, 2017
- *Le Chef de Nobunaga*, Mitsuru Nishimura et Takuro Kajikawa, Komikku, 2014
- *Touiller le miso*, Florent Chavouet, Éditions Picquier, 2020

FILMS

- *Dans un jardin qu'on dirait éternel*, Tatsushi Ōmori, 2019
- *Jiro dreams of sushi*, David Gelb and Jiro Ono, 2011
- *Kill Bill*, Vol. 1, Quentin Tarantino, 2003
- *Le goût du saké*, Yasujirō Ozu, 1962
- *Le voyage de Chihiro*, Hayao Miyazaki, 2001
- *Les délices de Tokyo*, Naomi Kawase, 2015, based on the book of the same name by Durian Sukegawa
- *Lost in translation*, Sofia Coppola, 2003
- *Sans Soleil*, Chris Marker, 1983
- *Tampopo*, Jūzō Itami, 1985
- *Tokyo Ga*, Wim Wenders, 1985
- *Your Name*, Makoto Shinkain, 2016

MAGAZINES AND REVIEWS

- *Les douceurs du Japon, évocations éphémères de la « Beauté japonaise » (Nihon no bi)*, Sylvie Guichard-Anguis. Dans Sociétés & Représentations 2012/2
- *Manger le Japon*, 2022 special issue of *Tempura* magazine

Contributors to this book

CLÉMENCE LELEU

Clémence Leleu is a freelance journalist who has specialized in Japanese culture since 2015. Her work mainly revolves around the societal and cultural issues of the archipelago. She regularly works for *Tempura* magazine. In *Japan. A Culinary Travel Diary*, she supplied the reports and most of the photographs.

ANNA SHOJI

Anna Shoji, born in Tokyo, is a market gardener. In 2015, she set herself up in the Tours region of France where she grows Japanese vegetables for chefs. She is a co-founder of the ecovillage Mura, which hopes to unite people around Japanese culinary culture. She wrote the recipes in this book.

ADRIEN MARTIN

Adrien is an illustrator and comic book author. His work is heavily influenced by his love of travel, Asia, and in particular Japan, and he makes use of every opportunity to represent the different aspects of each one. He created all the illustrations for *Japan. A Culinary Travel Diary*.

Thanks

Clémence Leleu

This book is a collective venture. So first of all I would like to thank Fanny Ecochard for thinking of me for this project and for giving me carte blanche to decide the content of the book, where our similar universes were found. A big thank you to my other editor, Élise Ducamp, for her dedication, her support and her useful feedback on my text. Obviously I would also like to thank my two partners without whom the book would not have been possible: Anna Shoji and Adrien Martin, who agreed to join me on this adventure and who brought their talent to it.

I would also like to thank all the people featured in the book who, through their testimony, their expertise and their perspective, give *Japan. A Culinary Travel Diary* its depth.

A special thank you to Ryoko Sekiguchi for her very particular view of Japan and the world, her availability and her encouragement. My thanks also go to Emil Pacha Valencia, editor-in-chief of *Tempura*, who since 2020 has permitted me to write detailed essays for each issue of the magazine. Thanks to his confidence and his requests, he helped sharpen my vision of Japan.

Then come those who gave me their unwavering support. Those who, in my everyday life, encouraged, reread, revived the flame of courage when it ran out and who have always believed in the success of this project. Pauline Riglet Brucy and Lisa Castelly, Guillaume and Roland Richard, Marie Forbin, Adèle Ponticelli, Jean Giraud and all the others whose friendship, encouraging messages and little jokes allowed me to complete writing this book. Without you *Japan. A Culinary Travel Diary* would not exist either. And finally thanks to Arthur Lecoeur whose blunder in booking plane tickets happily marked the beginnings of this story which links me to Japan.

I also thank the photographer Laurence Revol, who took my portrait for this book. She knows why.

A big thank you also to Delphine Constantini and Mélanie Martin, who styled the food photos. Without forgetting the models Claire Besset and Florie Cadilhac from the Blick studio.

Finally, thank you to my parents, Annie and Claude Leleu. They never knew me as a journalist, never heard me talk about Japan. Yet between these pages there is much of what they passed on to me. This book is dedicated to them.

Adrien Martin

I would like to thank Pauline, for her support every day and for allowing me to benefit from her perspective; Clémence for her confidence and the quality of her writing; and my parents, who passed on to me a taste for travel and their curiosity. Without forgetting my friends, too numerous to mention, and all those present throughout this book.

喫茶 サンルモン
COFFEE
!¥300
喫茶
サンルモン

Index of Recipes

Picture credits

All illustrations: ©Adrien Martin
Photographs: Jaquette, rabat (top): ©Laurence Revol; (bottom): ©Clémence Leleu
©Delphine Constantini: pp. 27, 43, 51, 55, 69, 85, 89, 95, 97, 98, 105, 107, 129, 137, 139, 147, 149, 159, 161, 163, 173, 175, 183, 185, 201, 205, 215, 224, 226, 245, 249, 257, 259, 292, 293, 294, 296.

©Clémence Leleu: pp. 13, 21, 23, 32, 34, 35, 37, 38–39, 47, 48–49, 61, 62, 63, 65, 78, 81 (bottom), 83, 91, 101, 116, 118–119, 120–121, 132, 143, 154–155, 165, 166, 168–169, 176, 192, 194, 207, 209, 219, 220, 221–222, 236, 250, 252, 254–255, 263, 265, 269, 271, 278, 281, 282.

©Unsplash: p. 64: Rob Maxwell; p. 100: Gabe Reuter; p. 119: Roméo A.; p. 142: Charles Deluvio; p. 143: David Klein; p. 189: Jeff Siepman; p. 357: Julien Miclo; p. 281: Kris Sevinc; p. 289: Yuri Shirota

©iStock: p. 46: tupungato / p. 74: Skyimages / p. 75 (centre): yajimannbo; (left): runin / p. 81 (top): Nikola Stojadinovic / p. 102: bonchan / p. 130: Kenishirotie / p. 131: kuppa_rock / p. 144 (top): Tomas Llamas Quintas; (centre): kyonntra ; (bottom): deeepblue / p. 145 (top): Yuuji; (bottom): Binoe / p. 178: EnchantedFairy / p. 179: tdub303 / p. 232: Razvan / p. 233 (top): 4nadia; (centre): Promo_Link; (bottom): supermimicry / p. 235: kuppa_rock / p. 241: kyonntra / p. 242: Techa Tungateja / p. 243 (top): mm; (bottom, left): HiroshiMaeshiro; (bottom, right): GI15702993 / p. 253: kazoka30 / p. 279: ShaneQuentin / p. 285: Nirad / p. 291: 5PH

Originally published in 2023 by Big in Japan, an imprint of Hachette Livre (Hachette Pratique), under the title *Japan Cantina. Carnet de voyage culinaire pour goûter le Japon du quotidien.*

Texts: Clémence Leleu and Anna Shoji
Illustrations: Adrien Martin
Food styling: Mélanie Martin
Design: Studio Blick

For the English edition:

A member of Penguin Random House Verlagsgruppe GmbH
Neumarkter Strasse 28 · 81673 Munich

Library of Congress Control Number is available; a CIP catalogue record for this book is available from the British Library.

Editorial direction: Claudia Schönecker
Project management: Veronika Brandt
Translation: Sylvia Goulding, Emily Plank
Copyediting and typesetting: Julie Brooke, Andrea Chesman, Sylvia Goulding - for booklab GmbH, Munich
Production management: Luisa Klose
Printing and binding: Toppan Leefung Printing Limited

Penguin Random House Verlagsgruppe FSC® N001967
Printed in China
ISBN 978-3-7913-9300-1
www.prestel.com